Investing for the Long Term

Founded in 1807, John Wiley & Sons is the oldest independent publishing company in the United States. With offices in North America, Europe, Australia and Asia, Wiley is globally committed to developing and marketing print and electronic products and services for our customers' professional and personal knowledge and understanding.

The Wiley Finance series contains books written specifically for finance and investment professionals as well as sophisticated individual investors and their financial advisors. Book topics range from portfolio management to e-commerce, risk management, financial engineering, valuation and financial instrument analysis, as well as much more.

For a list of available titles, visit our website at www.WileyFinance.com.

Investing for the Long Term

My Experience as an Investor

FRANCISCO GARCÍA
PARAMÉS

WILEY

This edition first published 2018

© 2018 John Wiley & Sons, Ltd

Registered office
John Wiley & Sons Ltd, The Atrium, Southern Gate, Chichester, West Sussex, PO19 8SQ, United Kingdom

For details of our global editorial offices, for customer services and for information about how to apply for permission to reuse the copyright material in this book please see our website at www.wiley.com.

Wiley publishes in a variety of print and electronic formats and by print-on-demand. Some material included with standard print versions of this book may not be included in e-books or in print-on-demand. If this book refers to media such as a CD or DVD that is not included in the version you purchased, you may download this material at http://booksupport.wiley.com. For more information about Wiley products, visit www.wiley.com.

Designations used by companies to distinguish their products are often claimed as trademarks. All brand names and product names used in this book are trade names, service marks, trademarks or registered trademarks of their respective owners. The publisher is not associated with any product or vendor mentioned in this book.

Limit of Liability/Disclaimer of Warranty: While the publisher and author have used their best efforts in preparing this book, they make no representations or warranties with respect to the accuracy or completeness of the contents of this book and specifically disclaim any implied warranties of merchantability or fitness for a particular purpose. It is sold on the understanding that the publisher is not engaged in rendering professional services and neither the publisher nor the author shall be liable for damages arising herefrom. If professional advice or other expert assistance is required, the services of a competent professional should be sought.

Library of Congress Cataloging-in-Publication Data

Names: Paramés, Francisco García, 1963– author.
Title: Investing for the long term : my experience as an investor / by
    Francisco García Paramés.
Description: Chichester, West Sussex, United Kingdom ; Hoboken : Wiley, 2018.
    | Includes bibliographical references and index. |
Identifiers: LCCN 2018003956 (print) | LCCN 2018011705 (ebook) | ISBN
    9781119430681 (pdf) | ISBN 9781119431206 (epub) | ISBN 9781119431190
    (cloth) | ISBN 9781119430681 (ePDF) | ISBN 9781119431213 (Obook)
Subjects: LCSH: Value investing. | Stocks. | Paramés, Francisco García,
    1963– | Capitalists and financiers—Spain—Biography.
Classification: LCC HG4521 (ebook) | LCC HG4521 .P265 2018 (print) | DDC
    332.63/22—dc23
LC record available at https://lccn.loc.gov/2018003956

Cover Design: Wiley
Cover Images: © Image Source/Getty Images; © Vladitto/Shutterstock;
© Phongphan/Shutterstock

Set in 10/12pt, SabonLTStd by SPi Global, Chennai, India.

Printed and bound by CPI Group (UK) Ltd, Croydon, CR0 4YY

10 9 8 7 6 5 4 3 2 1

*For María Ángeles, my rock and inspiration,
and for my parents, reading from heaven*

Contents

Foreword

Countless books have been written in the United States on the subject of investment which have helped to nurture a sensible approach to going about it. It's not easy to contribute something new to English-speaking readers. This book is an attempt to offer something similar to European investors, especially readers from the Spanish-speaking world, where investment shortcomings are much more pronounced. As such, most of the examples that are provided here are European or Spanish.

Even so, English-speaking investors will come across some ideas or elements which they may find interesting.

- Investment books seldom talk about the economy and even less so about Austrian economics; this book may prove enlightening in this regard. It outlines the basic tenets of the Austrian School and how they apply to investment.
- One of the main applications is the need to invest in real assets (real estate, shares in companies, commodities, etc.) to maintain the purchasing power of savings. These real assets are the only defence against currency depreciation when the latter is not supported by a strong anchor, such as the gold standard.
- Risk is misrepresented in the financial world; something which this book addresses, unpicking some of the myths.

My career path as an asset manager from a different cultural environment is also somewhat different from the norm. I have drawn some lessons from my own life story, experiences, the different obstacles and client attitudes I have encountered and the overall environment, which might prove applicable to the reader's own circumstances.

In sum, I hope that this book proves to be as interesting to English-speaking readers as it seems to have been to a Spanish audience.

Introduction

I never imagined I would write a book. Less still one on investment. But life has surprises in store for us all, and it's best not to squander them. It may sound obvious, but you have to turn problems into opportunities. Do so naturally, as a reflex and across all aspects of life – whether personal, professional (as an investor making the most of market turmoil) or more generally in the world around you.

When I first read Peter Lynch's *One Up On Wall Street*[1] at the start of my career, it seemed to provide such a clear and simple explanation of how to go about investing that there wasn't much more to add. The experience of various years did little to change my opinion. Other books that I encountered along the way, especially the classics, appeared to complement and reaffirm this view. It seemed that the path was already well trodden.

However, gradually – almost imperceptibly – things began to change. Perhaps because of experience, or a touch of vanity. Either way, in recent times it has struck me that none of these books were an exact reflection of the principles or the way of working that we bring to investing (I say 'we' because while this book represents my ideas and experiences, I have not been alone on this journey. My approach to investment has been refined and implemented alongside a team of colleagues with whom I have had the good fortune to work over the years, first at Bestinver and now at Cobas.) For example, they seldom ever talk of the right way of viewing the economy. A people-centric approach can be especially useful at certain crucial points in time. And so, gradually, the germ of an idea began to take root in my mind.

By coincidence, in October 2010 I was invited to give a talk to the Value Investing Congress in New York. I accepted, glad to have the opportunity to talk about our adventures in the cradle of modern investment. In preparing for that conference, I was forced to reflect on how our approach compared with that of other value investors. In the United States this style of investing is more common than in my home country of Spain. In doing so, I was able to pinpoint some differences, which form the hallmarks of our approach to

---

[1]Lynch (1989).

investing. Many of us go by the title of value investors, but none of us are doing exactly the same thing.

The conclusions from that analysis, which I explained in the conference, form the basis of our approach to investing. And there are indeed some significant differences from the rest. Perhaps most importantly, our guiding framework is based on an Austrian view of the economy and we take patience to the extreme, one of the key traits for investing.

However, had it not been for circumstances, this germ of an idea for a book would probably have remained just that, since I lacked sufficient time to take the project on. Being an investment manager is a full-time job and the effort involved in writing it would have meant spending time away from my family, something I have never been willing to countenance.

However, an enforced two-year 'gardening leave' following my departure from Bestinver provided a window of opportunity. Friends soon encouraged me to start writing and I began to give it serious thought, although it wasn't a straightforward endeavour. In addition to being rather shy, writing has never come easy to me – despite my lifelong love of reading.

However, I received two visitors in London at the start of 2015 who kindled the spark to embark on this project, although I was still unsure whether I would end up publishing it. Modesty is not easily overcome, especially when it is one's first foray into the literary world.

The first visitor was the son of a former client, Ángel Pardo junior, a philosopher, writer, and investor. We dined in a stunning brasserie in Chelsea, crystallising – albeit not in Stendhal's sense – the idea for a book and striking up a long-distance friendship which proved to be both profound and essential. He suggested that I free myself from the constraints and not worry about forcing the words. I should just start writing about what was going through my mind, letting the ideas flow; the book would come together later, of its own accord.

I liked the idea. A book on investment doesn't need a grand beginning or end, nor does it need a thesis, not even a murder. What's more, as somebody for whom writing does not come naturally, it freed me from the torment of an empty page or iPad screen. I would simply write what occurred to me, without any expectations. In fact, I had already sensed that the 'book' would come in handy for me, even if I didn't end up publishing it. It would serve as a collection of ideas, forgotten events, reactions, etc., helping to breathe new life into my investment outlook.

Ángel has played a key role in this endeavour, and I am greatly indebted to him. Not only did he light the fuse, but he also provided invaluable support from the side lines, proffering advice and, especially, a guarantee that somebody would read the manuscript and give their thoughts on it. Without his endorsement and my wife's, who was obviously the first to read it, the manuscript would never have seen the light of day, remaining little more than a few personal scribblings.

The second visit came from a possible editor, Roger Domingo, from Ediciones Deusto (Grupo Planeta). Daniel Lacalle had put me in touch after having successfully published several books with them. Not only was his publishing house the best fit for my venture, but Roger shared a similar approach to investment and the economy, which would help to smooth over any discrepancies that might arise. Furthermore, he was happy to let me write the book how I wanted, both in terms of structure and marketing. I had the reins, even the option not to publish, which was an essential prerequisite. Moreover, he offered me the option to publish an English version with John Wiley, which seemed like the perfect match, given their long history in the classics of investment.

Inspired by their support, I got down to writing and soon had a clear structure in mind, which has turned out to be a tribute to one of the most important books of the Austrian school (in every sense), Ludwig von Mises' *Theory and History*.[2]

The first part of the book discusses the backstory, my education and journey as an investor. The events that took place and how my colleagues and I responded to them. When all is said and done, I have lived through the end of the longest bull market of the twentieth century, the tremendous tech bubble at the start of the twenty-first century, and, alongside my colleagues, the biggest housing market and credit bubble in Spain's history and the subsequent bust along with other markets, amid the biggest global stock market crash since the 1930s.

This is a story that may prove of interest to others wanting to learn from the past. However, it is of relative value since ultimately, it's a personal tale which shouldn't serve as a precedent for anyone. For me it was also a good opportunity to reflect on forgotten events, some 20 years later.

In hindsight, perhaps the greatest achievement was managing to make the most of the almighty bull markets of 1996, 1997, and the start of 1998, with the Spanish stock market tripling in value in 36 months. Not only did we succeed in posting similar returns to the market, but we did so taking on very limited risk (holding high amounts of cash, some 20%), which enabled us to steer clear of the problems that were to come in the hangover from such a pronounced bull market.

The second part of the book explains the underpinnings of our investment process; the theory, in von Mises' words. After giving it some thought, the first chapter of this section – Chapter 4 – is dedicated to economics: the

---

[2]von Mises (1975).

Austrian School of Economics. It's not a typical approach for a book on investment, and chronologically it's not the first that comes to mind either, but now that I sit down to summarise these ideas, I believe it does make logical sense to start with the foundations.

A building is built from its foundations up and having the right economic reference framework is always advantageous. It won't always come into use in the investment process, but it provides peace of mind in terms of having some idea of the possible alternative economic scenarios – despite never quite fully knowing which of these scenarios will come to bear – and sometimes, only occasionally, it will help us predict what's going to happen.

The first floor of the building gets stuck into investment proper: Chapter 5 enters into battle, explaining the difference between real and monetary assets. Real assets are the only sensible option for the long-term investor. And as I explain, among the different types of real assets, there is a major advantage to investing in listed shares. If we are willing to accept the logical and empirical evidence, reading this book could be a turning point for those who are sceptical.

Some real assets, such as gold, have performed worse than monetary assets over the long term. However, the peace of mind that comes from knowing that real assets will always maintain our purchasing power is such that even the worst examples are preferable to the best monetary assets.

We dive into the world of stock market investing in Chapter 6, explaining how investors need to choose between passive, semi-passive, and active investment. The latter can be done through mutual funds or by investing directly in shares. It's no easy choice – the reader needs to work to choose the right path – and it will depend on how much effort we want to expend as investors. Only those who are prepared to dedicate the minimum amount of prudential time to investing are in the right position to choose active management, whether through funds or investing directly themselves.

Chapters 7 and 8 are for those who opt for the latter, setting out the types of stocks we should be seeking and how to go about finding them. It's hard going, with slim chances of success (beating the market), but anyone who wants to give it a go might be better placed to do so after having read about our experiences in selecting stocks.

Chapter 9 provides an appreciation for why all of this is possible, why opportunities exist and how, as humans, we create them during our moments of irrationality, when we fail to keep our emotions in check. We will try to see whether anything can be done about it. Ultimately, investment comes down to the psychological and social analysis of our fellow humans – ourselves included. Knowing how and why we act is crucial to the process.

These six chapters, from Chapter 4 to Chapter 9, form the basis of our investment process. It's a simple and intuitive process, but difficult to apply since it requires a set of personal characteristics which, if they aren't present from the outset, can be difficult to develop. Sometimes people are sceptical about books like this: Why publicly reveal a successful investment process? Why not keep it a secret? Aside from involving a certain undeniable element of generosity, the reality is that the 'recipes' are not at all easy to follow. Quite possibly we have to change ourselves before we can do anything, which is often a noble goal, but frequently quite impossible.

The chapters in the second part start with a general view of the economy, narrowing their focus towards stock selection, with each chapter honing in on the most important elements of the previous one. The reader should feel free to skip some of them if they are not interested in going into more depth, though – obviously – I wouldn't recommend doing so.

After a brief recap and a bird's-eye view of the future, we finish up with two appendices. The first is aimed at those readers who are unwilling to read the entire book – some presents can be a poisoned chalice. I would encourage them to spend at least a few minutes reading the 'Small Ideas', a brief summary of some of the book's key ideas, and reflecting on them. This might be enough. If they can't manage that, then I hope they will at least internalise the 'Guiding Principle', which is the most important point of all.

The second appendix gives an introduction to the references and further reading list, highlighting the books that have been of most use to me in understanding the problems discussed throughout this book.

I don't claim to have unearthed grand new revelations in the investment process; everything has already been invented. But I think the book as a whole is coherent, and it may be useful to younger or less expert readers who are starting out investing, and also to more seasoned investors, who I hope will also be able to take something away from it.

Investing for the long term means doing things differently: shunning conventional wisdom, fleeing from the obvious, swimming against the current. It requires reading, thinking, and a willingness to take risks and not make excessive concessions. We must be very alert to our surroundings. I may well not be very deserving of any of these attributes, since, as Kant notes, everything that has value comes with a price tag; in my case I'm fortunate that it doesn't cost me very much ...

Either way, I am not so vain as to think that my path is the only route, or even the best one. Clearly, there are various sensible investment processes. Nor do I aspire to be an example to others. My goal is simply to share my story, my experience as an investor, and try to provide some useful insights that might enable other investors to take a slightly better approach to their investment decisions. I consider myself blessed and in no position to be lecturing others, since both personal and wider life circumstances have been kind to me. To loosely quote Warren Buffett, if I had been born in an African village perhaps my tale would be of little interest.

That said, I would nonetheless be heartened if I end up serving as an example to some young reader or my own children. We are surrounded by dubious characters who can give a false impression of those of us involved in managing money, or who have achieved a degree of recognition. Some of us, perhaps the majority, are continually striving to do the right thing.

At the end of the day, to paraphrase Juan Ramón Jiménez, this book is written so that it can be understood by my family, so that it is accessible to all types of readers. I have tried as far as possible to avoid financial language, which makes incomprehensible something that should be easy to understand – how to approach investing without fear. I've done it, and it's turned out pretty well.

PART One

The Backstory

CHAPTER 1

A Bit About My Early Years

I will start at the beginning, resisting the temptation to spare my own blushes. I feel it would not be natural to share my experience as an investor without first revealing a little about myself. There won't be any major surprises, but I think it is the natural order of things. I feel this is the way to do it.

ORIGINS

I grew up in an average and pretty normal family. My father was a naval engineer, a civil servant. He retired as Director of Maritime Industries in the Ministry of Industry, after having confronted the once famous 'naval restructuring' of the 1980s and being Professor of Projects in the Naval Engineering School. My mother was a housewife, mother of five children and an excellent cook. I cannot clearly recall them wanting to impart great life lessons to me; perhaps they tried, but I proved not at all receptive and confounded their best intentions. My introverted personality inhibited such 'important' conversations.

Even so, when I look at how I approach life, with the benefit of time, I do see some important traits that I inherited from them. For example, I have this inexplicable belief in the need to do the right thing. My father 'did the right thing' regardless of the circumstances and, without a shadow of a doubt, I share the same conviction. Likewise, these days I find the need to pass on my mother's folk wisdom to my own children, even though I used to laugh about it. Clearly this comes from them, whether genetically or by imitating their behaviour, which was always exemplary. Either way, they live on in me.

My childhood studies were normal. I always passed on time, with the exception of the university entrance exams, which I passed at the second time of trying. My grades were never exceptional because, except for occasional periods, no particular topic appealed to me. Gym was the class that

I liked the most during this period, meanwhile physics was always totally incomprehensible. Recently I had another go, reading Richard Feynman, Physics Nobel Prize winner, but with no success.

Perhaps my aversion to physics was a premonition. One of the gravest errors of a cross-section of economic theory – as we will see – is applying natural science techniques, specifically physics, to social sciences, including economics, treating human behaviour as if it were an equation to be solved.

Overall, mine was a childhood without upheaval or apparent trauma, and not a hint of a financial whizz-kid, wheeling and dealing with my classmates. Nothing remarkable, like any other life.

However, when I turned 16 I developed a love of reading, which has gone on to become a core personality trait and a key constant in my life. Nowadays, when I see my 13-year-old son compulsively reading 500-page books, it surprises me how little I read at that age. Until 16 I didn't read books, because it wasn't part of my lifestyle, although I did at least read my father's newspaper nearly every day, and this helped me to stay informed about what was going on in the world.

In terms of global issues, I was especially interested in the existence of the Berlin Wall, which prevented people from leaving their country. I was astonished that people were prepared to die to change sides of the wall. It was then that I started to understand how freely organised markets are more effective at satisfying the needs of the masses, including the worse off. I sensed that what was happening on the other side of the wall was not pleasant, and it was incomprehensible to me how the intellectual world was not more critical of the wall and all it stood for in the face of such clear evidence. Later on I understood why; Aron, von Mises, and other thinkers cleared it up for me.

I became hooked on reading through the son of one of my father's friends. One night he spoke to me about how books represented a limitless world where it was possible to discover all that we were not seeing in our own placid lives. As a shy boy, rather introverted and something of a loner, it didn't require much effort to allow myself to be sucked into all types of stories. And from these conversations I was left with a name that will never leave my head: Proust. My friend had been a fan since the age of 14; I started a bit later.

This passion for reading is not particularly unusual in the so-called intellectual world of theatre, cinema or journalism, for example, but in the investment world it is a distinguishing feature compared with the average professional. The ability to gain exposure to an endless collection of people and stories, both real and imagined, fosters an open-mindedness that enables us to delve into the interests and preoccupations not just of these characters, but of the people in our own circle. Proust is an example of this, with his ability to dedicate various numbers of pages to the slightest perception of a secondary character or the etymological analysis of a name that attracts him. This came to be essential in my work.

During this period I read fiction, especially the great Spanish and French classics: Galdós, Cervantes, the generation of 1898, Stendhal, Victor Hugo, and countless other authors. Literature was the cornerstone of my reading. Later on, I gradually drifted away from fiction towards non-fiction, which has absorbed me during the bulk of my professional life. As a matter of fact, my non-fiction reading is very varied, with apparently little direct relation to my work: history, psychology, sociology, political science, etc. As we will see later, some of these topics have left an imprint on my personal and professional development.

As we have just noted, and will repeat later on, the right approach to the study of economics and investments is the study of man, which means that both novels and varied non-fiction are a good basis for building your own world view.

UNIVERSITY

Lacking a clear idea of what to do, I embarked on a course in Economics and Business Science at the Complutense University of Madrid. At 17 years of age I was pretty clueless, like most people at that age, and the best thing I could do was delay the important decisions for as long as possible. I did what I think is sensible in such cases: embarking on a diverse degree covering law, history, mathematics, accounting, business management, etc. A hotchpotch which could help me get my ideas straight and wouldn't close off any paths, except perhaps a career in building paths and bridges…

I went to a not especially prestigious public university and I did so for several reasons: failing the first round of university entrance exams, which took place in June, meant that I had little time over the summer to think about the future; and as I didn't have a clear idea, it didn't seem logical to force my family to foot any excessive costs. I also didn't believe that attending a private university was essential for a professional career. In reality, I thought of university studies as a formality that I had to get through, and I used part of the time available to learn languages – English, French, and German – again mostly in public language schools.

There is not much to highlight from the five years I spent studying at the Complutense University of Madrid because, evidently, it didn't clear much up for me. Whilst it didn't help me, at least it did plant the seed for what would later develop into my interest in the business world. More about that in a moment.

The first four years passed by inconspicuously enough. I combined my studies with language learning and military service, which proved very useful in getting to know the reality of my country, Spain. In my group of 10 sailors who shared a room together, there were two people who were illiterate, and only four of us out of the squad of 100 who had a university education. It is true that this was the Navy in Andalusia in 1984, but it also helped change my perspective on the world in which I was living, bursting my own little bubble. My country was no longer just my friends and my family; there was a wider world of people living very different lives from ours.

At the same time, I gave some consideration to trying to enter the diplomatic service. I didn't have a particular patriotic or political calling, but I found appealing the combination of exotic travel and, once again, the very wide variety of topics at the entrance exam. As can be seen, I have had a tendency throughout my life to try to leave as many options open as possible, and this is something I would undoubtedly recommend. However, in this case, I quickly abandoned the idea.

In the final year of my degree, something unexpected happened. It was a complete accident, arising from my love of sport, particularly basketball. On my visits to the library I had an enlightening encounter with a business magazine, which is no longer in existence. This encounter had great significance, both in 1985 itself – when the event took place – and later on in the future. The magazine was *Business Week*, and what caught my eye was the front cover, which featured no less than one Patrick Ewing, the star of university basketball and recent signing to the New York Knicks. Back then I found basketball, and especially the American professional league, NBA, a lot more inspiring than economics and business science, even though in those days we couldn't follow the games on Spanish television and had to make do with mythical photos.

The article explained the economic implications of Ewing's signing for the Knicks, which was probably the biggest up to that point in sporting history. But I also took the opportunity to read the whole magazine, which I found very engaging. Thanks to that, little by little, I began to gain an interest in the business world, which *Business Week* explained in quite an entertaining way. I cannot be sure whether this was a mere accident or the logical consequence of my passion for reading, but the truth is that this interest never went away. Up until then my focus had been on fiction, but gradually I started to take a greater interest in non-fiction, which I began to combine with literature. This seems to be quite a typical pattern, even taking it to the extreme where I only read non-fiction for years, thinking that literature – despite all I have said above – was not as worthwhile. These days I am more relaxed and have come to appreciate it again.

The truth is that it is important to try and look where others are not looking, and go beyond the superficial and commonplace. Doing otherwise only achieves mediocre results. In the following year, I came to realise that no one among my fellow students or in my first jobs even considered the possibility of regularly reading a foreign economic magazine or 'serious' literature.

It is worth mentioning that other than stumbling upon an interest in the business world, I learnt very little about the economy at university: useless neoclassical supply and demand charts, with a supposedly rational human being and a non-existent equilibrium, and little more. Thank goodness Hayek and von Mises came to my rescue nearly 20 years later, like economic superheroes. It is a real shame that economics teaching doesn't develop clear and simple concepts that are able to stand the test of time. Since some people want to give it an air of importance that it doesn't have, a façade of mathematical formulations has been erected to hide the lack of clarity and coherence of neoclassical economists, both monetarists and Keynesians, who dominate economics teaching.

However, it was a varied degree, which enabled me to begin to get a handle on potential areas of interest, or at least rule out possible paths to follow. My grades were mediocre to begin with, but gradually improved as I began to connect with the material.

Looking back, one of the most interesting conclusions I have reached after five years in a not especially prestigious public university, and many more years of professional experience, is that the importance attached to prestigious universities, and even university teaching itself, may be overstated. What you learn at 20 years of age is not as important as lifelong education – preferably when it is self-taught. Three or four years of being put on the right path by good professors may be useful, but the key thing is to have a spark of interest awoken in us at a particular point in time, which opens up an appealing and limitless path. It might be the case that some of the big universities help this happen, but I am not sure it's the case. And I cannot understand the current obsession, especially in the English-speaking world, with getting into certain universities. In my home country of Spain we are fortunate that there is not such a heavy emphasis on attending elite universities.

In my case the spark was ignited by an adolescent reader and a professional basketball player.

FIRST JOBS

In my last year of university I responded to various job adverts to practise the art of the professional interview. After the very first interview, I was offered a job at El Corte Inglés. I don't think I was a specialist in interviews, but if I do have any special qualities it is that I am natural and exude a certain air of being a responsible person. This unexpected success forced me to decide whether to start work before graduating in June. I decided to start in March and spent four months combining both work and study, and a football World Cup with Butragueño, the Spanish star, and Maradona.

I spent a year working at El Corte Inglés, the leading Spanish retailer (until Zara turned up), where I graduated in administrative work. This didn't offer me much on a professional level, but it was useful on a personal level. In my department at least, El Corte Inglés tried to hire university graduates for administrative tasks. It was an approach that obviously didn't work, and little by little the majority of us ended up leaving. Either way, starting out professional life doing relatively thankless tasks toughens one up for what might come in the future. To my surprise, I also discovered that a lot of people are happy doing a simple and uncomplicated job. It is possible that they are making a virtue out of a necessity, but this simplicity is something that has passed through my mind later in life, at moments of excessive responsibility.

On El Corte Inglés itself I can't say a great deal. I was there only 15 months, and my job position didn't afford me a wider perspective on the group. That said, there was a strange contradiction between the visually attractive shops, perfectly arranged and with impeccable service, and the somewhat outdated and highly hierarchical internal organisation. It is likely that things have changed after 30 years, enabling a transition towards more modern forms of distribution after the significant decline in popularity of the 'department store' concept around the world.

I certainly didn't see it as a job for life, meaning that I took it upon myself to do what you have to try at times of professional stagnation, when you are stuck without knowing where to go: think outside the box and change your life. This involves considering something radically different, tearing down previous plans. In my case, I went down the road of an MBA (Master in Business Administration). You might think that going from a company such as El Corte Inglés to studying an MBA is not such a radical change, but I can only attest to the sensation I had when visiting the MBA campus in Barcelona for the first time, of feeling very different.

Young people often ask me whether they should do an MBA, CFA, or other alternative. The response depends on each individual situation, taking account of their partner, ambitions to form a family, clarity of ideas on the future, work at that time, financial situation, etc. My case was clear: I was single and unattached, with a relatively uninspiring job and lacking clear professional ideas. I ticked all the boxes for doing an MBA.

IESE

After spending the summer months in the American multinational NCR (I had decided to change jobs, but I was accepted into IESE – Instituto de Estudios Superiores de la Empresa), I headed to Barcelona in September 1987 to do an MBA in what was and continues to be one of the best business schools in the world. Spain has an impressive number of high-quality business schools: IESE, IE, Esade. If only the universities could learn from them!

As a curious aside, I had to repeat the mathematics entrance exam. I guess I did the others pretty well, because otherwise they would not have given me the opportunity. As we will come to see later, good investment doesn't depend on exceptional knowledge of maths, but rather knowledge of dynamic business competition and a simple calculator.

I took out a loan with the Catalan bank, La Caixa, which had an agreement to finance IESE students (with an eye to their future earnings potential), and settled down in Barcelona. I felt very comfortable in Barcelona, both with the institution and the surrounding environment, made up of professors and students from 20 different nationalities. The self-sufficiency which I had experienced until then, due to the ease with which I had passed exams, gave way to something different: I discovered that some of my colleagues were brighter than me or, at least, were able to concentrate better. This had been true before, but I had always justified it to myself on the basis that I hadn't made a wholehearted effort. This excuse was no longer valid in Barcelona, where I did try to give the best of myself.

I think this ultimately helped me to focus on the future, knowing that I had to follow my own path, knowing that there will always be better and worse people than me, professional speaking (and personally as well).

The other hallmark that I was left with from the MBA was a certain dose of scepticism. Maybe it was the continual case study analysis, IESE's main teaching method, and the debate with other equally well-educated young people, which left my colleagues and I with a veneer of scepticism that I used systematically from that point onwards. Cases always have multiple solutions, and there is never a single response; no one is certain of being right, even less so when surrounded by people able to demolish their arguments. As investors, we are constantly being told very attractive stories. We are sold hopes, futures, triumphs, and our job is to choose only those stories or projects which are worthwhile.

I also had my first experience of a stock-market crash in October 1987. Strangely, back then, I viewed my flatmates, passionate stock-market investors, as irredeemable speculators. Clearly, I was still showing few signs of being a 'financial whizz-kid'. How was I going to get involved with money? How things change …

The clearest and most decisive conclusion from those two years in Barcelona was that analytical activity suited my personality. I was lucky to be able to apply the classic and essential 'know yourself' refrain. Others never find themselves, despite frantically searching. For me it was clear. I was not somebody suited to sales, or leadership, but rather study, reflection, and reading: in one word, analysis.

BESTINVER

Competitive and financial analysis looked like a professional field that matched my qualities, but I was still unsure which area of analysis I should focus on. The same type of analysis could apply to strategic advice, buying or selling a company, or investing in another, listed or otherwise.

The decision had to come from somewhere, and circumstances ultimately intervened.

I jumped directly from IESE to Bestinver, after two strokes of luck. I had already received an offer from a relatively prestigious consultancy firm – Coopers & Lybrand – but I went along to an interview with Bestinver after realising the night before that none of the other possible candidates were going to show up, as we were celebrating the end of term in advance …

I didn't think it was right to give such a bad image, and so I went to a very subdued interview, knowing that I wasn't overly interested. The added twist of fate was that Coopers had offered three positions to four people, assuming that one would fall by the wayside. No one dropped out and, as I was the last to reply, I was excluded. Let's just say that at the height of summer I was left with little option but to accept the offer from Carlos Prado and José Ignacio Benjumea to work with Bestinver as an investment analyst. In reality, it was not a conscious choice. At IESE I had not stood out enough to aspire to join McKinsey, Salomon Brothers, BCG, or any of the other big hitters at that time – which we all ultimately aspired to work for – and my decision was driven by circumstances. I took what was on offer to me in an area related to analysis.

At that time, Bestinver was the diversification arm of the Entrecanales family. I have to confess that I was impressed both by their red/maroon offices, which had a certain air of a house of ill-repute, in the prestigious La Pirámide building in the centre of Madrid, as well as by the company's Director General, José Ignacio Benjumea, who was amiable with me from the outset, as he has been over all these years. In any case, on top of this sheen of glamour, it struck me that Bestinver offered what I was seeking: a small environment, with interesting people, backed up by the discreet support of a very sound institution.

I was hired to help analyse the group's potential diversification investments. At the time, Bestinver had three areas of activity: diversification, which sought to channel profits generated by the family's construction activity towards new businesses, and where some investments had already been made; a stock brokerage service, which had been liberalised around that time and where the company had some presence; and a tiny portfolio management business.

It was a special time to start working. It was August 1989 and in autumn, Eastern Europe's totalitarian regimes began to topple. Having followed, from a very young age, media stories on the adventures of those who tried to escape, it was a time of widespread optimism, and we were keeping a very close eye on the news coming through to us on the office television. At the same time, Spain was heading at full steam towards entry into the European Union (EU). It was not a bad time to be young and setting out on a professional endeavour.

In the first few months I tried to scour the market to find private unlisted companies, seeking investment opportunities for the group and offering these companies the option of being listed on the stock exchange. I was allowed to do this without clear instructions and with a lot of flexibility; I guess they were not very clear about what they wanted from me. However, I didn't like the commercial part of the work one bit, essentially cold calling. This confirmed my lack of propensity for it and the limited analysis I was able to do on possible transactions did not offset this.

In fact, I wasn't very clear who my boss was and on my own initiative I started to study listed companies, helping the three brokerage agents and the small equity analysis team which fed them information. It's probably because of this that later in life I have put a lot of emphasis on my own initiative, free from guidance. This is my approach to management, when I have had to work with colleagues. If we wait for somebody to solve our problems by giving clear instructions, it is more likely that Godot will show up first.

MY INITIAL ANALYSIS AND INVESTMENTS

Acerinox, the leading stainless steel giant, was the first company I visited and analysed at the end of 1989. Back then it struck me as being an exceptional company, and that remains the case to this day. However, I guess I was too timid and I recommended 'holding'. Little by little I began to realise that I could add value to the analysis, and in my free time, which I had quite a lot of given the lack of a clear remit, I set myself the challenge of becoming acquainted with all the companies listed on the Spanish market.

At that time the CNMV (Spain's National Securities Market Commission) produced a book with the quarterly results of all listed companies. I reviewed them all, from A to Z. I think that the first one was Agrofuse, a company involved in the farming business, which we never invested in. Throughout 1990 I spent my time doing this, with the good fortune of not having to respond to pressure from a boss, or a structure that demanded short-term results or output.

At the start of 1990 I read a review of Peter Lynch's book *One Up On Wall Street*[1] in *Business Week*, which I had continued to read regularly since university. The book explained the fundamentals of value investing (or sensible long-term investing). In fact, as I have already mentioned, until very

---

[1]Lynch (1989).

recently I still believed this book to be so complete and clear that it wasn't possible to add much to what had already been said.

Value investing aims to invest sensibly over the long term, estimating companies' capacity to generate future earnings and paying a competitive price for them. This sounds self-evident and something all investors should do, but they don't, so in reality, value investors are simply sensible investors.

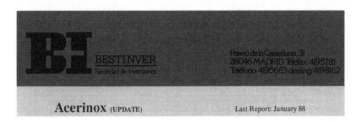

Acerinox (UPDATE)   Last Report: January 88

Acerinox (update) last statement: January 88
Date: 30 November 1989
Price: 1,305% (13.050 ptas) / 30 November 1989

Consolidated Group (millions of pesetas)	1987	1988	1989 (F)	1990 (F)	1991 (F)
Sales	46,509	76,660	85,000	101,200	116,500
Share capital	6,050	7,323	8,639	8,639	8,639
Net profit	5,078	10,306	8,600	14,100	16,730
Net cash flow	12,188	16,347	12,600	18,600	21,230
Earnings per share (pesetas) (*)	625	1,286	995	1,632	1,937
Free cash flow per share (pesetas) (*)	1,684	2,039	1,459	2,153	2,457
Gross dividend (pesetas per share)	182	200	200	225	250
PER (*)	20.9	10.1	13.1	8.0	6.7
RPCF (*)	7.7	6.4	8.9	6.1	5.3
Dividend yield (%) (*)	1.4	1.5	1.5	1.7	1.9

Market capitalisation (millions of pesetas):	112,738	Price/book value			2.2
LAST TWELVE MONTHS: QUOTATION FREQUENCY (%):	95	Maximum (%):			1,860
Average daily volume (shares)	14,762	Minimum (%):			1,067.5

(*)Figures adjusted for rights issue. (F) Forecast.

Income Statement

	1987	1988	1989 (F)	1990 (F)	1991 (F)
Net sales	46,509	76,660	85,000	101,200	116,500
Cost of selling	20,749	40,934	53,550	61,700	69,900
Gross margin	25,760	35,726	31,450	39,500	46,600
Personnel cost	4,837	5,831	6,500	7,400	8,100
Other costs	6,217	7,032	7,800	8,500	9,200
Depreciation	7,110	6,041	4,000	4,500	4,500
Provisions	112	2,469	400	500	600
Exchange rate variations	102	(571)	—	—	—
Other income	494	479	500	2,500	500
EBIT (earnings before interest and taxes)	8,080	14,261	13,250	21,100	24,700
Interest expenditures	1,938	859	1,300	1,000	800
Pre-tax income	6,142	13,402	11,950	20,100	3,900
Taxes	1,064	3,096	3,350	6,000	7,170
Net income	5,078	10,306	8,600	14,100	16,730
Net cash flow	12,188	16,347	12,600	18,600	21,230

Thanks to Lynch I discovered the other investment maestros: Graham, Buffett, Philip Fisher, Templeton, etc. I wrote to Omaha and they sent me all Warren Buffett's letters to shareholders that had been published at the time. I have always said that his timeless wisdom, outside of the MBA network, is the best Master's degree for a student of the business world. Not just professionally, but also personally. We will turn to him in more detail later on.

Overall, 1990 was a key year in my training as an investment analyst and manager, during which a series of very significant factors came together:

1. I had found the type of work that suited my key personality traits – analytical capacity and patience. It was a relatively quick and pretty clear process.
2. In Santos Martínez-Conde I had a head of analysis with a very clear 'value' approach. Although at that point he was unfamiliar with the American maestros, he applied fundamental valuation to all investment opportunities. I spent 18 months working with him until he left in

January 1991, and he left an opening as head of analysis which I asked to fill. He is now Chief Executive Officer at Corporación Alba, the March family's investment holding company.

3. I had total freedom to analyse the companies which I considered to be of interest, at my own pace. This rounded out my education, as we will see.

4. I discovered Peter Lynch and Warren Buffett. And all the rest.

5. I had my first practical lesson on volatility and 'uncertainty'. On 2 August 1990, Iraq invaded Kuwait, provoking a global crisis which had implications across the markets. The S&P 500 fell 20% in three months, from peak levels in July prior to the invasion to lows in October. This period of uncertainty proved to be an optimal time for buying shares. On 17 January 1991, a coalition of states invaded Iraq, provoking an upward movement in the stock markets and a recovery of pre-invasion peaks in less than a month. As the classical investors had always maintained, buying bad news was the best way to take advantage of 'uncertainty'.

Using this guidance I sensed that there was a clear gap in Spain for applying what Americans called 'value' investing. The stock market in Spain was dominated by large banks and by the heirs to the old stock and exchange brokers, notably Asesores Bursátiles and FG. However, sensible fund management was scant.

This is essentially how I laid the groundwork of my training. These lessons have remained with me until now, and I have never had cause to doubt them. I would have liked to have given a bit of 'spice' to this part of my story, describing my doubts, qualms, and ups and downs, but I can't, because the natural doubts that we all face before taking on a profession rapidly came to an end that year on the basis of a single year of experience. I suppose in that sense I am one of Stendhal's happy few. I was 26 years old and I had a clear vision of my long-term future.

When young people ask me how to get started with investing, I always say that they have to start right now. There are two options. The first is that some charitable soul in the markets will come along and offer you a work opportunity related to investment analysis or management. This makes life easier, provided that bad habits are not picked up, which can later prove hard to shake. The second, more likely, option is that you have to self-teach, working in other jobs to support yourself while learning about investing correctly in your spare time. Fortunately, there are a lot of resources out there these days to help you.

I was lucky enough to spend a year mid-way between the two, I was paid by somebody but I was allowed to choose how I spent my analytical time. Either way, the crucial thing is to create your own portfolio from the outset. The amount that we invest is irrelevant, the key is organising an effective process, which suits us and, if possible, actually works. How are we going to convince others to give us an opportunity if we don't believe in it ourselves!

Another key landmark was in February 1990, when I bought my first shares. Up until then I had never even considered it. As I have already mentioned, unlike other investors I never had an entrepreneurial spirit as a child, young person, or young adult. On the contrary, it struck me as a world inhabited by speculators, far away from my own world, which tended to be somewhat intellectual. I bought Banco Santander shares. Back then it was a much easier-to-analyse bank than it is now: its business was growing in Spain, thanks to its aggressive commercial policy – that year it launched the first deposit war with the 'superaccount' – and its small-scale forays abroad; it was trading at a reasonable price – nine times earnings – which didn't reflect its past or future growth capacity. I recall being nervous throughout the morning until the order was finally confirmed. It was a tiny order – just 50 shares – but it marked a turning point in my life. (Furthermore, this also shows that I am not genetically ill-disposed to investing in banks, despite not having done so from 1998 to 2012.)

This was the start of my portfolio of personal investments. I cannot comprehend how somebody who analyses the markets, providing buy or sale opinions or managing money, can refrain from becoming a shareholder in the companies they like. In my case it was an unstoppable urge: I analysed companies and if I liked them, I had to buy them, even if only in small amounts.

Sometimes there are legal restrictions in place, but there shouldn't be a problem provided you are transparent. Later on, when tax-free fund transfers were established, I gradually wound down my portfolio in order to invest in funds, which was the logical thing to do (before then I worried that if I ever fell out with Bestinver and decided to change company, I would be liable to pay tax on the corresponding capital gains when selling my funds).

This first purchase was the start of the process of building a portfolio of stocks. It seemed like an ideal moment. The environment was very positive on the back of the fall of the Berlin Wall and Spain's entry into the EU, and reasonable prices meant I could buy good assets at a good price. I even decided to take on a bit of debt. I calculated my savings capacity over the following two to three years and, taking account of repayment of the loan from La Caixa which funded my Master's degree at IESE, I asked for three loans, each worth 1 million Spanish pesetas ($6,000): from my father, my friend Miguel del Riego, and my bank.

It is the only time that I have had to take on debt to invest. I didn't have any family commitments and I did so modestly, after estimating my probable income and with at least two very flexible backers. I have always urged a lot of caution when taking on debt. There can be exceptions – this is one example – but always on the basis that we can withstand very negative scenarios, losses of more than 50%, without suffering a risk of default.

I started investing this money in different Spanish stocks on a small scale: Ence, Tafisa, Nissan Motor Ibérica, Cevasa, Inacsa, Tudor, Fasa Renault, etc. The advantage of being a small investor is that with little money you can take on positions which have an impact on a group of stocks. This portfolio convinced me that I liked managing money and that I could do it reasonably well. I also made a very serious error, which – luckily – didn't cost me too much money or pride: Nissan Motor Ibérica.

Nissan Motor Ibérica was the Spanish subsidiary of the Japanese multi-national automobile manufacturer, Nissan. It had an attractive position in industrial vehicles, with various production facilities on Spanish soil and sales across Europe. Thanks to Lynch's teachings, I believed I had good knowledge of how to invest in cycles and how to identify growth companies. I saw Nissan as a growth company from Spain to Europe, with new vehicles on the way, especially for passengers, where it currently did not have a market presence. Its recent track record backed up the growth idea.

However, the slowdown in the Spanish economy following the hang-over from the 1992 festivities – the Barcelona Olympics and the Seville Expo – saw cyclical stocks begin to suffer significantly. Sales in my wonderful growth company collapsed, turning it into a vulgar cyclical company.

During the fall in its share price in 1990 and 1991, I had systematically increased my positions, with Nissan Motor Ibérica stock at one point reaching 40% of my personal portfolio. As we will discuss later, increasing positions in a stock in freefall is one of the hardest decisions an investor can make; sometimes you never recover the full extent of the fall. Though it is true that in cyclical companies, sooner or later the situation will change, meaning that despite everything, persisting with the purchase normally bears fruit.

Investment in Nissan Motor Ibérica

PURCHASE			
Date	No. shares	Price (pesetas)	Total (pesetas)
18 April 1990	100	814	81,400
10 December 1990	400	378	151,200
27 December 1990	500	339	169,500
18 February 1991	700	495	346,500
19 February 1991	50	500	25,750
	1,750		774,350
SALE			
27 January 1994	1,750	260	455,000
LOSS: 319,350			

Losses on Nissan Motor Ibérica accounted for 40% of the investment, on top of the opportunity cost of three good market years.

The company eventually had major problems, nearly going into bankruptcy. Only a rescue takeover by the parent company in 1994 enabled losses to be limited at around 50% of the initial investment.

I learnt an important lesson from the excessive focus of my portfolio on Nissan: even when we are totally convinced of our convictions we can get it wrong, making it vital to diversify our investments. Mercifully, thanks to the success of my other investments, I didn't lose confidence in my ability to choose stocks and I was able to amply cover the losses on Nissan.

PETER LYNCH

Peter Lynch's *One Up On Wall Street* was crucial reading in my initial training. It taught me extremely useful tools and helped me to solidify many of the concepts which at that time were in an embryonic state. Through him I discovered all the other major investors: Warren Buffett, John Neff, John Templeton, etc.

That is why it is worthwhile giving a quick summary of the 10 universal lessons that I drew from his book:

1. Invest in what you know. We always say the same thing and it is worth reiterating. As Lynch says, a non-investment professional can amble through a shopping centre and discover good shops with good products. Perhaps they are listed and trading at a good price. A clear example is Inditex, possibly our biggest oversight, especially considering that I was born 30 km from their headquarters.

2. Investment professionals are subject to what Buffett calls the institutional imperative: we have the tendency to copy what everyone else does to minimise our own personal risk, but not the customer's. I have seen this apply, throughout my life, to boardrooms, CEOs, politicians, resident communities, etc. To paraphrase Keynes (occasionally he said sensible things), as people we prefer to be wrong together than right alone.

3. The stock market is a risky game, knowledge can reduce risk by enabling probabilities to be properly assigned. There are also gamblers who, through their hard work, are able to turn the probabilities in their favour and consistently obtain great returns. An example was the writer Charles Bukowski with horse racing.

4. You have to self-analyse. Do I have a house? Do I need the money? Do I have the skills to invest? These questions are easy to articulate but hard to answer. Buying a house is a good starting point in life. It is true that shares perform better over the long term, but a house is an asset that we understand very well and know how to value (let's forget about real-estate bubbles for the time being). We will go into more detail on this in Chapter 5. Investing the savings we don't need is self-explanatory, this is the only way to withstand the ups and downs of the markets. We will talk about the skills needed for investing later on, but suffice to say that this is the hardest question to answer, in some cases it will take years to get an answer and sometimes the question will have no response or the answer will be erroneous.

(continued)

5. There is no need to predict the economy, barring exceptional circumstances, nor the markets in the short term. It is about investing in companies. The quality of the company and its price is the other essential point; this enables us to step aside from short-term speculation and focus on what really matters.

6. Different types of companies have to be treated differently. Companies can be classified in different ways, and Lynch's classification is very useful: slow growers, stable growers, fast growers, companies with hidden assets, turnarounds, cyclicals. This is obviously a simplification, and some companies belong to various categories, but it is a good starting point. Each company warrants a different approach, and our expectations should adapt accordingly.

7. The characteristics of an ideal company: boring or disagreeable, with no analysts following it or institutions investing in it, which doesn't grow, which has a repetitive purchase product, which is a user of technology, in which the employees of the company buy shares.

   Sure enough, if a company's stock fulfils these requisites, it will be easy to make something on it. Tobacco companies have been a clear example of these types of shares.

8. On the contrary, eschew the new Microsoft or new Coca-Cola: companies that blithely diversify, with rumours or the flavour of the month.

9. There is an exceptional long-term correlation between earnings and share prices. The charts in Lynch's book illustrate this with marvellous simplicity.

10. And best of all is his 'cocktail party' theory. As the market rises, the guests at a cocktail or dinner party become more interested in fund managers, asking you for investment tips. But when the markets are euphoric and we are close to the top of the cycle, the guests start to recommend their own ideas, which may have been successful for a period. Then comes the crash and you fade into the wallpaper ... Until the new cycle begins.

We have all been in versions of this type of situation in bars, with family, and we will continue to experience them. Thankfully.

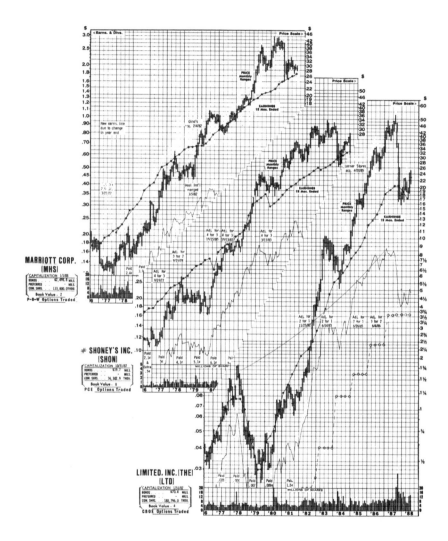

Lynch's charts, which relate earnings and share prices, perfectly illustrate how the long-term share price faithfully mirrors earnings developments. We have tried to reproduce these charts for Spain, as can be seen on this and the next page.

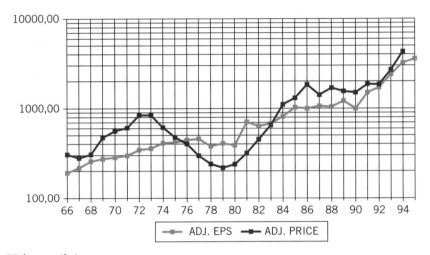

Hidrocantábrico

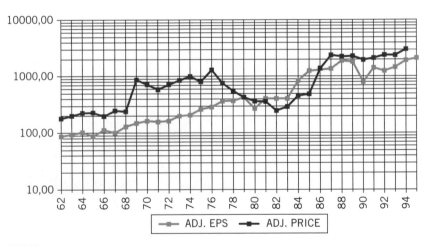

CEPSA

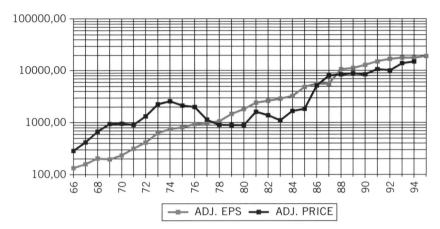

Banco Popular

CHAPTER 2

Going Solo (1991–2002)

1991–1998: I START INVESTING. BULL MARKET

Meanwhile, movements were afoot at Bestinver. Over the course of 1990, our diversification arm began to lose steam and at the start of 1991 the team in charge, led by José Ignacio Benjumea, upped sticks to set up a private equity project funded by the Rockefeller Foundation. Jorge Mataix and Luis Gabarda stayed behind as co-director generals. Santos Martínez-Conde, the head of analysis and portfolio management, also went with them. I mustered the nerve to ask the two co-directors whether I could take over responsibility for managing the Bestinver portfolios.

I felt I was capable of rising to the challenge, after having spent a year studying the Spanish stock market and analysing nearly all the key sectors. Luckily, there was not a lot of money to manage, which meant it wasn't completely preposterous for me to take on the responsibility – some two or three million euros, if memory serves me. If the amount had been larger it would have been unthinkable for them to entrust me with this responsibility; I was only 27 years old, with just a year of experience under my belt.

Despite some reluctance on the part of José María Entrecanales, who saw a certain 'wetness behind the ears', they conceded and I started life as an asset manager in 1991.

That same year we launched our first fund, Tibestfond. It was a cash fund that never amounted to much and later became Bestinver Renta, offering a decent alternative service to liquidity. We managed equities via mandates or private investment portfolios. At the start, it was just a handful of portfolios and next to no money, attracting no public attention.

1993–1994: UP AND DOWN (OR UP AND AWAY...)

At the end of 1992, we launched Bestinfond, which in time went on to offer one of the highest returns in Europe. Initially, it was a family fund, focused on the Spanish stock market, which gradually attracted external clients over time thanks to the returns it achieved. Ten years later it would go on to become the embodiment of our ideal mix of global and Spanish stocks.

It was an important step for all involved and required a cautious approach. After three years analysing stocks, studying the investment strategies of the masters – Buffett, Graham, etc. – and a little of market history, I was already certain of the style of investment I wanted to apply. But it needed to be very well explained and serious errors had to be avoided; the goal was to buy attractive shares at a time when they were unwanted or not valued by the markets, without worrying too much about general economic or stock market developments.

It is worth remembering that global stock markets had been tracking upwards for 10 years. The process had begun at the start of the 1980s, when Paul Volcker, Chairman of the Federal Reserve, broke the American economy's inflationary spiral once and for all. There was a brief interruption with the major shock of October 1987. However, this didn't lead to long-lasting losses in international markets and the indexes continued to rise for some time after.

In Spain, however, the stock market did perform somewhat more erratically from 1987 onwards. The economy experienced patchy growth, culminating with a recession in winter 1992–1993 caused by the hangover from excessive spending in previous years. May 1993 brought about the third peseta devaluation in quick succession, which, together with an improvement in the external environment, enabled the economy to recover.

We were therefore fortunate. After these somewhat bumpy years, exacerbated by the first Gulf War, the Spanish stock market found itself at the same level in December 1992 as it had been in December 1987, 35% below the 1989 peak. When a market stagnates for such a long period of time it tends to be storing up future gains. The prices of large caps, banks, electricity, etc. were extremely attractive and there wasn't much need for us to focus on small companies, which – while obviously offering more value – needed more careful explaining to clients. And we already know that it's not the same thing to get it wrong with Telefónica as it is with an unknown company.

Bestinfond's initial portfolio (see the table on the following page) was heavily invested in large caps, over 70%. Telefónica, Bilbao-Vizcaya, Banco Santander, Bankinter, and Iberdrola accounted for nearly 50% of our total equity investment. However, we had already begun to uncover some of the small-cap gems which would go on to become star performers for us over time, such as Electra de Viesgo, Hullas del Coto Cortés, and Vidrala. And who could forget Acerinox.

1993 was a positive year for global stock markets and it was exceptional for the Spanish market. The IGBM (Madrid Stock Exchange General Index) rose by 46%, supported by a sharp cut in interest rates in Spain. The yield on Treasury bills fell from 13.5% to 7.75% in less than 12 months. Bestinfond also performed very well, rising by 44%, especially bearing in mind that we were holding high levels of liquidity during the first three quarters,[1] nigh on 50%! We only lowered some of this liquidity towards the end of the year to end up with 30% cash. Continual price rises over the course of the year made it impossible to fully invest; it is generally not a wise idea to chase prices while they are rising.

Bestinfond's Initial Portfolio (31/12/1992)

STOCKS	Investment
Bankinter	18,495,840
Bilbao-Vizcaya	47,268,000
Pastor	10,764,000
Popular	10,780,000
Santander	34,872,797
Enher	8,308,000
Cantábrico	11,407,500
Iberdrola	16,900,000
Reunidas	3,888,750
E. de Viesgo	6,842,750
Campofrio	2,550,000
Ebro	3,792,000
Aumar	1,950,000
Acesa	17,100,000
Finan. Alba	3,750,000
Vidrala	4,500,000
Cubiertas	31,955,000
Metrovacesa	5,700,000
Acerinox	1,533,600
Hullas C. Cortes	10,603,800
Indo	3,000,000
Tabacalera	12,090,000
Telefónica	30,780,000

---

[1]Liquidity is the level of Treasury or cash not invested in shares. At the time I was still not fully aware of the dangers of liquidity, which back then was reasonably well remunerated at around 10% per annum. Furthermore, we tended to only hold high liquidity for very short periods, with the market adjusting almost immediately to facilitate rapid reinvestment.

(*Continued*)

STOCKS	Investment
TOTAL EQUITIES	298,832,037
Treasury bills	1,960,094
Debt repos.	252,277,797
TOTAL PUBLIC FUNDS	254,237,891
TOTAL DOMESTIC PORTFOLIO	553,069,928
TOTAL PORTFOLIO AT COST	582,224,810
PORTFOLIO CASH VALUE (pesetas)	553,069,928

Source: CNMV.

Generally speaking, it is harder to outperform the indexes in bull markets, but with half the investment we secured similar results to a benchmark index, delivering a strong increase in value – not at all bad for our first year operating as a public fund focused on equities. We ended the year reducing our position in large caps to 40% of the portfolio. Around this time some old friends began to appear, such as Elecnor, Citroën, Lingotes Especiales, and Unipapel. That year some of them went up in value by over 100%.

Then came 1994. Alan Greenspan hiked interest rates by surprise and the markets had a tough year overall. We started the year with a conservative portfolio and made the most of the fall from February onwards to increase our investment in equities, which accounted for over 90% in the second quarter, reaching 95% in the second half of the year.

The IGBM ultimately suffered a decline of 11.7% in 1994, but Bestinfond went up in value by 5.28%, proving to be the best-performing mutual fund in the Spanish stock market that year. The large caps had suffered the most and our limited exposure to them enabled the portfolio to perform well. However, banks – Santander, BBVA, Popular, Argentaria, and Bankinter – still accounted for between 30% and 40% of the portfolio that year. Seen from 2016, and knowing a bit about our philosophy, this might seem odd, but with the EU progressing solidly, following the signing of the Maastricht Treaty in 1992, Spain's economic outlook was very robust and the banking sector was an easy way to capitalise on the opportunity.

1994 was a key year. We showed that we could keep our trunks on in both a bull market such as 1993, as well as in 1994's bearish market. When the tide went out we weren't swimming naked, as Buffett has often warned. The stock market went up and the fund went up; the stock market went down and the fund kept going up. We won our first management prize and future clients started to take note of us, our net asset value (NAV, the share price at which the fund trades), and the fund's performance was being published daily in Spain's main economic press.

Left, Francisco García Paramés

These two years cemented trust among our client base, especially the most important ones – the Entrecanales family – forming a solid basis with which to weather the events that were to come our way over the next 20 years.

1995–1997: EUPHORIA RUNS WILD

The markets performed exceptionally over the following three years from 1995 to the end of 1997. Once the Gulf War had died down, which had temporarily delayed the benefits to be derived from the fall of the Berlin War, the market economy subsequently spread across the world. There were few major uncertainties and we experienced the final glorious 'autumn' of the long bull market initiated two decades before, at the start of the 1980s.

This positive cycle started with the liberalisation policies embraced by the United Kingdom and the United States. Following the calamitous 1970s, the UK and US governments finally turned their backs on expansionary public spending policies (which culminated with the Vietnam war and President Johnson's 'great society' in the United States and the negative effects of numerous post-war nationalisations in the United Kingdom: the 'winter of our discontent' and the UK's IMF loan). Furthermore, this liberalisation gradually spread – to a greater or lesser extent – across the West (underlined by President Mitterrand's policy U-turn in France).

The first quarter of 1995 was still negative. The IGBM fell by 5.66%, against a backdrop of political instability in Spain – the GAL plot, effectively state-sponsored terrorism, was in full swing – and another peseta devaluation. But in June the Fed once again cut interest rates and markets embarked on a breath-taking 36 months. The IGBM jumped from 268.85 points on 31 March 1995 to 888.67 points on 31 March 1998, more than tripling in value in three years.

While it was true that the market hadn't done much since 1989, it is equally true that the bull market went back a long way: the Madrid market had multiplied in value by 12 since 1980, as Spain began to leave behind the debilitating crisis of the 1970s. All in all, an exceptional performance in three unbeatable years. As of June 2016, some 20 years later, the IGBM stood at 780 points. The banking crisis is partly to blame for this disappointing performance, but the extremely high starting point – coming off the back of previous price increases – conditioned future developments.

Our portfolio obtained spectacular returns during those three glorious years in absolute terms, tripling net asset value, though lagging a little behind the overall market. As I have already noted, when the market rises quickly, it becomes quite a lot harder to outperform. It is always easier to create relative value from falls.

Nonetheless, it is worth pointing out that in our case the increase in value took place while holding a high average level of liquidity throughout the period – around 25%. This gives additional merit to the returns achieved, but is also an indication that we were facing a lot of uncertainty. In fact, ever more expensive share prices led us to gradually increase liquidity over the period. We were already struggling to come up with sufficient ideas to invest 100% of assets in the stock market, meaning that by the end of the year we were holding 19% liquidity, which we maintained and increased slightly over the remainder of the upswing.

Another transformation was taking place in the portfolio, with the gradual disappearance of large caps. By the end of 1996, they accounted for just 20%. Meanwhile the list of secondary stocks began to lengthen: Electra de Viesgo, Cubiertas, Fiponsa, OMSA, CAF (Construcciones y Auxiliar de Ferrocarriles), BP Oil … (BP's Spanish subsidiary, for which, oddly enough, we received two takeover bids: we took part in the first, repurchasing later and subsequently BP launched a public tender offer, which we also participated in).

In December 1996, Federal Reserve Chairman, Alan Greenspan, made his famous remarks on the 'irrational exuberance' of stock markets. The price rises during previous years had meant that shares were now becoming seriously overpriced. The markets fell briefly during the following days, but later regained momentum.

Spanish elections in 1996 saw the centre-right come to power for the first time since the transition to democracy in 1979, and it became increasingly clear that the first stage of Monetary Union was about to get underway, providing an additional stimulus to the markets.

We kept liquidity at a very high level in 1997, some 30%. Little by little we completely unwound our holdings of large caps: Banco Santander, Repsol, and the like. We continued to focus on the medium caps which had been left behind, particularly increasing our positions in ERZ and Enher, very defensive electricity stocks. Selling Banco Santander was a poignant moment for me, it having been the first share I bought back in 1990. After seven years the market price now reflected its capacity to generate earnings over the long term. I had begun to have reservations about the bank and now, nearly 20 years later, the bank's shares are trading at similar levels…

Still, the market did not see any clouds on the horizon. Only towards the end of 1997, while on honeymoon in Italy, did some insipid warning signs emerge out of Southeast Asia, but the market shrugged them off. The biggest bull market of the twentieth century had been running for 15 years and it appeared as though nothing could stand in its path.

1998: THE END OF THE CYCLE

Gradually we woke up to the reality of our position in the centre of the storm, at the worst moment for any sensible investor: the end of a long upswing. And everything pointed in this direction.

In the first quarter of 1998 the IGBM was revalued by 40.9%, while Bestinfond remained at 22.12%. 40% in a quarter after two years of increases of 41%! I am not sure whether there has been a similar quarter in the history of the market, but at the time it struck me as total lunacy.

We continued with the process of selling shares, meaning that by the end of the quarter liquidity had climbed to 32%. Never before (except at the very outset) had we held so much liquidity.

It was also the first time that our approach came under real scrutiny; our returns were significantly below the market. Indeed, at the start of 1998 we began to have issues with some clients. It wasn't easy to espouse an investment philosophy in those markets. Many investors had obtained and were continuing to obtain significant returns from investing their own money, and they thought that we were the ones in the wrong. As Peter Lynch explained in his cocktail party theory, these are the times when clients tell you where you have to invest. The only way to cope with end-of-cycle euphoria is with time and patience.

When I speak of patience it is not just about waiting for the shares we have invested in to rise, but also being able to sit tight until expensive stocks fall to more attractive prices. And this can be even harder still.

I felt obliged to call on some clients personally to reassure them, explaining that it was a highly critical moment, which required taking maximum precaution. Ultimately, some clients ended up leaving the fund and for the first time I had to stand firm in the face of external irrationality.

By the summer of 1998 we had taken an extreme liquidity position in the fund, representing 31% of total assets. In fact, liquidity would have been over 60% had it not been for our investment in the subsidiaries of the electricity company, Endesa.

We had just under 30% of assets invested in Electra de Viesgo, ERZ, Enher, and Saltos del Nansa – good distributing utilities with superb generating assets, which were mainly hydraulic. These were top-class electricity assets at very reasonable prices given the market conditions, which is why to date they have been the most significant investment in a single 'area' that we have made in 25 years.

This one-off focus on a single sector was influenced by a relationship that I struck up with Xavier Cuadrat, a professor of sociology at the Complutense University of Madrid. Xavier is a market enthusiast who started investing his savings at the beginning of the 1980s, riding on the coat tails of the long bull market. He had and continues to have (though I don't see him much these days) the trait of foraging into the heart of companies. He goes to AGMs in far-flung places, speaks with whoever he can, and visits assets wherever they may be, combining visits to Romanesque churches with water dams.

I too was already doing a similar type of thing (I remember attending Prim's AGM – a company which distributes medical products – and having the sensation of gate-crashing a baptism or communion for one of the family's children), but he made me even more aware of the need to take this route. I ended up visiting the impressive dams at the Tajo and Duero rivers and going down Hullera Vasco-Leonesa's coal mines.

Bestinfond Portfolio (30/06/1998)

STOCKS	Investment (millions of pesetas)	% Total
CAF	276	2.54
Electra de Viesgo	1.037	9.54
Reunidas de Zaragoza	1.082	9.96
Elecnor	494	4.55
Ence	0	0.00
Enher	1020	9.39
Acerinox	103	0.95
Cevasa	146	1.34
Cevasas Nuevas	0	0.00
Fasa Renault	281	2.59
Frimancha I. Cárnicas	4	0.04
Grupo Anaya	352	3.24
H. Cantábrico	94	0.87
Hullas Coto Cortés	163	1.50
Hullera Vasco Leonesa	72	0.66
Koxka	94	0.87
Iberpapel	88	0.81
Indo Intern.	38	0.35
Lingotes especiales	41	0.38
Liwe España	0	0.00
Oscar Mayer	254	2.34
Papelera Navarra	526	4.84
Prim	115	1.06
Roberto Zubiri-A	6	0.06
Saltos del Nansa	14	0.13
Uniland	39	0.36
Unipapel	340	3.13
Dchos. lingotes Esp. Serie A	16	0.15
Dchos. lingotes Esp. Serie B	17	0.16
TOTAL EQUITIES	7.475	68.80
TOTAL INTERIOR	10.865	100.00
TOTAL PORTFOLIO	10.865	100.00

Source: CNMV.

SHADOW REPORT ON ENDESA AND ITS SUBSIDIARIES

Summary of Appraisals

Exchanges according to the criteria used by minority shareholders in Enher, ERZ, Viesgo, and Saltos del Nansa, and to the proposal made by Endesa (only for subsidiaries where there are major differences):

Minority Shareholder Criteria

> 1 Enher × 2.57 Endesa
> 1 ERZ × 3.66 Endesa
> 1 Viesgo × 2.54 Endesa
> 1 Nansa × 8.04 Endesa

Endesa Criteria

> 24 Enher × 25 Endesa + 200 Ptas
> 1 ERZ × 2 Endesa + 38 Ptas
> 14 Viesgo × 23 Endesa + 345 Ptas
> 5 Nansa × 19 Endesa + 171 Ptas

According to the valuation models described later on, we obtain the following share price for the Endesa Group:

Endesa Group Valuation	Millions of pesetas
ASSETS	3,969
Electricity holding Assets	992
Subsidiary valuation	1,765
Parent diversification	219
International parent	436
Other parent assets	557
PARENT LIABILITIES	1,000
Net debt	795
Pensions	205
NET EQUITY	2,969
No. shares (millions)	954,8
VALUE ENDESA/SHARE (pesetas)	3,109

Using the exact same valuation criteria, we obtain the following valuation for their subsidiaries:

Valuation Subsidiaries	Valuation (billion pesetas)	Valuation (pesetas/share)
Enher	501	8,016
ERZ	220	11,340
Viesgo	154	7,897
Sevillana	560	1,877
Fecsa	428	2,055
Gesa	134	11,814
Nansa	25	25,000
Elcogas	8	—
Unelco	200	6,529

This knowledge gave us the confidence to commit to making such a significant investment in what was basically a single idea.

As a side note, it is worth pointing out that Endesa ultimately launched an operation to merge all its subsidiaries using a very self-interested exchange equation, which failed to reflect the true value of the subsidiary's assets (see tables above). Unfortunately, unlike on other occasions when we were able to successfully convince the parent company to improve its offer for their Spanish subsidiaries – PSA-Citroën and Renault (although they were delisting tender offers, where CNMV had the last word) – we were not able to change their minds. For Endesa it was an important operation, which helped to compensate for the loss in value of their Latin American investments, meaning that they dug in on their preferred exchange equations, supported by an 'independent' valuation from Deloitte, who did not cover themselves in glory on that occasion. We weighed up taking it to court, but decided against given the uncertainties involved with a long-drawn-out process, which would have done little more than distract us.

ACTIVISM

I have always taken the view that I am not an activist shareholder, and that I only invest in well-managed companies requiring few changes. Though there are two exceptions to this:

- When the situation is clearly unfair, such as the one above or what happened to Ciba in 2008 (More on this later).

- When there is a dispute between two 'factions' of shareholders, obliging us to take a stance. When this happens it is usually because we have got it wrong and the company is not on the right track. Koenig & Bauer, a world leader in the manufacture of printing machines, is a recent example of this; a group of minority shareholders tried to force through a change in the management team.

Either way, I only get involved in 'activism' when I have a significant stake; when my investment is small, I let larger shareholders lead the way. At the end of the day it's about making efficient use of my most scarce resource, which is my time.

Under normal conditions I limit myself to insisting on the virtues of share buybacks, since if I invest in a company it's because I think the market is undervaluing its assets. So, reducing the number of shares at this market price makes economic sense. Otherwise, if I am asked about issues related to management, I politely respond that there are limits to my knowledge and I turn down opportunities to participate on management boards.

I do this for various reasons:

- I don't have the time. With a diversified portfolio of shares, there is no way I could handle the enormous demands associated with being a director in a listed company.
- I don't have the knowledge. Each company and sector is unique, making it difficult to enter into depth in the management. I would love to acquire this level of knowledge, but it would reduce the time available for other companies.
- It would limit my management flexibility, restricting the purchase and sale of shares to specific time periods to avoid falling foul of insider trading rules. This restriction could run counter to my interests and those of our shareholders.
- This has always been my position, which new Spanish legislation has 'reinforced' by barring fund managers from naming directors in companies in which they are invested, to avoid influencing the management! Say no more: bureaucracy in action.

Either way, it is worth bearing in mind that I have tended to be quite susceptible to family-run companies, which have historically accounted for more than 70% of our invested assets. This allows us to delegate control of management and the managers to the family. Who better than the family owners to ensure that the managers are looking after the shareholders' long-term interests. However, you obviously also have to watch out for nepotism, with unqualified family members becoming heavily involved in the management. We will look into this in the second part of the book.

END OF THE CYCLE

In the summer of 1998 the crisis and the conditions that would trigger it were already brewing. 1997 had already produced a flicker in Asia of what was to come. Many developing economies – such as Thailand, Malaysia, and Indonesia – were growing, based on strong imbalances, particularly external, and were dependent on a continual flow of external investment to finance growth.

These problems worsened in 1998, broadening to other countries such as Russia (also affected by the falling oil price) and Latin America. This culminated in one of the largest and most prestigious hedge funds in the world, Long Term Capital Management (LTCM) – led by an array of Wall Street professionals and Nobel Prize winners in Economics – running into dramatic liquidity problems and requiring a rescue. Furthermore, the Fed injected an exceptional amount of liquidity into the system through successive interest rate cuts.

The rescue averted the crisis of the summer of 1998, but the liquidity injected into the system sowed the seed for a still larger crisis two years later.

Fortunately, the markets seized on this as a good excuse (they always find one) to correct some of the excessive prices. Between the beginning of July and the start of September, the Spanish index (which had risen by 50% from January) fell by around 40%, while our funds retreated by 10%. This afforded us the opportunity to reinvest the bulk of our liquidity at much more attractive prices. We ended the year with liquidity of 10%. We obtained overall returns in 1998 of 30%, below the market returns of 37%, but a respectable difference given that the volatility and the risk level of our investments had been much lower. This is crucial and bears repeating: we took on much less risk.

It's my personal belief that the 20-year bull market came to an end in the summer of 1998. The Dow Jones had risen from 790 in 1982 to 9,000 by the summer of 1998, multiplying more than 10-fold, the biggest increase in prices in history over such a length of time.

Buffet explained it all very well in an article published in *Fortune* on 22 November 1999. Over 17 years he had obtained an annual average return of 19% from investing in shares, an astonishing achievement for this period. Yet he now saw the outlook for the next 17 years at a maximum of 4% per year. He may not be a prophet, but 17 years on the Dow Jones had clocked up a 2% annual real return.

While most indexes went on to hit record highs in March 2000, by that time there were also numerous attractive companies on offer; but back in summer 1998 it was practically impossible to find value in any of the markets. The cheapest sector in Spain was trading at a P/E ratio of 17, and the

Spanish stock market as a whole had an average P/E ratio of 25. The banks traded at five times book value ...

Our approach during this long bull market was to try to take advantage of opportunities in the market, generally with secondary stocks, while at the same time preparing the portfolio for what would sooner or later happen: a sharp downward adjustment in prices. The Fed kicked the can down the road in 1998 with its liquidity injection, but it couldn't be avoided months later.

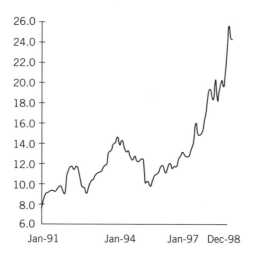

IBEX P/E Ratio

Market Valuation

	1997	March 1998	April 1998	May 1998
Growth in EPS (%)	13.5	13.0	14.2	14.2
Return on own funds (%)	12.2	12.8	13.0	13.0
Dividend yield (%)	2.4	1.9	2.0	2.0
Long-term interest (%)	5.6	5.1	5.1	5.0
P/E ratio (x)	20.5	25.6	24.4	24.3
IBEX 35	7,255	10,209	10,025	10,005
IGBM	632	889	871	875

Source: AB Asesores Morgan Stanley Dean Witter Research.

Valuation of Banking Sector (prices to 29/05/1998)

Banks		Relative Return	%	Growth in EPS	P/E Ratio	Relative P/E Ratio	Price/CF (cash flow)	Dividend Yield (%)	Relative Return
1	15,168.7	1M	−3.2 97	28.0	31.2	1.1	14.4	1.3	1.6	0.9
2	5.0	3M	−6.3 98J	21.9	25.4	1.1	17.0	0.2	2.0	1.0
3	n.m.	12M	23.7 99J	17.2	21.7	1.0	16.2	0.2	2.3	1.0

Source: AB Asesores Morgan Stanley Dean Witter Research.

	Last Price			%		EPS	P/E	CFPS	P/CF	Divid.	Yield (%)
Argentaria	4M										
1	1,581.5	12,910	1M	2.0	97	514	25.1	573	22.5	295	2.3
2	4,690	14,350	3M	−0.3	98J	600	21.5	700	18.5	314	2.4
3	n.m.	7,200	12M	11.0	99J	689	18.7	811	15.9	341	2.6
Bankinter	3M										
1	411.9	9,950	1M	−3.2	97	433	23.0	480	20.7	228	2.3
2	3,343	11,880	3M	−10.7	98J	477	20.8	521	19.1	286	2.9
3	n.m.	6,800	12M	−24.0	99J	533	18.7	570	17.4	320	3.2
B.B.V.	2M										
1	5,147.0	7,610	1M	−2.3	97	194	39.3	416	18.3	96	1.3
2	1,147	8,060	3M	−4.2	98J	259	29.4	439	17.3	129	1.7
3	mm.	3,366	12M	43.6	99J	310	24.5	432	17.6	155	2.0
B.C.H.	4M										
1	1,829.6	4,965	1M	−2.7	97	129	38.6	271	18.3	64	1.3
2	1,097	5,190	3M	−6.0	98J	176	28.1	315	15.8	88	1.8
3	n.m.	2,262	12M	34.8	99J	217	22.9	347	14.3	109	2.2
Popular	3L										
1	1,360.5	12,020	1M	−5.7	97	595	20.2	711	16.9	300	2.5
2	2,641	15,240	3M	−22.1	98J	656	18.3	746	16.1	329	2.7
3	n.m.	7,647	12M	−2.4	99J	719	16.7	815	14.7	359	3.0
Santander	2M										
1	4,377.6	7,630	1M	−5.4	97	231	33.0	882	8.7	122	1.6
2	1,141	8,210	3M	−5.1	98J	283	27.0	450	17.0	134	1.8
3	n.m.	3,700	12M	15.1	99J	335	22.8	460	16.6	167	2.2

1. Market capitalisation (billions of pesetas):
2. Book Value/Share
3. Net Debt/Own Funds
Source: AB Asesores Morgan Stanley Dean Witter Research.

With the benefit of hindsight, I believe those years were probably the most important of my professional career. It's no simple undertaking managing to survive at the end of the longest bull market in the twentieth century, managing to post a reasonable return while being conscious of the dangers on the cards for the following years. Not only was it necessary to be well acquainted with the markets and companies, but also with oneself and the environment. And all of this needed to be managed appropriately. In such heady market conditions, clients – who have been successful with their own individual investments without having to put in much effort – think they know better than you.

Surviving that storm unscathed prepared me to overcome the crises that were to come later, the 2000 dot.com crash and the 2008 financial crisis. Seen from the perspective of the late 1990s, the latter seemed almost like child's play.

1998–2002: DOWNSWING. GLOBAL PORTFOLIO

So far this account has only focused on our portfolio in the Spanish stock market. Up to that point Bestinfond had only invested in Spain.

The start of 1998 was therefore a key milestone, with the launch of Bestinver Internacional. The main proponent was Javier Colomina, the managing director at the time, who was insistent that this was the way to go. I accepted the challenge, albeit with a healthy dose of scepticism.

It was certainly true that to manage in the Spanish stock market it was necessary to take account of the global environment and the pricing of comparable companies (for example, there's no sense in analysing Telefónica in isolation). However, I always believed – and still do – that you have to focus on what you do well. And at that time what I knew how to do was navigate the Spanish market. I was not at all certain whether I would be capable of investing globally.

But we got down to work, and the first year proved to be an absolute disaster ... not so much in terms of philosophy, or experience, or laying the groundwork, but definitely in terms of results.

Lacking the necessary certainty and conviction to create a portfolio off the bat and faced with the added difficulty of a very overvalued market, we invested heavily in fixed income for most of the year, at around 50%. We diversified our investment in equities among funds and other products, such as commodity-backed bonds.

Our equity position at the end of the cycle was designed to make the most of low prices in Asian markets and commodities (I am struck by a certain déjà vu as I write this in late 2015!). Investment in Asian stocks through funds or structured products accounted for more than 20% of the portfolio; exposure to oil and other commodities another 20% (oil was trading at 15 dollars per barrel); and finally, less than 10% was invested in a limited group of shares in small European companies.

Commodities have never had much weight in our investment, they are too exposed to market-imposed prices, but at that time – as in 2015 – there were opportunities worth exploiting.

With such a peculiar structure and a lack of sufficient conviction, the fund was destined not to perform in the short run, and that's what happened. Hampered by a further decline in crude oil from 15 dollars to below 10, and by a lack of recovery in Asian markets, the year ended with a 14% loss. A great start to the fund's life! Especially bearing in mind that global indexes rose by 10% that year.

Being able to overcome these types of situations is critical for an investor wanting to get things right in the long term. It's not just critical but also inevitable: there are always going to be bad runs. No one avoids them. You have to ride them out. To do so successfully requires three things. First, having earned the confidence of investors and the environment in general. Second, being resolute and unwavering in your philosophy. Third, praying like crazy for it to be over with quickly!

For us the small scale of the fund, three million euros, and the limited number of shareholders played to our advantage. It gave us a certain amount of room to experiment, provided it didn't blow up in our faces. We tested the patience of our investors and shareholders, but miraculously the international portfolio rose 43% in the first half of 1999, well above global indexes, thanks to the recovery in Asian markets and oil prices. This enabled us to comfortably recoup the first year's losses.

Bestinver Internacional Portfolio (30/09/1998)

STOCKS	Investment	% Total
TOTAL MONETARY ASSETS	11	2.51
Government bonds 11512	10	2.28
Government bonds 11462	0	0.00
Total temporary purchases	10	2.28
TOTAL SPANISH FIXED INCOME	21	4.79
TOTAL SPANISH EQUITIES	0	0.00
TOTAL DOMESTIC PORTFObIO	21	4.79
Treasury bills Germany	85	19.41
Bonds Den Danske Bank	27	6.16
Bonds Gohnan Sachs Petroleum	17	3.88

(*Continued*)

STOCKS	Investment	% Total
Argentaria PFD 7.2 Serie C USD	9	2.05
Federal Home Loan Bank	15	3.42
Bonds Fnma 5% 16-02-01 Dem	27	6.16
DSL Bandk 6.25% Mat 29-12-99	27	6.16
B. Birds Notes on Nikkei USD	46	10.50
Bonds BNP Finance 4% GRD	15	3.42
TOTAL FOREIGN FIXED INCOME	268	61.19
GT Berry Japan Fund-B	20	4.57
Asian Capital Holding	23	5.25
JF Asean Trust	7	1.60
Cie Financ Richemont-Uts A	12	2.74
Sgs Soc Gen Surveillance- B	4	0.91
Outokumpu	7	1.60
Metaleurop, S.A.	15	3.42
Enterprise Oil Pic	5	1.14
Premier Oil	12	2.74
Banca Populare	6	1.37
Saga Petroleum serie A	24	5.48
Saga Petroleum serie B	8	1.83
Chile Fund	6	1.37
TOTAL FOREIGN EQUITIES	149	34.02
TOTAL EXTERNAL PORTFOLIO	417	95.21
TOTAL PORTFOLIO (millions of pesetas)	438	100.00

Source: CNMV.

Not only that, but little by little we managed to invest the fixed income in attractive companies, finishing 1999 with an equity investment of 80%. 25% was still in Asian funds and commodities, but 50% was already in small and medium-sized global companies. Dassault Aviation, which went on to be one of our firm favourites, entered into the portfolio at this time, as well as others such as the Swiss companies Bel and SGS.

We were able to invest in small companies in 1999, because the markets had embarked on one of the most extreme episodes of schizophrenia in their history: the overpricing of everything related to new technologies (TMT) and the underpricing of traditional companies. Thus, while in summer 1998 it had been impossible to find good companies at a decent price, by 1999 this was now an option.

In 1999 our international fund was still very small compared with our overall size – three million euros (compared with 176 million euros of total assets under management and a total of 80 million euros in Spanish stocks; the rest were fixed-income funds) – and was yet to earn its stripes.

Our eggs were still firmly placed in the Spanish stock market basket. And 1999 was not an easy year. Not by any stretch of the imagination.

Bestinver Internacional Portfolio (31/12/1999)

STOCKS	Investment	% Total
Government bonds 11355	0	0.00
Government bonds 11595	62	12.53
TOTAL PUR. ASSETS	62	12.53
TOTAL SPANISH FIXED INCOME	62	12.53
TOTAL DOMESTIC PORTFOLIO	62	12.53
Bonds Goldman Sachs Comodity	0	0.00
B. Birds Notes on Nikkei USD	48	9.70
Ctystp 9.5% USD	27	5.45
TOTAL FOREIGN FIXED INCOME	75	15.15
Sgs Soc. Gen. Surveillance-B	8	1.62
Outokumpu	14	2.83
Metaleurop, S.A.	19	3.84
Eridania Beghin	9	1.82
Dassault Aviation	12	2.42
Enterprise Oil Pic	6	1.21
Premier Oil	16	3.23
Somerfield	12	2.42
Boskalis CT	12	2.42
Opg	10	2.02
Vedior	7	1.41
Dimon Incorporated	13	2.63
Codan Forsikring DKK	9	1.82
Beln Sw	19	3.84
Barry Callebaut AG	11	2.22
Holzmann (Philipp) AG	0	0.00
Krones AG Pfd DEM	8	1.62
Schmalbach Lubeca AG	16	3.23
Metsa-Serla OY B ORD	0	0.00
CNP Assurance	24	4.85
UAF	15	3.03
Schweitzer Mauduit Intl. Inc.	11	2.22
Invesco GT Japan Fund-C	38	7.68
Asian Capital Holding	27	5.45
Chile Fund	9	1.82
Fourmi Japan II	33	6.67
TOTAL FOREIGN EQUITIES	358	72.32
TOTAL EXTERNAL PORTFOLIO	433	87.47
TOTAL PORTFOLIO	495	100.00
TOTAL PORTFOLIO (thousands of euros)	2,975	100.00

Source: CNMV.

1999: THE LOW POINT

If 1998 was a tough year for the Spanish portfolio, 1999 and the first quarter of 2000 were something else.

During the first three quarters, the markets were very muted. The index fell 0.5% and our fund declined by 3.5%, very bearable losses. 30% of the assets remained linked to Endesa, due to the merger of its subsidiaries. It was not an ideal situation, and we weren't comfortable with it, but we had to wait a few months to unwind the position in Endesa.

We were clearly avoiding large caps and particularly Telefónica and telecommunications, because they were extremely overpriced. The portfolio was made up exclusively of medium and small caps. We started the fourth quarter with liquidity of over 20%, because the previous months had not given us enough time to fully reinvest the cash generated from selling Endesa.

Thus, when the stock market rebounded by a surprise 17.36% in the fourth quarter, our fund fell by 7.65%. A difference of 25%! As I explained earlier, in the first half of 1998 we had lagged the market, but at least our clients had obtained positive returns. This time around it was different, our clients lost money when the stock market went up ...

Yet, during this time of great unease, I never lost confidence in the virtues of our strategy. I had already read extensively on the history of markets and I was convinced that the situation would turn around soon. Books such as those by Kindleberger, MacKay, and John Brooks, and specialist articles and analysis, were very useful reminders of past bubbles.

It was widely remarked that telecommunications and the development of the Internet were going to change our way of life, removing any trace of our previous existence, leaving it obsolete, but I was certain that it wasn't going to be a pleasant or profitable process, the inflated investment in this segment of the economy would lead to the typical excesses seen in the past.

Of all the nonsense that was said during this period to justify the boom, there is one piece that is particularly worth recalling, because it came from 'one of ours': *Barron's*. In December the prestigious American weekly *Barron's*, probably the best among those dedicated to investment, devoted its front page to Warren Buffett,[2] criticising his lack of exposure to the TMTs (Telecommunications, Media, and Technology): 'To be blunt, Buffett, who turns seventy in 2000, is viewed by an increasing number of investors as too conservative, even passé. He may be the world's greatest

---

[2]'What's wrong Warren?', *Barron's*, 27 December 1999.

investor, but he hasn't anticipated or capitalised on the boom in technology stocks in the past few years'.

If this was happening to Buffett after an incredible 40-year track record, I could sleep easy at night.

Not only was I unwavering, but I believed that an extraordinary and unexpected opportunity was presenting itself, of the type that only crops up in our memories or our wildest dreams. Between 1997 and 1998 I had viewed the investment outlook with concern in the face of sky-high share prices, but the dichotomy that was opening up in 1999 and 2000 between TMT and 'traditional' stocks had the makings of an enormous relative return, which is what happened.

Either way, in December, we sent a special letter to our clients trying to convey a sense of composure and asserting that the quality of our stocks would ultimately see out the technology frenzy. We predicted that Telefónica, Terra, etc. would suffer losses of 70–80%, as proved to be the case. It was the first time we had written this type of letter, but it wouldn't be the last. Some nine years later we had to once again resort to special communications with our clients.

Madrid, December 1999

Dear client,

In 1999 the returns obtained by our equity funds – Bestinfond, Bestinver Bolsa, and Bestinver Mixto – were not up to our, nor our shareholders', expectations. The excellent returns of the past are no solace to clients who started investing in these funds in 1999. We may well end the year with slightly negative returns on these funds and there is a reason for this: in our opinion, the group of stocks in which we have invested have the potential for very strong growth and price increases, but this has not yet been reflected in the share price. The market is currently engaged in trading in technology stocks: Telefónica, Terra, etc. We intend to avoid these stocks which can create (as happened 20 years ago with Telefónica) losses of around 70–80% on your investment.

Our primary concern is to maintain the value of money over time, although to do so in some years we may suffer slight losses and we have to avoid getting involved in speculative actions. Our focus is elsewhere and we hope that newer clients will bear with us, so as to be able to enjoy the benefits that this policy offers over the long run.

In any case, now more than ever, we are at your disposal to clarify any queries concerning our funds or our investments, which are – of course – yours.

Yours faithfully,
Francisco García Paramés
Investment Director

As an aside, I should point out that we did actually make a small concession to the bubble. In February 2000, as a sop to some clients who felt they were missing out on the biggest steal in history, we bought a bond for their private portfolios which was 100% guaranteed and linked to the Nasdaq, the technology index. It was a tiny concession, which did not do any harm, given that it was completely guaranteed. There were no losses and everyone came out of the experience happy.

Why Invest for Others? Why Invest at All?

By contrast, I did have some concerns regarding a more existential issue: whether I was happy managing other people's money or not.

There are various pros and cons, but the drawbacks were particularly obvious at that time: you have less to worry about and complete independence if you only manage your own money.

But there is also much to be said for it. Firstly, it is a good business, and if you manage things well, the same level of effort can yield exceptional results. Costs are reasonably stable, meaning that profits move practically in line with revenue. Secondly, there are lots of investors out there who need help. How do you turn them down? While it's true that the market offers a range of alternatives, by default everyone believes that their own strategy and portfolio is the best one out there. If so, how can we refuse to let family members, friends, etc. enjoy the benefits? Thirdly, we have never gone out of our way to actively attract the clients who knock on our door. It requires a certain initiative and interest on their part, meaning that they tend to be people who are very attractive, both on a professional and a personal level. Indeed, many of their contributions have helped refine our management, forming a large family with a single destination (a bit like a nation ...). Fourthly, hard times tend not to last long; at least this has been our good fortune, as is being illustrated.

These compelling motives quelled my doubts at that time and I continued to manage other people's savings. Nor can I say that I am plagued by these concerns at present, now that I have had the opportunity to start from scratch and decide how to focus my investment approach, relatively free from past constraints. The four arguments are still valid, although back then the first factor – being a profitable business – was more important to me. Nowadays, the emotional commitment that I have built up with a large number of people over a long time is clearly the driving factor, and it's what gives the work a meaning that it didn't have at the outset. It is extremely satisfying to observe how effective management of people's savings has an impact over the years. I am aware that for many clients I have been a key source of support to them in their lives, allowing them to have greater independence and more alternatives in their personal and professional decisions.

In reality, my thoughts often revolve around the bigger question of why do I do what I do? What drives me to do it? Sometimes I have the sensation that it is fate, how things had to be. When I was very young I was inclined to presume that things would go well for me, I had a degree of certainty in my own capabilities; I didn't know what form it would take nor how, but I couldn't conceive, nor did I want to, of anything else. I envisaged a peaceful life for myself, with a career focused on business – I didn't detect any artistic streak – and a family with children. I have always been intensely independent, but breaking new ground was not part of the plan (though now that I think about it, perhaps I have in some areas).

As I have already mentioned, being an analyst suited by introspective and shy personality, which – nourished by reading – formed a good basis for my personal development. I find the work itself rewarding. It is well known that when you have the sensation of mastering something it creates an affinity, and it's not necessary to have a preconceived idea of destiny. Things just turn out that way.

A path revealed itself to me. One that had to be followed because it emerged out of my upbringing and my personal education. I am not talking about the path that is expected of you, less still a politically correct one, but a path which you believe is right and essential. Inevitable. Unwavering. Each day a step, each step more assured. A career path.

But beyond being interesting work and a good professional career, I also find a certain overarching meaning that overwhelms me and forces me to look outside and consider the impact of my work on those around me.

At the same time, I have always had a desire, almost an urge, to be right, to find the truth; not my own truth but a shared truth, though it may not always be understood as such by others. I am not talking about metaphysical truth, which I have never been able to possess, but more of the tangible variety, despite my aversion to physics.

It comes down to truth and, let's be honest, recognition. I can't deny it. It's not the be all and end all, but ultimately we are talking about humanity; life itself.

In any case, I have always been free to make my own decisions. My family, specifically my wife María Ángeles, have always respected and supported all the decisions I have taken. If I had decided to leave investment behind for something else she would have accepted the change, taking on the new situation with unerring conviction in my principles.

After this digression, I still don't know how to respond to the question. I don't have a meaningful response for why I do what I do, but I know that I will keep doing it until the end.

2000–2002: BACK TO NORMALITY

The frenzy went on for another two months, but in March 2000 the tables turned and the market set off on a downward path that lasted for three years, with an accumulated loss of 40%.

During these difficult times, as already mentioned, our Spanish portfolio was dominated by small and medium caps. Our main positions were in Corporación Mapfre 8%, Aldeasa 8%, CAF 6%, Elecnor 6%, and Mapfre Vida 5%. They were trading at an average of nine times earnings, a P/E ratio of nine, and were some of the stars that enabled our portfolio to post an accumulated return of 49% over three years of bear markets. For example, CAF went up in value from 14 euros in 2000 to 440 in 2010 (see Spanish Portfolio on 31/03/2000 on the following page).

When I am asked whether equities are expensive, I always give the same response: there are cheap and expensive stocks. The stock market is not some uniform mass; it is made up of lots of companies that have to be weighed up to determine whether they are expensive or not at a given time. It's true that there is usually a correlation between stock movements, and when some are expensive the rest usually are too. However, there are continual exceptions to the rule, as occurred in 2000–2002. This is exactly what enabled us to obtain exceptional returns in a bear market.

2000 also marked another turning point, we completed the transformation of the international portfolio to focus on stock selection. By the end of the year our hand-picked stocks accounted for 75% of total assets, with the remainder in Asian funds and liquidity. In a world of doing everything at breakneck speed, we had taken three years to invest the portfolio in our stocks, preferring to take our time and do things right. From then on we always selected our own stocks.

2000 was also a good year for the international portfolio, both in terms of absolute returns and relative to the MSCI index. Gradually we were building up the confidence to take the lead, and even began recommending the fund to our clients. The period of apprenticeship and experimentation had come to an end.

Spanish Portfolio: Bestinver Bolsa (31/03/2000)

STOCKS	Investment	% Total
Government debentures 8% (30-5-4) 11488	2	0.12
TOTAL OTHER ASSETS FIX. INC.	2	0.12
Government debt 11512	69	4.17
Government debt 12247	0	0.00
TOTAL PUR. ASSETS	69	4.17
TOTAL FIXED INCOME	71	4.30
Catalana de Occidente	106	6.41
Corporación Mapfre	150	9.07
Fiponsa	27	1.63
Informes y proyectos	7	0.42
Adolfo Domínguez	86	5.20
Aldeasa	146	8.83
Aumar	0	0.00
Campofrio	40	2.42
C.A.F.	123	7.44
Dinamia	88	5.32
Elecnor	99	5.99
Cepsa	0	0.00
Cevasa	56	3.39
Hidrocantábrico	77	4.66
Hullas del Coto Cortés	26	1.57
Hullera Vasco Leonesa	11	0.67
Iberpapel	53	3.21
Indo	18	1.09
Inacsa	0	0.00
Koipe	66	3.99
Lingotes	15	0.91
Miquel y Costas	80	4.84
Natra	47	2.84
Papelera Navarra	97	5.87
Prim	42	2.54
Uniland	11	0.67
Unipapel	111	6.72
TOTAL EQUITIES	1,582	95.70
TOTAL DOMESTIC PORTFOLIO	1,653	100.00
TOTAL PORTFOLIO	1,653	100.00
TOTAL PORTFOLIO (thousands of euros)	9,935	100.00

Source: CNMV.

MY ENCOUNTER WITH HAYEK

I had already read quite a bit about markets and I had seen for myself the regular ups and downs, but I hadn't found a theoretical framework which could give an effective account of them.

When I first read Frederich A. Hayek at the end of 2000, I was intrigued by the boldness and clarity of his ideas. His ideas came at a time between wars, and in the post-war 1940s when liberal (libertarian) economic thinking (and liberty in general) was on its knees. One of his most well-known books, *The Road to Serfdom*,[3] spurred me to dedicate five years of reading to economics books, particularly the 'Austrian' school. This is the name given to the school of economics that caught my attention, initially dominated by Austrian and German thinkers.

I was immediately hooked by the fact that they employed the language of my world, with actual, real people taking personal and professional decisions. Here there were no Martian mathematical models, but rather the planet earth – paradise or valley of tears – life and our part in it. My route to discovering them was somewhat unorthodox, going from daily interaction with the markets and applying my own intuition to a logical and compelling theory. I had finally come very close to finding the truth that I sought, and studying these thinkers helped me develop a deeper understanding of my environment from then on.

I crowned my 'Austrian' years in 2005 with Ludwig von Mises' *Human Action*.[4] On the way I discovered Murray Rothbard, mainly through his *History of Economic Thought*,[5] Huerta de Soto, Jesús (a particular highlight was *Money, Bank Credit and Economic Cycles*[6]), and Hayek himself, with *The Fatal Conceit*[7] and many others.

I was struck by the obviousness of their reasoning, with its common characteristic of being surprisingly well expressed, but, above all, I was attracted by how deeply rooted their ideas were in the concrete world around me, on earth, and not on another planet...

Everything they explained fitted perfectly with what I was seeing with my own eyes, every day on the markets and in the street. And without mathematical formulas to befuddle the understanding.

---

[3] Hayek (1994).
[4] von Mises (1995).
[5] Rothbard (2000).
[6] de Soto (2006).
[7] Hayek (1998).

That is how I came to be acquainted with the Austrian school of economics, and through these authors and their peers I found a 'theoretical' framework which has served as an essential additional support to being better prepared for the shocks to come. We will discuss the key ideas of the Austrians in Chapter 4.

THE FINAL TAKE-OFF: 2000–2002

How did we manage to obtain a 49% return in a market losing 40%? The starting point was crucial. At the beginning of 2000 the biggest market divergence in history was taking place; within an expensive market a whole series of stocks were trading at ridiculous prices.

Long-term returns come from reading, studying, and analysing, but they also depend to a large degree on what everyone else is doing and the scale of the blunders being made by the markets (other mere mortals) around us. If the market is behaving rationally, it's difficult to outperform and our returns will be broadly similar. It's much better therefore for volatility to be very elevated, provoking a degree of irrationality, which opens up opportunities that wouldn't emerge in a more stable environment.

1996–2000 was one such period of extreme irrationality, providing a suite of opportunities for independent-minded asset managers.

Perhaps it's true that good things come to those who wait – because a bit of luck is always essential – but it's equally true that these crazy market situations come around sooner or later. Irrationality is always lurking in the wings, waiting to pounce on humanity. You have to be on the alert, because invariably it will attack. We will come back to this in Chapter 9.

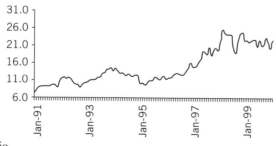

IBEX P/E Ratio
Source: AB Asesores Morgan Stanley Dean Witter Research.

Spanish Market Valuation

	1999	January 2000	February 2000	March 2000
Growth in EPS (%)	16.9	16.2	16.2	19.1
Return on own funds (%)	16.0	15.8	15.9	16.3
Dividend yield (%)	1.8	1.9	1.7	1.7
Long-term interest (%)	5.4	5.8	5.6	5.4
P/E ratio	21.4	20.3	22.5	21.5
IBEX 35	11,641	11,009	12,686	11,935
IGBM	1,008	989	1,124	1,084

Source: AB Asesores Morgan Stanley Dean Witter Research.

Sector and Market Returns

	P/E Ratio (x)		Absolute Return (%)			Relative Return (%)		
	31/03/00	2000J	1M	3M	12M	1M	3M	12M
Banks and Insurers	23.3	19.6	2.6	5.2	18.7	6.4	−2.1	−5.1
Electricity	19.0	18.2	5.7	17.2	10.3	9.6	9.0	−11.8
Media	38.6	37.2	−12.4	7.0	86.3	−9.2	−0.4	49.0
Oil and Chemical Industries	22.0	12.8	10.0	−2.9	23.5	14.1	−9.7	−1.3
Retail trade	22.7	19.2	−5.4	−11.5	−9.9	−1.9	−17.7	−28.0
Contractors	18.6	15.0	10.0	4.8	−8.6	14.0	−2.5	−26.9
Food	13.1	11.4	15.5	16.2	−20.5	19.7	−6.0	−36.4
Real-Estate Properties and Hotels	20.8	19.1	6.5	10.1	0.5	10.4	2.4	−19.6
Various	22.6	16.2	13.5	21.8	31.8	17.7	13.3	5.4
Market	25.2	21.0	−3.5	7.5	25.1	−5.1	4.8	−1.0

Source: AB Asesores Morgan Stanley Dean Witter.

At the same time, the value market was not as well developed 15 years ago as it is now. There weren't as many asset managers in Europe and Spain scouring the markets for price inefficiencies. The success of certain fund managers has contributed to developing a more independent style of asset management, which at that time was thin on the ground.

All said, at that point in time I was able to apply our analysis to a market distorted by the technology bubble. If this hadn't been the case, our subsequent results would have been much less exciting. This is why I always maintain (and we insisted on this in 2008–2009) that falling prices are good for us in the long term, since we believe that we know how to make the most of them.

However, inefficiencies don't last for ever and bit by bit the market woke up to the overpricing of large companies, especially technology firms, and to the value contained in our stocks, enabling our funds to capitalise.

It was against this backdrop that the events of 11 September 2001 took place; yet another blow against peaceful political and economic development. The brutality of the attacks, which revealed mankind in its worst light, had important political and military implications. However, as we know, the economic impact was limited; Americans responded with admirable resilience, and continued fighting for a better life.

Alongside great suffering, this day was separately a key moment for me. Over lunch with José Manuel Entrecanales, which was interrupted by news of the attack, I received his approval to change the economic conditions governing my relationship with Bestinver.

The year before I had proposed changing my remuneration (and that of future managers) to put my relationship with the company on a sustainable footing, linking my compensation to the company's economic results. I had considered the option of linking it to the returns achieved by the funds, but while this is common practice in the sector it was rather complicated, which is why I thought it would be simpler to link them to the company's results. This meant my interests were clearly aligned with Bestinver shareholders.

You might think that this was an incentive for unfettered growth, with my personal interest driving me to increase assets under management and profits. Perhaps, but bear in mind that first, we didn't do any marketing beyond our annual conference setting out our investment philosophy and dealing with individual clients' concerns and second, our agents were not set sales targets – this had to be clearly articulated when we took on two external sales directors, as it's not very common in a company. Third, our distribution network was almost non-existent, with no fees offered to external distributors. The only increase in assets, and therefore results, that we could have derived from the good results from funds that attracted new clients.

I was told that José Manuel had to go to quite a lot of effort to convince his father and uncle, and thanks to this we reached an agreement which kept me at Bestinver for another 13 years. Despite the later success and growth in assets, the terms of my remuneration remained essentially unchanged from then on, despite being well below the market average.

Returning to management. At the start of the century, our portfolio in Spain remained dominated by small caps, which had been a key feature since 1997. Outside of Spain our portfolio was invested almost entirely in equities, our strong suit, with European companies making up 50% of the portfolio and American companies another 30%, with now only around 10% of the portfolio in Japanese funds.

The focus on European equities went on to be a key characteristic of the global portfolio from that point on. The geographical proximity of European markets, which also tend to be less efficient relative to the American markets, makes it easier and more natural to invest in Europe.

The advantage of proximity is an obvious one. A fund manager once remarked that the probability of a fund obtaining a good return is inversely proportional to the distance travelled by the fund manager in selecting the stocks. Perhaps it is a bit of an overstatement, but there is some logic in this. The closer to home we are, the more insights and criteria we will have to analyse a situation. Nor should we overlook the advantages of being able to travel easily to where a company is located and build good relationships with its managers and shareholders. Just think about the housing markets that we know best. We know our own street perfectly, we have a pretty good idea about our city, things start to become hazy at the country level, and we are completely lost if asked about the opposite side of the planet.

It's not so evident that the European market is less efficient than the American one, but my experience is that it's another clear reason for preferring Europe. It's worth remembering that the investment tradition in the United States goes back a very long way and is very ingrained, with a wide range of actors at all levels. After having had some bad experiences there, nowadays, whenever I find a stock that looks to be trading at an attractive price, I always ask myself what I am seeing that the Americans aren't.

In Europe, the financial sector has traditionally been dominated by the banks, who draw strength from their brand image and distribution capacity through an extensive branch network. It doesn't always yield financial efficiency, but it leaves little room for other actors.

This physical proximity to Europe hasn't prevented us from gaining global exposure; a large proportion of European companies are global, with sales across all markets and currencies. This also provides us with a natural currency hedge, without having to use the standard hedging instruments.

Predicting short-term currency movements is very difficult; it is also expensive – hedging costs are non-negligible – and distracts from the focus, which for us has always been on different companies' long-term competitive advantages.

It is therefore a waste of time going to a lot of effort thinking about possible currency fluctuations. Over the long term, countries tend to copy each other's economic policies, especially in developed countries, and currencies tend to converge towards purchasing power parity: the purchasing power of each currency, or more graphically, the *Economist*'s Big Mac index, which tells you what it costs to produce a burger in each country. I recall our first meeting with BMW, during which the CFO showed us a chart comparing the performance of the dollar against the Deutsche Mark and later the euro. After lots of ups and downs in between, it was at the same place in 2006 as it had been at the start of the 1970s ...

After an excellent 2000–2001, with both portfolios posting positive results in a sinking market, 2002 was an exceptional year for our Spanish equity portfolio and a bad year for the global fund. In Spain we delivered our best ever relative performance against the index, +8% compared with −23%, a difference of 31%. This rounded off three superb years of very positive results in absolute and relative terms, nearly 100% outperformance of the index.

Not only this, but at the end of the year we highlighted in our quarterly report that large caps were once again looking appealing, and that it was a good time to buy them and, therefore, buy into the market. By then we already had 10% of the portfolio in IBEX stocks, which represented a major change from 1997 when we did not have any significant positions in large caps.

This forecast proved spot on, and in the four years to come – from 2003 to 2006 – the IGBM rose by 145%. There's no such thing as a crystal ball for markets, but when most stocks are expensive, the market will deliver mediocre returns at best. By contrast, when prices are reasonable, there's room for upside surprises.

In contrast, 2002 was a bad year for our international funds, with a loss of 26.95%; the worst result for any of our funds to that point. It was little consolation that the reference index registered even larger losses of 33.02%. The bulk of the losses took place in a disastrous third quarter, where we suffered a fall of 25%. While we were certainly hurt by dollar depreciation (we still had 30% of assets in the United States), we had also made some errors. This included investing in Flag Telecom, whose insolvency provoked significant losses (sometimes Peter Lynch gets it wrong; my wife worked at Flag and we were supposedly familiar with the business. I hope the same doesn't happen with her current employers, Telefónica!). Either way, the fall meant that we were holding six companies in the portfolio who had more cash than their market capitalisation. Benjamin Graham would have been pleased; it was a good omen.

Fortunately, the international portfolio was still small and there weren't too many of us who got our fingers burnt. Bestinver Internacional had 12 million euros in assets, meaning that a limited number of investors suffered losses. We were still primarily a fund manager in the Spanish stock market.

By way of conclusion, it is worthwhile recapping the state of play in December 2002, after 10 years of managing funds in the Spanish stock market and five years with international equities. The results might be of some reassurance to the multitude of asset managers who have started up in recent years and are struggling to get going.

Over 10 years, from 1993 to 2002, we obtained a return of 570.65% on our Spanish investments compared with 289.39% achieved by the IGBM. We only registered one year of losses, in 1999, and took on significantly less volatility than the market. Even so, we were only managing 148 million euros, with growth of 40 million in 2002. What's more, a significant part of the assets under management belonged to a single family shareholder.

Over five years of international activity, from 1998 to 2002, we posted a 28.03% return compared with a decline in the benchmark MSCI index of 10.2%. At that time, our global funds handled 11.9 million euros.

Overall, our two equity activities amounted to 160 million euros in December 2002. Nothing to be sniffed at, but when other asset managers complain about a lack of growth and difficulties in attracting money, I explain to them that it took years for us to gain investors' approval. For better or worse, time is the only way to tell who's right or wrong, and clients need to be confident in their decisions.

At some point a spark will come along and ignite the fuse, and you will be carried away by a wave of exuberance. This is what happened to us from 2003 onwards.

CHAPTER 3

Investing as a Team (2003–2014)

2003: A NEW MANAGER

2003 ushered in another milestone. After 13 years of going it alone, the asset management team doubled in size. We went from being one asset manager to two.

To be fair, Mario Serna had been supporting me as an analyst for nearly two years, but he didn't have any prior experience and was still learning the ropes. Over the years, a number of analysts had done an excellent job for Bestinver Securities and the equity broker, but they focused on analysis for foreign clients who invested through the securities brokerage. I was involved in hiring some of them and even managed them at times, but they were all young graduates who helped me only intermittently and on specific issues, for example making the case for the valuation of Endesa and its subsidiaries. Their main job was supporting the broker rather than the asset manager.

I confess that I made a mistake with Mario, which I may have been guilty of in the past and later on too. I led by example, without setting aside time to specifically instruct him or apply a coherent approach. This might have been enough for some people – I think the young people who spent time on the asset management side had a satisfactory experience – but perhaps it was not for everyone. This might be why Mario decided to call it a day when Álvaro arrived. Fortunately, he turned out to be the only departure from the asset management analysis team over the next 10 years.

The decision to take on another fund manager was far from easy. I was after an established asset manager; somebody still young, but who already had some experience under their belt. And as I was used to making my own decisions, with a system that worked for the clients and myself, it was a challenge to transition to a more consensual approach. However, it was becoming a necessity to have support from somebody else – particularly in the international area – to help improve decision-making and reduce client risk.

The results so far had been excellent, but the losses in 2002 arose partly from having too many companies in the international portfolio, with a lack of complete control over multiple evolving scenarios. It was too much for one person to be on top of the details of the 150 companies in the portfolio, plus the 30–40 companies in the Spanish portfolio, and the hundreds of potential candidates under consideration (see the appendix at the end of this chapter).

In Spain there were around 100 possible investments on offer, which was feasible at the time after 13 years of accumulated experience. But we needed to apply the same processes we had used in Spain – where our error rate was extremely low – to the selection of global companies, making it an imperative to devote more resources to analysis in this area.

The decision to recruit Álvaro Guzmán de Lázaro was straightforward, as it has been for all our major appointments. He was introduced to me by a common friend and ex-analyst from Bestinver and Beta Capital, Antonio Velázquez-Gaztelu. They visited one day to discuss the virtues of Repsol and we met a couple of times afterwards for lunch. It soon became clear to me that Álvaro was a good fit for the job. I wasn't about to launch a routine recruitment process or such like. In fact, we never did for key positions. Álvaro started working with us in the spring of 2003.

He was the right fit for the company. He completely understood and shared our philosophy and he had experience applying a similar management style for a family portfolio. By day he worked as an 'ordinary' analyst at Banesto Bolsa, but at home he spent time on his passion – finding top-notch stocks for his own portfolio, which required a lot of personal effort and persistence.

Álvaro is a more typical example of how to start investing than I am. If no one is prepared to pay you to invest – which is logical for the young and inexperienced – then you have to go for it in your free time. The amounts invested are an irrelevance. Indeed, my case is even starker than Álvaro's, I started with just 50 shares in Banco Santander. The key thing is to learn the process, survive the emotional ups and downs, and build confidence in your ability to invest effectively and convey that confidence to others. Believing that we can invest and being able to prove it, even with small sums, is a crucial first step. Nowadays, the Internet offers the opportunity to self-teach, learning from and copying other investors.

One of Álvaro's major contributions was to standardise the models of the companies in which we invested. Something that I had not done. Up until then I had kept all the ideas in my head, believing that if anything slipped out then it was probably with good reason. This was more than likely not the best approach, but it seemed to work for me. Fortunately, the arrival of Álvaro – and other colleagues later on – meant that everything was fully documented on paper or digitally.

Collectively, we formed a team that worked well. We had few disagreements over the choice of stocks, and any differences were resolved 'democratically'. I didn't think it was right to impose criteria on the team, so the decision to buy into a company had to be unanimous. We didn't invest if there wasn't consensus. Álvaro and I didn't always see eye to eye on certain macroeconomic issues, but these weren't pivotal for our type of investment. I think we only disagreed on two or three stocks, which strikes me as a good outcome.

His arrival meant we could travel to Europe more frequently to visit our companies and improve our knowledge of them. And gradually, the quality of our international fund improved. By the end of 2003, European stocks now accounted for 67% of the international portfolio.

The fund rose by 32.7% in 2003 (compared with an 8.83% increase in the index), enabling us to recuperate our 2002 losses.

BULL MARKET: BUBBLES

By the start of 2003, IBEX 35 stocks accounted for 20% of our Spanish portfolio. Three years of tumbling markets had opened up some tantalising opportunities, such as Repsol or Aguas de Barcelona, which embellished our usual suspects: Mapfre, CAF, Elecnor, etc.

But while the Spanish market was attractive, we were far from blind to the clouds that were gathering over the economy and that would go on to have a dramatic impact within a decade. As can be seen from an interview I gave to Javier Arce in the magazine *Futuro* (see below) in May 2003, the real-estate bubble was starting to seriously concern us.

'For example, in the real-estate sector, we are seeing the creation of a bubble, which is going to do a lot of damage some time in the next five years … When the economy grows by 2 and real-estate lending by 20, a bubble is being inflated … We have a typical supply-side crisis resulting from interest rates which are too low for the economy … This is one of the reasons why we don't have a single bank share'.[1]

---

[1] *Futuro*, May 2003, pp. 21–28.

THOSE WHO LIVE FOR VALUE (JAVIER ARCE)

According to Francisco Garcia Paramés, Bestinver's investment director, at current prices now is a good time to return to the stock market. But investors shouldn't be fooled, the returns on offer are around 6%. Forget about the past.

The IBEX 35 lost 28% of its value last year. The third consecutive year of tumbling prices. Nobody should therefore be surprised that the vast majority of the 10 million Spaniards with a stake in an equity mutual fund lost money. Everyone? Well, not quite everyone. There were two funds, which by turning their back on telecommunications, banks, or large-scale real-estate developers, delivered an 8% return to their shareholders. Both are managed by Bestinver, an Acciona group company (controlled by the Entrecanales family), and have posted positive results during the last three disastrous years for the stock markets. The numbers speak for themselves, making Francisco García Paramés, Bestinver's investment director – with a portfolio of 3,000 shareholders and 430 million euros – an ideal person to ask whether, in light of current prices and the economic situation, now *is* the time to return to the stock market. And how should it be done.

He has no qualms about revealing his preferences: companies without debt, undervalued, with a history of impeccable trajectory behind, and that already give dividends more profitable than Treasury bills. Nor in confirming that now *is* the time to invest 'provided you are willing to live with returns of 6%. But not if you are expecting strong returns'. The conversation also throws up a concern and a warning: he is convinced that we are inflating a housing market bubble, which will burst sooner or later. 'There are inevitably going to be problems here'.

You are living proof that money can be made in a bear market.

Truthfully, our conservative philosophy means we tend to do rather well in bear markets. It's lean times when the value of what we do comes to light, because when the stock market is rising, everyone benefits. For example, we never bought into the whole Internet boom, Terra and the like ...

Provided you are willing to live with returns of 6%, now is the time to return to the stock market.

What should people with shares in Terra do right now?

Terra's now trading at 4 ½, closer to our valuation – between three and four euros – but either way I would sell. I would sooner invest in Treasury bills than in Terra. We have always valued it at between four and five euros, even when it was listed at 11 euros.

What happened to make people think that Terra was worth more than Repsol?

That's the markets for you. 400 years ago the same thing happened in the Netherlands, 300 years ago in England: it's difficult to hold back from such strong psychological movements. You need to have a very clear focus. If the leading lights of the industry bought into it, then it's understandable that the average investor, who reads the newspapers, also jumped on board.

Francisco García Paramés believes we should distrust anyone offering large returns and that investors themselves are responsible for avoiding a repeat of the Gescartera case.

You talk about the newspapers. There is a lot of economic information … but what about its quality?

I am obliged to read the papers, but I confess they sometimes put me on edge. There is less nonsense around these days because there has been a lot of humble pie, but a few years ago the information was ludicrous.

Not without ulterior motives?

No, but that's only normal. For example, in the real-estate sector we are seeing a bubble, which some time over the next five years is going to do a lot of damage, but if you look at the agents involved, the guy selling homes is not going to tell you that prices will fall, nor will the stock market broker.

The problems are to be found in companies whose executives act like owners while holding 2%.

Real-estate companies are insistent that homes are selling and people are buying.

The fact that people are buying is relative. When the economy grows by two and real-estate lending by 20, what's happening is that a bubble is being inflated. What people do is put five million [pesetas] into a home worth 50. In principle, the bank will provide the remaining 45 when the development is complete, but since over two years these 50 will have become 65, that five million turns into 15. Another Terra.

(*continued*)

But here in Spain, except for basically 1993, housing prices have never fallen.

There is always a first time for everything. In Japan prices have declined by 75% over 12 years; in Hong Kong they have fallen by 65% since 1998. In four years in Spain we have built 550,000 houses, and in the United Kingdom, which is having its own bubble, they have only built an average of 200,000 over the last five years, like France or Germany, with double the population. And since the markets are all about supply and demand, there is a significant excess of homes in Spain. We have a typical supply-side crisis resulting from interest rates which are too low for the economy and a clearly recognisable bubble is being created.

A bubble being inflated to a large degree by financial institutions willing to accept these valuations.

What's going on in the banking sector is a version of Warren Buffett's institutional imperative, the tendency to copy one another. If all banks are increasing lending volumes, then as managing director of a bank I can't be left behind. And when the downturn comes, everyone is affected. We take responsibility for the risks associated with our decisions, we don't pass them on to the client saying that if the stock market goes up, great and if it doesn't, well, what's wrong? Haven't you read the newspapers? Haven't you seen the news? What do you want from me? I am doing what everyone else is doing. Banks shift the risk on to their shareholders. That is one of the reasons why we don't have a single bank share.

None whatsoever? Since when?

Since about four years ago, because we saw this coming. In Spain we're going to go from building 550,000 houses to 150,000; it's inevitable.

The Bank of Spain has been warning about this issue...

We're talking about 10% of GDP. The only thing I can do is hold stocks which are relatively insulated from it.

The chairman of Spain's number one real-estate company claims there will be a slowdown when the stock market recovers.

One day the music stops but you don't really know why. Why did the Nasdaq hit a high in February 2000? Any old news story will do. The triggers are unpredictable. The same thing happens on the stock market; it's enough to know whether a stock is expensive or cheap. The when and why a price is going to rise are much harder to predict.

The Spanish stock market has an average P/E ratio – amount paid for each euro of dividend – of 14. Is that cheap?

Yes, it's around the historical average. If I recall, the historical average for the US Standard & Poor's is 15. We're around that.

So it's the time to invest.

Provided you are willing to live with 6% returns. But not if you are expecting massive returns. 6% annual is what you can get from a P/E ratio of 15, which is economic growth plus inflation. Nothing more.

Can it go any lower?

Large caps are closing in on what we think is fair value, but our portfolio has an average P/E ratio of between nine and 10.

What's in your portfolio?

We have Mapfre, Aldeasa, Aguas de Barcelona, Elecnor, CAF... those are the top five stocks. They account for a third of our portfolio, then – of course – we have a lot of other stocks.

Which stocks gave you the best returns last year?

Natraceútica, a Valencia biotech company. Also Viscofan, Uni-land. All of them did pretty well; these are equities with a P/E ratio of nine and 10, so as long as things stay on track...

This is the key factor, buying cheap.

Buying things below what we think they are worth. You end up with companies with a low P/E ratio and a high dividend yield; the average for us is 4%. Double what Treasury bills are paying. And sustainable dividends, because our portfolio is pretty defensive; companies that are unencumbered by debt and aren't affected by the cycle. No banks, construction, real estate... The companies which everyone is talking about, following, and analysing are pretty well priced.

Aside from Telefónica, banks...

The banks would be fine if it weren't for the housing bubble. Right now the NPL ratio is at a low point, half a percentage point, but the historical average is 3% and Banesto reached 10%. Germany is a case in point: its housing market maxed out six or seven years ago and right now Commerzbank is worth 500 billion pesetas, 10% of BBVA. They were slaughtered by bad debts. And when everyone is lending 20% more after a 100% price increase... then there are going to be problems.

In the real-estate sector, we are seeing the creation of a bubble which is going to do a lot of damage.

(continued)

What would you recommend shareholders in Iberdrola and Metrovacesa to do?

Sell.

At current prices, it seems likely that we will see more M&A, even cross-border. Transactions that couldn't be completed because of the overpricing of Spanish banks, for example, will eventually be pushed through.

Here in Spain, people are paying prices of two times book value, while banks such as Hypobank or Commerzbank are trading below book value. A merger for them would majorly dilute their capital. And cross-border mergers are politically very sensitive, not just from an economic perspective.

How much money do you need to invest in one of your funds?

Until recently any amount was enough, but we have just put in place a minimum of one million pesetas (6,000 euros) and a 3% redemption fee for the first year. This is because the new law, which allows for switching between funds, could see people start to use them like a current account. And we don't advertise, nor are we particularly concerned about growing, so if somebody invests with us we want them to be in it for the long term.

Achieving an 8% return against the backdrop of last year ought to be the best calling card.

Yes, we have a huge amount of inflows, simply from people knocking on our door. Last year we grew from 280 to 400 million euros.

Is there a lot more rotation because of the new legislation which allows investors to switch funds?

We are seeing transfers, around 300 in the last three or four months. People bringing their money to us.

The Ministry of Education has leaked a draft regulation for mutual funds, but it doesn't look like there are going to be substantial changes…

It's basically about information issues, what you have to report and how frequently. We have to publish our portfolio every three months, but as it's pretty stable, that's no big deal.

What's your opinion on the new code of good governance that is being pushed for in listed companies?

I think it's a very good idea, but when the next stock market boom comes around it will soon be forgotten. As per usual. It's what always happens. You see it when you read books by investors from 100 years ago; they talked about the exact same issues we're talking about now.

The language hasn't changed, nor have the problems. Meaning that the way you earn and lose money is also the same. The stock market crash of 1929 led to the Chairman of the New York Stock Exchange being incarcerated. We haven't reached that point yet. Things are improving; so far we have only imprisoned several directors in some companies.

It's enough to know whether a stock is expensive or cheap. The when and why a price is going to rise are much harder to predict.

The Americans are trying to make it a requirement for institutional investors to sit on company management boards and get involved.

We ultimately only invest in companies managed by people we trust, who have a track record of good management over the last five years and who will likely continue doing well over the next five. We take every precaution possible, and over the last six or seven years we have set a very high barrier in terms of our demands, not just for the business, but also what you could call ethics. For example, you're unlikely to see strange things happen in a company where a family owns 60% of the capital.

As is the case for Ortega and Inditex, and your own group, Acciona, controlled by the Entrecanales family.

60% of a group like this is 220,000 million pesetas, what would be gained from deceiving minority shareholders? Nothing.

There are cases such as the Albertos.[2]

(continued)

---

[2] A long-running fraud case in Spain. The Albertos referred to two cousins, Alberto Alcocer and Alberto Cortina, who were accused in 1993 of falsifying the conditions of the sale of building land in Madrid's Plaza Castilla to Kuwaiti group KIO at the end of the 1980s. The Albertos held a 40% stake in Urbanor, the company which sold the land to KIO. They were accused of falsifying the sale documents to deceive minority shareholders in Urbanor into thinking that the sale had been made at a lower price than the actual sale price, pocketing the difference themselves. In March 2003, shortly before this interview was conducted, they had been condemned by Spain's Supreme Court to over three years in jail, and to pay out 24.4 million euros in compensation. This turned out not to be the end of the story, with various legal challenges and rulings continuing over the course of the decade.

Obviously there are all types of people. We are talking about probabilities rather than certainties. And my experience is that family companies, backed by strong assets, are less of a risk.

Except for this one case?

Yes, an exceptional case. A company where 10 billion pesetas disappeared. And it's no longer listed.

Faced with the problems with executives that you mention, their shareholders are now discovering that the compensation and retirement agreements for the two senior executives amounts to 150 million euros and they feel powerless...

Well, in this specific case a lawsuit has been brought against them, but it's true that controls are quite lax.

So, if people like you who control good blocks of shares just give up their voting rights and don't take part in AGMs...

Yes, but we try to ensure that we carry out a rigorous prior screening. Going back five years ago, we already judged the IBEX 35 to be expensive, so we have invested in 35 small companies. We have successfully exited from 22 of them at what we considered to be a fair price. Family companies where we haven't come across any problems. The problems are to be found in companies whose executives act like owners while holding 2%.

But you appealed to the CNMV on one occasion and successfully negotiated an increased price for a public tender offer, so it appears you are willing to go further than silently collecting dividends.

In the two or three cases where we have come across such problems, we absolutely have responsibilities to our clients.

From your perspective, do you think individuals can make sound investment decisions with the information available to them?

Nowadays, investors have access to the same information as professionals. I know private investors with little economic information who have managed to accumulate their own portfolio of assets in the stock market...

This is ultimately crucial.

Absolutely fundamental. Because losses like we had this year with Ahold – we invested more than 1% of one of our funds – happen all the time. That's why it is crucial to know who's behind the company, who the managers are, who you can trust or not... and this is within the grasp of any small investor with the necessary patience and desire.

It doesn't seem as though the auditors have improved on the trust-worthiness of the chartered accountants of yesteryear.

Not at all. A stock-market boom blows everything completely away, all the safeguards. Levitt, the former Chairman of the SEC, warned about this for years: a bull market is a bull in a china shop. And if you look at some of the takeovers that were made, some undertaken with a lot of safeguards, you realise it doesn't matter; that type of market is voracious. The story goes that in 1720 there was a company which floated on the stock market and was supposedly very lucrative but couldn't reveal what it did. It was sold and it turned out to be just a front. Four years ago a colleague showed me a prospectus for an American company which also didn't tell you what it did. It didn't have an investment project, but it hoped to have one soon. 300 years on…

Regarding audits, some people argue that it wouldn't be a bad idea for each company to pay a quota for the proportion of its audit costs to a fund managed by the CNMV, which could then allocate auditors by lottery.

It doesn't sound like a bad idea, but I honestly haven't given it much thought. We try to avoid these problems by steering clear of questionable companies.

A guarantee fund has been established for securities companies after the Gescartera scandal.[3] Do you agree with it?

I don't. I think we're mature enough to see through anyone offering a 15% annual return. If it no longer matters who does well or not, it's only going to encourage more people of the same type: 'Don't worry, the first two million are guaranteed anyway'. I think everybody should accept their share of the responsibilities; investors also have to do their homework.

---

[3] Another famous scandal in Spain during the early 2000s. Gescartera was essentially a Ponzi scheme masquerading initially as a portfolio management company and then as a stock-broking company. It claimed it could deliver returns of 10% per month. Needless to say, the funds disappeared with various false documents being used to dupe the supervisors. The case raised questions over the CNMV's role as a watchdog, and the sky-high returns on offer seemingly duped various high-profile institutions, such as the Catholic Church and the National Police retirement fund.

We recommended steering clear of Spanish banks and real-estate companies, but the warning clearly went unheeded and the bubble continued unchecked for nearly a decade. Unfortunately, it crashed back down to earth years later. 2003 saw a continual increase in our assets under management, reaching 225 million euros in the Spanish funds and 47 million in the international fund by the end of the year.

We had finally earned the necessary confidence of potential investors after 10 years of hard work and results.

2004–2005: THE REAL-ESTATE BOOM IN FULL SWING

We had forewarned of the dangers of the housing market bubble in Spain. And in 2004, we had yet further evidence that the fundamentals underpinning Spanish economic growth were far from sound, based on lending rather than saving and productivity growth.

The European Central Bank, copying its American counterpart, had set short-term interest rates at 2% in 2003. This was too low for the needs of the Spanish economy, given that inflation was running above these levels. As can be seen on the following chart, Spain and Ireland, the two European countries with the biggest housing bubbles during that decade, were being offered negative real interest rates for three and four years, respectively. (The situation was not dissimilar in 2015 and 2016 but, fortunately, it was not transmitting to the economies in the same way, to the great bemusement of the central banks.) These negative interest rates provoked excessive lending growth.

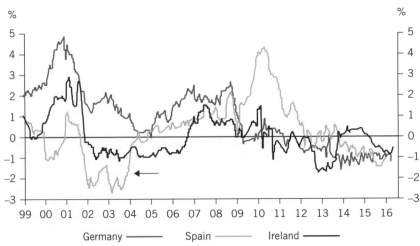

Real interest rate (ECB repo rate less CPI inflation rate)
Source: Macrobond & HSBC.

It was logical with funding at 2% and real-estate asset inflation of 10% that all economic agents wanted a piece of the 'free for all'. Furthermore, banks were prepared to lend up to 100% of the investment, a rarity in normal times. This explains why there was so much overnight real-estate wealth: developers invested with third-party money, creating companies for each development. If it worked, they won; if it didn't work, they closed down the company with the losses going to the banks and on to the rest of the country. They never lost out.

Nor did the politicians or civil servants responsible for zoning the land. These individuals, whose decisions determined when and where construction would be carried out on each bit of land, and therefore who got rich from their decisions, were the true creators of unjust wealth – both for third parties and, frequently, for their own benefit. It's no surprise that Texas, which is the only place in the United States where construction is unrestricted, has the most accessible housing in the country in relation to wealth.

After several years of low interest rates, it was not until the last quarter of 2005 that rates finally began to rise in Europe.

The real-estate situation was of major concern to us, and we began to allocate the Spanish portfolio very conservatively, investing only in defensive and/or exporting companies. This would be a constant over the following seven years, until 2012. Furthermore, by December 2004, we had increased liquidity to almost 15% of the portfolio. This rose further to an average of 20% during 2005, the highest proportion since 1998. One of the biggest sales that year was Cevasa (a pioneer in the private development of state-subsidised housing for rental), one of our favourite stocks, with rental real-estate assets which had clearly been undervalued until that point. Our block of shares was bought by one of the many real-estate companies which later went to the wall.

GOING SHORT

As always, our warning of the bad times to come was premature, but at least we slept soundly. This is one of the advantages of never short-selling. Some readers will wonder why we didn't short the banks and real-estate companies if we were so convinced. If we consider the five years from 2003 until 2008 (in reality, the bubble in Spain held up surprisingly well during the global financial crisis and didn't burst until a bit later), a short position on these securities would have left us facing devastating losses, which would have put in question our very survival as investors.

A short is a bet that the price of an asset will fall. It can be done via derivative products, options, futures, and so on. We have never engaged in this type of investing:

1. Because we are optimists, and we think that things will always improve. Humanity is living in a golden era and it will continue if people are left to work in peace. It doesn't fit with our personality or long-term objectives.
2. Because time plays against investors with short positions, since quality real assets tend to gain in value. A good share, cheap and with potential, will increase in value over the years. It only requires patience for the market to wake up to it, and if it doesn't, we can increase our investment further still (or not, but we get to decide and the losses are limited to the investment made).

   By contrast, time is against you when you have a short position. If the price of the asset goes up, you can face major losses, making it necessary to take on more guarantees and increased exposure to this risk, although the investor may not want to do so.

   We have already mentioned that we were downbeat on the Spanish real-estate and banking sector over this period. If we had bet against the sector we would have suffered for nearly 10 years until those involved faced the music, and we might not have survived. Michel Lewis describes this agony to perfection in his book *The Big Short*.[4]
3. Because short positions are exclusively short-term investments, and movements over this timeline are practically impossible to predict. Holding a short position in the long term is, technically, almost impossible.

In sum, we want to sleep soundly and we want the people who have placed their trust in us to sleep well too.

GLOBAL PORTFOLIO

By December 2004, European companies accounted for 80% of assets in the global portfolio. And we had reduced the number of companies from 150 to 100, focusing our investment on fewer stocks thanks to an increase in the quality of our analysis. Spain's excesses didn't seem to be so pronounced elsewhere and we found value, meaning we were fully invested.

---

[4]Lewis (2011).

Bestinver Internacional Portfolio (31/12/2004)

STOCKS	Investment	% Total
TESORO DE ESPAÑA	11,001	4.98
TOTAL PUR. ASSETS	11,001	4.98
TOTAL FIXED INCOME	11,001	4.98
TOTAL DOMESTIC PORTFOLIO	11,001	4.98
Abrazas Petro	923	0.42
Amer Nat Ins	2,098	0.95
Ares	643	0.29
Avis Europe	1,676	0.76
Bally Tot Fit	804	0.36
Banque Privée Edmond	0	0.00
Barry callebaut	2,912	1.32
Batenburg	517	0.23
BE Semiconductor	641	0.29
Bell Holding AG	885	0.40
Bell Industries	902	0.41
Bilfinger	0	0.00

STOCKS	Investment	% Total
Boewe Systec AG	2,515	1.14
Bonduelle	719	0.33
Brantano NV	2,835	1.28
Bucherindstr	5,869	2.66
Buhrman	7,768	3.52
C&C Group	925	0.42
Camaieu SA	6,782	3.07
Carrere Group	1,311	0.59
Compass Group	1,281	0.58
CSM NV	0	0.00
D Ieteren SA	487	0.22
Dalet	143	0.06
DassaultAviat	3,063	1.39
De Telegraaf	1,511	0.68
Delhaize	0	0.00
Dentressangle	1,196	0.54
Devro plc	951	0.43
Dolmen Computer	1,051	0.48
Econocom	4,870	2.20
Edel Music	841	0.38
Engineering	1,062	0.48
Escada AG	7,937	3.59
Esprinet	4,101	1.86

(continued)

STOCKS	Investment	% Total
Etam Develop	2,955	1.34
Fairchild Corp	315	0.14
Fairfax Finci	4,730	2.14
Faiveley SA	2,463	1.11
Finlay Enter	2,369	1.07
Fleury Michon	899	0.41
Fuchs Petrolub	1,078	0.49
GFI informatique	1,290	0.58
GIFI SA	3,340	1.51
Guerbet SA	1,173	0.53

STOCKS	Investment	% Total
Hagemeyer	3,467	1.57
Head	767	0.35
Heineken Hld	1,215	0.55
IDT Corp	1,098	0.50
Imtech NV	819	0.37
ISS A/S	459	0.21
Kanaden Corp	862	0.39
Kindy SA	1,096	0.50
Kinepolis	6,908	3.13
Kone	0	0.00
KonniklijkeAhold	2,112	0.96
Konniklijke Boskalis	0	0.00
Lafuma	1,105	0.50
Lambert dur Chan	1,324	0.60
Macintosh NV	6,114	2.77
Maisons Fra Conf	809	0.37
MarionnaudParfm	2,947	1.33
Matalan	0	0.00
Medion	2,162	0.98
Metallwaren Hldg	6,319	2.86
Metsa Serla	1,294	0.59
MGI Confer SA	1,055	0.48
M-RealOY3	0	0.00
Nipponkoa	1,968	0.89
Nutreco NV	6,314	2.86
OCE NV	6,681	3.02
Okumura CORP	0	0.00
OPG Groep NV	5,687	2.57
Orchestra-Kazib	882	0.40
Panana Group	1,049	0.47
Passat	1,696	0.77
Pierre Vacances	935	0.42
Pinkcroccade	0	0.00

STOCKS	Investment	% Total
Playboy	0	0.00
Regent Inns plc	1,645	0.74
Rentokil	0	0.00
REpower Systems	1,484	0.67
Rite Aid	5,168	2.34
Roto Smeets Boer	5,624	2.55
Roularta	2,137	0.97
Sabate SA	863	0.39
Sasa Industrie	1,303	0.59
Shire Pharmaceuticals	1,308	0.59
Signaux Girod	904	0.41
Sligro Food Grp	1,737	0.79
Smoby	1,405	0.64
Stef Tfe	348	0.16
Sthn Egy Homes	1,820	0.82
Tommy Hilfiger	1,275	0.58
Tonnellerie	2,038	0.92
Trigano SA	0	0.00
Unilever	951	0.43
United Services	2,535	1.15
Varsity Group	2,355	1.07
Vet Affaires	4,297	1.94
Vetropack	3,501	1.58
VM Materiaux	1,203	0.54
VNU N.V.	928	0.42
WamerChilcott	0	0.00
Wegener	7,212	3.26
Wolters Kluwer	0	0.00
Zapf Creation AG	962	0.44
TOTAL EQUITIES	209,978	95.02
TOTAL EXTERNAL PORTFOLIO	209,978	95.02
TOTAL PORTFOLIO (thousands of euros)	220,979	100.00

Source: CNMV.

However, in contrast to the Spanish portfolio, we were still reticent about increasing the concentration in certain stocks in our global portfolio. For example, in the fourth quarter of 2004, only five stocks accounted for more than 3% of the total: Camaieu, Kinepolis, Wegener, Escada, and Burhman. As a side note, in June 2005 we bought our first position in BMW, which – after many ups and downs – has proven to be an exceptional investment over time.

We focused mainly on European mid-caps, which proved to be pretty rewarding, despite some clear duds such as Escada itself, Boewe Systec,

Smoby, Schlott, Regent Inns, Alexon, Clinton Cards, and some others whose names are painful to remember. In all of them we lost practically our entire investment. However, these failures helped to improve our investment over the long term, because rarely do you fail to draw some useful conclusions for the future. It's preferable to reach such conclusions reading about others' experiences – it's probably essential and reduces the likelihood that one of our errors will be fatal – but making our own errors is inevitable and even to some extent desirable, to avoid dropping our guard, keep learning, and stay alert.

Despite these problems, the results during these two years were very positive – 19% and 30% – and outperformed the benchmark indexes. As can be seen, it's possible to obtain very acceptable returns despite suffering a few setbacks, and there are probably two keys to this: getting it right more often than not, and being very careful about the scale of errors.

We usually got it right, the 30 or 40 serious errors that we made accounted for 10% of our investments out of a total investment in 500 companies over time. That's a tolerable percentage.

The size of positions should follow Eugenio D'Ors' maxim: 'Experiments should be made with lemonade and not champagne'. The stocks with the highest weight, over 5%, should command our total confidence to avoid the risk of serious damage. The riskiest bets should be kept to a prudent size, never more than 1–2%.

2006–2007: ON THE BRINK...

2006 was the last year of an undisputed bull market. In Spain we started with 20% liquidity, but we took advantage of market retrenchment in the second quarter to up our investment, which brought liquidity down to 10%.

During this second quarter, we bought Telefónica shares for the first time in 10 years. Post-correction it was now trading at a tasty price and we continued buying throughout the year, reaching 8% of assets in the Spanish portfolio by December, something we had never done before. The country meanwhile remained captivated by the real-estate dream, which was covertly absorbing the financial and political system.

It was another vintage year for the international portfolio, +24% while being invested up to the legally permitted maximum and with BMW now among the top three holdings, together with Fuchs Petrolub and Metall Zug. A good trio of aces.

However, the most scarring event of 2006 had nothing to do with investing. On 7 March, four of us from Bestinver plus two pilots were involved in an aircraft accident in Pamplona. As incredible as it may sound, it was the only time in 25 years that we used a private aircraft to travel. One Bestinver colleague, Alfredo Muñoz, director of finance and operations, and one of the pilots died. María Caputto, deputy sales director, Ignacio Pedrosa, sales director, the second pilot, and myself survived.

Despite the enormous emotional shock, it only had a small impact on the company's investment. With Álvaro in place we already had the necessary support to ensure continuity and our portfolio was always geared to investing in the long term, meaning I was able to spend a while coming to terms with what had happened. In reality, I wasn't out of action for long and within about two weeks I was able to start reading. My injuries were not significant and I received the full support of everyone, including José Manual Entrecanales and the entire Acciona group.

The advantage of enforced time out of the office was that I had no option but to start using remote IT tools. Little by little I began to adapt to the new emerging technologies, including the iPad, which I now struggle to escape.

In 2006 we reached the high point in terms of the continual and massive inflows of clients prior to the 2008–2009 crisis, hitting six billion euros in assets under management. This meant that our assets had increased by 20 in three years. It was absolutely extraordinary, giving us a 40% market share in the mutual fund sector reports registered on Inverco, the grouping of mutual funds for Spanish markets.

We had never been growth focused, but working without specific targets we had managed to attract more interest than we could possibly have imagined. Over the years we had two commercial or client relations directors, Ignacio Pedrosa and Beltrán Parages, neither of whom were ever assigned growth targets. We didn't get involved in any active promotional activity, with next to no advertising (except for a small campaign in 2000, Crisis? What crisis?, highlighting this year's good results), nor did we have any distribution agreements (except for some very small-scale ones which dated back to before 2000 and were maintained as a token of gratitude for confidence in us when we weren't well known).

There are various reasons why we adopted this passive approach. Firstly, when a client makes an active decision to come to us it creates a much stronger bond of trust, as it is a conscious decision made in the absence of pressure. This builds in some resilience during difficult times. Secondly, growth creates the need to set limits on the amount managed, so what business logic is there for sharing profitability within limited capacity with distributors? None whatsoever. Thirdly, we have frankly been fortunate to find ourselves in a position of not needing to do so. Under other circumstances, perhaps we would have taken a different decision.

Either way, we were caught off guard by the pace of growth and it wasn't until much later that we were able to get on top of the situation and provide a good service. Initially we lacked the physical space to respond to all the indications of interest, leading to inevitable backlogs and delays. It wasn't until we were able to double our capacity, expanding to another floor, that we got the situation under control.

2007

With the wind in our sails, we confronted 2007, a transition year following sustained positive performance. As we saw in the 1990s, the transition from a bull to a bear market tends to be one of the more challenging for us because our portfolio, which is geared to being conservative, fares less well in the dying throes of a bull market.

Fortunately, we started the year by taking on a third fund manager, Fernando Bernad. Once again it was a straightforward hire. He was introduced to us by Álvaro, who had worked directly with him at two different times. He was a great help to us from day one, thanks to his extensive prior experience in our type of management. In fact, he had even been responsible for a small asset manager, Vetusta, which was no longer in existence. His arrival enabled us to expand the analytical team, taking advantage of his ability to manage and organise them. Álvaro and I lacked the time, and perhaps the desire, to manage and coordinate the work of a large team of people. We had clear ideas about where we added value and we wanted to avoid upsetting our working conditions.

Every decision to strengthen the team is a hard one. Each new person increases capacity and adds value, but they are also an added restriction, given that we have to set aside time to train them. You end up losing a degree of freedom, and sometimes the role of asset manager gets confused with people manager. Therefore, we have always selected learned fund managers, such as Álvaro and Fernando. It's a different story for analysts, where we have always picked academic high flyers with limited experience, so we can train them as we see fit. This approach wouldn't have been possible without Fernando, who played a key role in their training, putting together a sound team that – over time – was able to contribute good ideas.

From this point on we hired Carmen Pérez Báguena and Mingkun Chan, who joined Ivan Chvedine, who was already working for us as an analyst. Collectively we formed the sextet which was forced into pitting its wits against the crisis.

At the start of the year, in March, I sent a letter of thanks to Warren Buffett. I made the decision in Tenerife when I discovered that he had bought shares in Posco, the Korean steel company. We had recently been involved in Arcelor and I liked the parallel. In the letter I thanked him for being a source of inspiration to me, an investor stranded in a country like Spain, with little investment tradition. I also suggested that he buy BMW preference shares.

He replied almost immediately, two days later, asking for ideas about investing in Spanish private companies. Not a single company came to mind that would fit with his philosophy, so I didn't respond. This, unfortunately, ended our short-lived correspondence.

Another key milestone took place in the spring, when I joined a week-long seminar organised by IESE in China. I was already positively inclined to the country, remembering Jim Rogers' superb books. As a retired asset manager he had travelled the world, first by motorbike and then by car, carrying out an 'on the ground' comparative analysis of the various countries he visited. His main conclusion was that China held the key to the future, which he justified with the following arguments: the Chinese people's fervour for improving their living standards; their capacity for work and saving; and reasonable protection of property rights, with less bureaucracy and corruption than similar developing countries.

It was with great interest then that we visited Chinese companies, subsidiaries of foreign companies, investors, and academics. I also separately arranged to visit the China offices of the companies in our funds. It was a unique experience, which deepened my understanding of the country's economic development and decision-making process. I began to read avidly a wide variety of books on China, ranging from fiction to academic and journalistic non-fiction. Particular highlights were *The Second Chinese Revolution* by former Spanish ambassador to China, Eugenio Bregolat,[5] and, especially, Peter Hessler's *Country Driving*,[6] which provided an enlightening description of the daily life of Chinese people.

Over the years, and following various trips, including a family visit with summer camp included, I discovered for myself that China's development was substantive and based on a capacity for work and saving which allowed them to overcome any obstacle put in their path. The image of an economy that was supposedly under the remote control of the Communist Party was far from the reality. A whole spectrum of activity was completely free from government interference, providing a degree of flexibility unknown to Europe, Japan, Brazil, and other developing countries. This freedom, combined with very significant competition in non-strategic sectors, allowed for strong growth without inflation. And even in economic areas which were effectively controlled by the Party – electricity, transport, basic resources, etc. – the Chinese enjoyed what the legendary President of Singapore, Lee Kuan Yew, described as the best bureaucracy in the world, thanks to an essentially meritocratic system.

What's more, up until 2009, this development was not based on debt. That is, until the global crisis forced a relaxation of monetary rules. Years later the debt level is now elevated, but the assets underpinning it are real and substantive. I don't deny that there may have been some bad investments

---

[5] Bregolat (2007).
[6] Hessler (2010).

in infrastructure, but the essence of China's development remains the population's enormous capacity to adapt to a changing and highly competitive environment.

That said, we didn't start investing in China, but we still thought it was essential to be well informed about the country. This led to the hiring of Mingkun Chan, who we signed from IESE. It was not an easy choice, given the quality of the field: 17 all-Chinese candidates. The other finalist had won a debating tournament ... on Japanese TV!

CORPORATE SOCIAL RESPONSIBILITY: AFRICA SUPPORT FUND

In 2007 we also launched the Africa Support Fund, which – aside from making a tiny contribution to easing the social and economic plight of some African communities – was a response to an issue which plays on the mind of everyone who invests in public companies and which undoubtedly should be addressed: corporate social responsibility.

I take a similar view on this to Milton Friedman: a company's or project's goals should be set by its founders. If the goal is to alleviate poverty in a specific part of the population, or support the less able, or foster cultural activities, then success should be measured by the impact achieved by the company. And this should be carried out by the entrepreneur, free from unwanted third-party interference.

If the aim is to offer a product or service to society as efficiently as possible, in return for compensation, then the entrepreneur should also be left to do as they see fit, always being mindful of current regulations. If, as is natural, the aim is to maximise the difference between the value of sales and costs (profits), then there is no need to put roadblocks in their path forcing them to pay costs that don't apply to them. If profits are excessive, another entrepreneur will always – and I mean always – come along, helping to push down surplus profits.

The goal in both cases should be set by the entrepreneur. Anything that obliges them to mix up objectives leads to confusion or even conflicting goals, which sends a very opaque message to society, inhibiting correct price formation, which is the key signal for other people to act.

I remember a well-known banker who was awarded an honorary degree by a prestigious university on the basis of the generous donations made by his bank. Meanwhile, he spent his time ripping off shareholders for his own personal gain and giving classes on ethics.

We require the companies we invest in to respect the letter of the law – however little we may like it – and maximise our shareholder return. As shareholders we will use the earnings we obtain in pursuit of our own personal objectives, which may include 'social' goals. Marking a clear separation between corporate and personal goals helps to make things much clearer, enabling both activities to be carried out in a beneficial way.

When we launched the Africa Support Fund, in collaboration with José María Márquez and África Directo, we were careful to stress the separation between the role of commercial and 'social' enterprises. The fund went on to have a lot of success and we have financed hospitals, schools, medicine, water treatment systems, treatment for albino children, etc. A large number of projects across more than 20 countries, with a total investment of around 3,500,000 euros.

I believe this project helped set the logical foundations for social responsibility by shareholders in companies, which is what matters. However, while this type of aid is vital and must be sustained, it needs to be complemented with other types of long-term support. The most durable type of support should involve local entrepreneurs applying accepted techniques, ideas, or technologies to their own developing country, or coming up with new approaches. Activity funded by the inhabitants of the affected country with their own money is the most tenable alternative. This is the most sustainable you can get and, what's more, it doesn't distort domestic markets in the places where help is being provided.

As far as possible, support should be provided along these lines. However, the real problem arises when politicians and officials plunder their own country's resources or the wealth generated by entrepreneurs, decimating their work and wiping out incentives for private initiative. There are various global schemes aimed at addressing this issue, such as the Transparency Charter promoted by Paul Collier. As they begin to bear fruit, they should constitute a major step forward in the development of these economies.

Patient capital is another option providing a bridge between straight donation and pure market approaches. An example is the Acumen Fund, which carries out impact-oriented financial investment. They seek returns from social projects, which are used to fund new projects.

There are a lot of ways to help, but it's crucial to avoid contamination between objectives. This only serves to confuse both the saver and the beneficiary, and distort exchange relations within both the donating and the recipient country.

Construction of the St. Anthony Primary School in Kamwenge, Uganda

Kilisun for people with albinism

Africa Support Fund (euros)

Country	Total (country)
Angola	202,000,00
Benin	73,427,00
Burkina Faso	7,200,00
Burundi	58,500,00
Cameroon	130,000,00
Congo Brazzaville	5,350,00
Eritrea	110,000,00
Ethiopia	64,000,00
Kenya	106,500,00
Mali	28,850,00
Malawi	699,076,00
Niger	5,000,00
Mozambique	24,540,00
Dem. Rep. Congo	44,300,00
Tanzania	684,013,50
Sierra Leone	139,041,00
Sudan	411,660,00
Uganda	527,107,29
Zambia	35,000,00
Total (year)	3,355,564,79

Source: Africa Direct.

Back to the markets. The first half of 2007 started well enough, but problems began to emerge in the summer in some structured products (using derivatives: options, futures, etc.) backed by real-estate mortgages, signalling that a change of cycle was in the air. We have almost always steered clear of structured products (the only exceptions being bonds indexed to commodities and Japan in 1998 and the 2000 Nasdaq bond). They are hard to understand and you feel as though you are being charged hidden fees, which makes them less attractive.

The likely result therefore tends to be somewhat similar to inflation and little more. Likewise, we have hardly ever invested directly in derivatives, options, and futures. These instruments shift the investment focus to the short term (long-term hedges are excessively expensive, although cheap in the short run) and we believe that short-term movements are totally random. The best hedge for a portfolio is to construct it with sound stocks at a fair price.

I say 'hardly ever' because during 2000–2001, as a one off, we did try to cover our dollar investment. At the time, more than 30% of the assets in the global portfolio were in dollars, with the dollar trading at its highest level for 30 years, below one against the euro. After hedging against a possible dollar depreciation for a couple of quarters, the regulator, CNMV, got in touch to remind us that as we didn't have a 'risk control unit' we couldn't keep going with this hedge. We gave some thought to creating such a unit, but decided against it, given the cost and the limited occasions on which it made sense to use derivatives.

We have always maintained an excellent relationship with the regulator, but that time they were wide of the mark. We complied with the letter of the law, but it cost our clients a loss to the tune of 10% of their assets when, in subsequent years, the dollar depreciated by 40% to reach 1.35 against the euro in 2005.

Returning to 2007, while we were clear about the (grim) prospects ahead for Spain, having set out a very defensive portfolio – in fact, we had broadened our sights to Portugal to try to limit the exposure to Spain – we were not as well prepared for a global crisis, despite having no explicit exposure to the financial sector. We were not as alive to the American real-estate boom and its implications. We didn't know how to apply the same perspective we were applying to Spain to places such as Miami or Las Vegas.

Meanwhile, we sincerely believed, and were later proven right, that our portfolios were robust – with good companies and reasonable prices. We have been asked many times why we didn't prepare for the fall by holding more liquidity, but in reality we were content with our global portfolio. There was no problem with our companies, but rather with other highly overindebted companies which provoked a temporary liquidity freeze that indiscriminately dragged down the whole financial system.

Our most significant investments in that period went on to perform superbly over time, both in terms of results and share prices. Only Alapis and Cir/Cofide turned out to be disappointments. The first because of fraud, which ended up with the incarceration of their chairman (take away: don't invest in companies that invite you to all their events and where the chairman travels with a legion of bodyguards); the second because of the catastrophic situation of the European electricity sector in recent years.

The second half of 2007 was already proving difficult; our funds posted negative returns, both in absolute terms and in relation to the market.

We've said it before and it's been illustrated several times in this account: the worst time for us is a change of market from bull to bear. The type of companies we invest in at these times are defensive, and we typically hold above normal liquidity. This time our liquidity was at normal levels, but we were coming off the back of an exceptional run of performances by our funds, which led us to drop our guard a little and be less vigilant than we should have been.

Out of curiosity, in autumn 2007, I tagged along to the Investor Day of one of the big Spanish banks just to see how the banking sector was bearing up. I was able to confirm their complete ignorance about the state of play in the housing market. I discovered that they had absolutely no idea of what was about to hit them. The commercial director brazenly forecast that 500,000 to 600,000 homes would be built per annum over the next five years.

If one of Spain's largest banks didn't have a clue about what was going on, it only confirmed my overall impression that the financial sector was going to be badly affected, particularly the cajas (or savings banks). The high degree of political interference was a particular problem for the latter, and rumours were continually circulating about fraudulent lending activity and attempts to cover up the scale of the problem. When people talk about nationalising the banks to avoid a repeat of the past, they show gobsmacking myopia about what happened to the cajas, which were controlled by the regional political establishment, yet again demonstrating how political intervention is an aggravation in a financial crisis.

We ended the year with one of the most significant developments for a long time regarding our product range: we set up a hedge fund in the autumn, which was essentially a concentrated fund. It was designed to be the crème de la crème, reflecting our best ideas, capable of outperforming the other funds but subject to somewhat greater volatility. Time has shown this to be the case, with the hedge fund obtaining some additional percentage points of return over Bestinfond.

After initially starting out with a fee schedule that was similar to the competition, we changed the fees for the hedge fund because we thought it was unfairly punitive on the client, creating an innovative new system. The fixed fee was identical to the fund reflecting our model portfolio, Bestinfond, and any excess returns obtained by the hedge fund over this fund were split 50–50 between the client and the asset manager, a highly satisfactory solution for all parties.

2008: THE BIG FALL

Despite being very well prepared in the Spanish portfolio and not having invested in financial companies in the global portfolio, the first quarter of 2008 got off to an exceptionally bad start, registering declines of 6% and 12% in the NAVs of the Spanish and the global portfolios, respectively. This happened despite receiving three purchase offers in the global portfolio, notably for Corporate Express, an important company for us with a weight of 3.5%. It was a bad omen for the rest of the year.

However, the main problem during the quarter was not so much the results the funds were posting, but the outflow of investor money. Funnily enough, the bulk of our outflows took place at this time and not after the Lehman Brothers collapse in September. And this was because many of the overwhelming number of investors who had arrived in previous years were clearly not prepared to endure stock-market volatility. In fact, there were numerous cases of people buying funds using bank loans, which were also being given away lightly for non-real-estate-sector activity too. Thus, the bulk of the year's redemptions, which ultimately amounted to 20% of assets, took place in that first quarter.

Redemptions during those three months were running at around 20–30 million euros a day, but we were able to handle them without major issues with the help of the purchase offers we'd received, the offloading of some significant blocks of shares, and investments from our shareholders, who took advantage of attractive market prices to carry out investment in the funds.

LIQUIDITY

Some people have accused us of obtaining good results through exposure to illiquid stocks. As we have seen, this was not always the case, with extended periods of investment in large caps – in reality we're agnostic about company size, we are solely interested in their business and valuation. However, the supposed problem of a lack of liquidity in secondary stocks is a non-sequitur. The crucial problem which can make life difficult is getting the valuation wrong. When you get it right and the share is trading at a discount, there is always going to be a counterparty. Sometimes you have to offer a small discount, say 5%, but on other occasions you obtain a higher price than the market. Illiquidity trading (being prepared to buy a share that has little trading volume and wait patiently for the market to price it correctly) is one of the most simple and reliable options around.

By contrast, the supposed liquidity in large-company stock can evaporate from one day to the next. We suffered an example of this with Ahold a few years earlier. We valued the company at 13 euros and seeing as it was trading at nine euros, we thought it was an attractive proposition as a member of the EuroStoxx 50, the index of large European companies. The issue was that the accounts didn't reflect the reality and when this was uncovered, the share price opened the next day at three euros. So a large and liquid company lost 66% of its value overnight and, needless to say, there was no liquidity either at nine euros. Our error was in the valuation.

What grated with us was that in this particular case there had been some warning signs – as almost always happens – which should have alerted us. In particular, their decision to buy a chain of Spanish supermarkets, Superdiplo, where we also had a stake and considered that Ahold had overpaid. But there's no room to hold a grudge in investment and years later we bought back into Ahold, with a degree of success.

Meanwhile, the list of small companies which we sold at their target price is endless: Cevasa, Inmobiliaria Asturiana, Fiponsa, Tudor, Grupo Anaya, Fuchs Petrolub, Camaieu, Hagemeyer, Buhrman, etc. In some cases the market itself woke up to the underpricing and brought them up to a fair price; in other cases another company bought them outright; there can be a multitude of possible drivers, but they all help to eliminate this inefficiency. The biggest exception we faced was the previously mentioned sale of Endesa's subsidiaries. The latter very shrewdly made use of a merger process which required an exchange to take place if an 'independent' evaluator gave the green light to the exchange equation, as proved to be the case. If they had launched a share purchase, we wouldn't have participated. This happened with Camaieu, the French clothing distributor, where we only consented to the third buyout, which took place two years after the first attempt. Anyway, we didn't lose money on Endesa's subsidiaries, we simply missed out on lost earnings.

The latest and most recent example of the false liquidity problem took place when I left Bestinver, followed by my colleagues in 2014. 25% of assets were redeemed in a quarter, but they were able to sell the necessary shares on a bear market without having to resort to discounts, except on a handful of occasions.

2008: CONTINUATION

Returning to 2008, the second quarter saw the two portfolios lose another 6%. While the Spanish portfolio fell less sharply than the index in the first half of the year, the loss in value was broadly similar in the global portfolio. The markets afforded some respite in April and May, with strong recoveries of around 20%, following JP Morgan's decision to purchase the insolvent Bear Sterns, one of Wall Street's leading investment banks.

Redemptions continued but the pace slowed significantly relative to the first quarter, which – together with the recovery in the market facilitating necessary sales – went a long way to steadying our nerves. Strangely enough, throughout the whole year building work was taking place in the office and the entire team was working in the same room, instead of our normal offices. I suppose this also helped us to hang in there.

In the global portfolio we reinvested in Ciba part of the sales from the share purchases. It was a global leader specialised in chemistry and went on to reward us with a welcome surprise not long after. Buffett had bought Rohm & Haas in the summer, a chemical company with similar characteristics to Ciba, at a much higher price than Ciba's multiples.

To add fire to the flames on the financial problems in the United States, rising commodity prices and especially oil – which stood at 140 dollars a barrel – led to a spike in global inflation expectations. Oil, which 10 years before had been trading below 10 dollars a barrel, had multiplied by 15 over the decade, while the stock markets had not done much at all, with a return of around 0%. You could already sense where the value would be in the future.

Our funds dropped sharply again in the third quarter, with the Spanish portfolio shedding 12% and the global portfolio 9%. After a relatively calm summer, September unleashed the biggest economic turmoil in recent decades. Lehman Brothers collapsed on 15 September, followed days later by serious problems at AIG, Merryll Lynch, etc.

THE FINANCIAL CRISIS

The general feeling among public opinion is that the financial crisis was caused by malicious Wall Street bankers, whose greed broke the idyllic social order created by a healthy and diligent society. They undoubtedly have their share of the blame, but blaming them is like pinning drug problems on the guy pushing on the street. We all know that those who are ultimately – or principally – responsible are the big traffickers who put the drugs on the market in the first place, and the consumer, while the dealer pays for the harm caused by their own weakness. In the case of the financial crisis, the people ultimately responsible were those who artificially lowered interest rates or bent legal obligations, providing access to lending to people failing to meet the necessary minimum conditions.

In Spain, we were clean of the Wall Street virus and the CDOs (mortgage 'chunks'), all of which is brilliantly explained in *The Big Short*; yet, we had the same problems, if not worse than the Americans. What we did have in common with them was the interest rate.

The underlying problem is that the price of money (the interest rate) is not determined by the market, as happens with clothing or food; instead it is decided by so-called state experts on the basis of limited information (we will go into this in more detail in Chapter 4). What would we think if the price of clothes was decided by a panel of experts? It's happened in some countries and we know the outcome.

Returning to interest rates, how could a policy of artificially low interest rates not create perverse effects? Clearly somebody was going to try to make the most of it, and the Wall Street operators were in a privileged position to use the means on offer to them by the political class, in this case the Federal Reserve.

These low interest rates, which were also the driver of the Spanish crisis, dated back to 1998, when LTCM was bailed out for fear of being 'too big to fail'. After that there was the dot.com crash, the 9/11 attacks. and the second Iraq war, giving the Fed plenty of excuses to keep base rates below 2% for the three years from 2002 to 2005. In spring 2003 short-term interest rates stood at 1%, the lowest since 1958, against a backdrop of over 2% inflation. In other words, negative real interest rates for three years. Accordingly, in a period of two years from 2004 to 2005, house prices in the top 10 American cities rose by 38%, according to the Case–Schiller index.

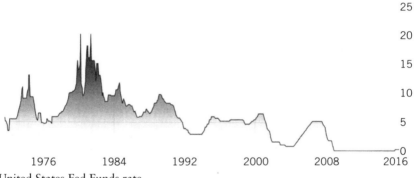

United States Fed Funds rate
Source: Federal Reserve.

But it wasn't just the Fed who were to blame, the US Congress also played a part. (If the problem had been limited to low rates, perhaps the crisis might have been avoided. From 2008 to 2015, interest rates have been close to 0% without apparent harm; it appears as though the money has not trickled into the system in the same way as before.) It's incredible looking back at some of quotes from Barney Frank, the Democrat congressman in 2003 then responsible for the policy on Government-Sponsored Enterprise (GSE), Fannie Mae, and Freddy Mac, the financial institutions responsible for guaranteeing mortgages: 'I do think I do not want the same kind of focus on safety and soundness that we have in the OCC (Office of the Comptroller of the Currency) and the OTS (Office of Thrift Supervision). I want to roll the dice a little bit more in this situation toward subsidized housing'.[7]

Frank was not so much worried about the solidity of the system as driving up home ownership among the least well off, which is why he didn't let up on his efforts to oblige banks to follow his ethos, without worrying about people's repayment capacity. Previously, in 1992, the GSE had been subject to the affordable housing law, which required that 30% of guaranteed mortgages be provided to underprivileged households. This proportion rose to 50% under Clinton in 2000 and to 55% with Bush in 2007. As a result, a significant proportion of subprime or low-quality mortgages were guaranteed by quasi-governmental organisations controlled by the US Congress (according to the SEC).

The Community Reinvestment Act (CRA) was also important. This was old legislation from the President Carter years, which was strengthened by the Clinton administration and which required non-discrimination against minorities in the provision of loans, effectively obliging banks to grant them. In this regard, the words of another politician are enlightening, Andrew Cuomo, US Secretary of Housing under Bill Clinton, in regard to the judicial decision requiring banks to grant mortgages to the less well off: 'The bank will take on more risk with these mortgages… it will give mortgages to families who wouldn't otherwise have been able to access them… Lending amounts to 2.1 trillion dollars in high-risk mortgages and I'm convinced there will be higher incidence of default on these mortgages than on other loans' (in Thomas Woods, *Meltdown*[8]). And he slept easily after saying it. On investigation, the GSEs guaranteed 1.7 trillion dollars of high-risk mortgages.[9]

Simply put, in the 15 years leading up to the crisis, Congress and the American executive actively promoted house buying among the underprivileged. A laudable objective if it had been done prudently, without surpassing desirable limits, but that's not how it went down.

---

[7]Barney Frank to the House Financial Services Committee on 25 September 2003. During the same period he was quoted as saying: 'The more people in my judgement, exaggerate a threat of safety and soundness, the more people conjure up the possibility of serious financial losses to the Treasury, which I do not see. I think we see entities that are fundamentally sound financially and withstand some of the disaster scenarios'. (Referring to the semi-public entities sponsoring mortgages), 10 September 2003.
[8]Woods (2009).
[9]Gene Epstein, 'The Fannie and Freddie Chronicles', *Barron's*, 7 January 2012.

The global financial crisis would not have happened if two of North America's leading political institutions had refrained from interfering in monetary price formation (via interest rates) and mortgage lending conditions (through legislation encouraging people with low repayment capacity to take on debt).

In this context, some of the American commercial banks, Wall Street – people who, by the way, have little to do with our way of working – and the ratings agencies responded overly aggressively, as they are inclined to do when taking advantage of any loophole liable to generate fees, issuing confusing and opaque products. This was enhanced by an incentive system which favoured short-term asymmetric 'bets' of the type where, if the trader gets it wrong, it's the institution they work for that takes the hit, but if they get it right, they stand to make significant personal gains.

China also played a role in pushing down interest rates through major purchases of American bonds.

These factors compounded the problem that had been created, taking it to an extreme. But neither Wall Street banks nor the Chinese governance can be held primarily responsible for something that took place elsewhere and for which they were solely accomplices to the previously mentioned political institutions.

Who did and didn't see the crisis coming? While Barney Frank and the rest of the pro-intervention political and academic establishment championed lending to people with doubtful repayment capacity, there were some exceptions. An example is the libertarian congressman Ron Paul who at, the same time, on 10 September 2003, told Congress that:

> *The credit line to the GSEs … distorts the allocation of capital. Even more importantly, the credit line is a promise made in the Government's name to carry out a large-scale, immoral and unconstitutional income transfer from American workers to GSE debt holders.*
>
> *Ironically, by transferring the risks of generalised mortgage losses, the Government is increasing the probability of a painful real estate crash.*
>
> *Despite the long-term damage inflicted on the economy by Government intervention in the housing market … in the short-term it is generating a boom … which will not last forever.*

I suppose being a doctor helped Ron Paul to have a clear perspective on things. Meanwhile, one of the most influential living economists, Nobel Prize winner Joseph Stiglitz, issued a report in 2002 on the GSEs. In this report, prepared with Jonathan and Peter Orszag, he concluded that with new capital standards the risk of severe shock was less than one in 500,000.[10] Another Nobel Prize winner, Paul Krugman, also of the interventionist bent, was still claiming in 2008 that the GSEs had nothing to do with the real-estate crisis.

CIBA: SALVATION AT THE DARKEST HOUR

By enormous coincidence, the same day that Lehman Brothers announced its bankruptcy, 15 September 2008, we received a purchase offer for Ciba, the second largest position in our global portfolio, accounting for 8%. Basf, the German chemical company, was seizing the moment to buy assets at a good price. Ciba shares had been trading at 25 Swiss francs in the summer, rising to above 30 on the back of rumours, which was formalised on the 15th with an offer of 50 francs. We valued the company at around 100 francs (Basf's own advisors, in the document accompanying the purchase offer, estimated the company's value at 80–87 francs in their fairness opinion), and initially turned down the offer.[11]

After waiting several weeks, and observing the market collapse, in November we decided to sell our entire stake to Basf. Since Ciba had gone up in value by 75% and the rest of the portfolio had fallen by 25%, it now represented 20% of our portfolio. This entailed a degree of risk, and offloading the shares would provide us with some liquidity firepower at an ideal time. The alternatives had now become extremely attractive, making it increasingly less appealing to hold on to Ciba shares and fight for a higher price. The ability to detach oneself from building emotional connections with investments is a major asset; it's better neither to become besotted with a specific stock or company, nor to despise them either.

---

[10]Stiglitz *et al.* (2002).
[11]Perella Weinberg Partners, 'Fairness Opinion for the attention of the Board of Ciba Holding Inc.', 13 September 2008.

We must be able to adapt to different circumstances. Despite the potential for a further 100% increase in the price of Ciba shares, we decided to offload our holdings, giving us the opportunity to buy companies with potential for 200% upside. The extra liquidity would also give us a cushion to withstand a worsening of the crisis.

This is yet another example of the importance of focusing on stock picking over attempting to predict what will happen in the world. We live under constant uncertainty and will continue to do so until the only sure thing in life comes knocking. I remember listening to these happy words for the first time when I started working in the financial markets in 1990, and I haven't stopped hearing them since. Want to guess what moment we are in right now? You got it – a time of great uncertainty.

Despite tumbling prices, by October 2008 our investors were no longer withdrawing much money. Our investors are a sensible bunch, and we were already talking about falls of over 25% from 1 January, such that the desire to sell began to dissipate. Throughout the year we went to great lengths to communicate and be transparent. We held telephone conferences, we started publishing the target values for our funds, and we broadened the information set out in our quarterly reports and other client communications.

On 30 September we sent another letter to clients, along similar lines to that of December 2000. In this new letter we stressed that our portfolios were extremely conservative and that the American housing market adjustment was now quite well advanced. The letter, and other efforts to communicate, appeared to have the desired effect.

Madrid, 30 September 2008

Dear investor,

Recent events have had a significant impact on various financial institutions in Western Europe and especially the United States. The crisis has the same origins as its predecessors: an over-leveraging of the financial system endorsed with the tacit or explicit support of the corresponding authorities. As we have been warning for some time now, such excesses always come unstuck, to the detriment of nearly all concerned.

However, we would like to reiterate that while in the short term it may seem as though Bestinver funds have been affected by the situation, the long-term impact will be minimal, providing us with an opportunity to take advantage of the turmoil. This is due to several factors:

- Our exposure to the banking sector has been non-existent for some time now and will continue that way, this is no coincidence, but rather a prediction of the credit bubble bursting.
- Over 90% of our companies have minimal debt or none at all. They don't need credit to operate; some of them have net positive cash.
- Customers of our companies are dispersed around the world, meaning they can focus sales efforts on more attractive markets (China, Brazil, Germany, etc.).
- We should not lose sight of the fact that global growth in 2008 will be around 3%. It could slow in 2009 but remain positive, given the strong stimulus to growth from Continental China, which is based on sustainable factors such as savings and productive work, both of which have been in short supply in some western countries. Despite the steady flow of negative news coming out of the western world, various other countries are growing sustainably, without accumulating debt.
- The extreme surge in commodity prices, which has had such a negative impact on some of the companies in our funds, is starting to revert. This will provide a very significant boost to Western consumers, which will soon be reflected in their purchasing power.
- As we noted back in January, the biggest negative impact on our funds is coming from the lack of liquidity affecting some co-investors in our companies. This will be short-lived and will ultimately reveal the enormous value in our investments. We are publishing target values each month on our website and they have been on a steady upward path since the start of the crisis.

The end of the 'crisis' is unlikely to come until house prices stop falling in the USA. In some areas, price declines have reached around 50%, meaning the end may well be in sight. The North American economy's major asset is its impressive flexibility. An incredible adjustment has taken place in less than 18 months which will provide a much more solid base for the years to come. We sincerely believe that the long-term effects will be positive.

Either way, we remain convinced – however surprising it may seem – that equities are the best asset for preserving value at a time of financial crisis. Patience and composure will enable us to reap the rewards in the medium term.

In October, we will expand on all these points in our quarterly letter, which forms part of our commitment to explaining our work to the best of our abilities.

Francisco García Paramés
Chief Investment Officer

Transparency has always been an essential part of our relationship with clients. It's true that there have to be some limits – the competition is always peering over our shoulder – but within these limits we try to be as helpful as possible. This enables our clients to better understand our work, which helps us.

As a consequence, over the crisis as a whole, from summer 2007 to spring 2009, redemptions amounted to a little over 20% of assets under management. This was primarily due to institutions pulling out, as they have a harder time withstanding outside pressure than families.

In the last quarter of 2008, not only did the crisis fail to let up, but it worsened, and the falls were even more pronounced: 15.7% on the Spanish portfolio and 20.9% on the global fund! Our overall losses came to 35.16% and 44.71%, respectively. 5% better than the market on the Spanish fund and 5% worse at the global level.

October was particularly painful. We posted losses of 15%, but there were days of 10% price falls, followed by short-lived rebounds. As it happened, my third daughter was born on 9 October, in the midst of the worst days.

Her arrival helped put the crisis firmly into perspective, easing the tension around us and creating some distance from what was going on. The continued declines had created a surreal sensation, almost as if it was all a big wind-up. Álvaro brought the latest positions to the hospital and we tried to make the most of the movements in share prices.

By the end of 2008 the Spanish portfolio was trading at a P/E ratio of six and the global portfolio was at 3.4. These were obviously the lowest prices we had ever encountered, and wouldn't be repeated for a long time. The potential upside was enormous, 150% and 340%, respectively.

2009: IMMEDIATE RECOVERY

2009 started in a similar vein to the end of 2008, with more losses which continued into the first week of March. But some positive signals were already beginning to emerge, and with the change of year I gave serious consideration to borrowing to invest; the first time I had thought about it in 18 years. Any investment, even more so with equities, should be made with surplus savings, money that's not needed for daily life. Debt should be a small component of any investment. It's true that a housing investment could be underpinned by a mortgage worth 50% of the value of the asset – at most – but investment in equities should involve very modest amounts of debt, never more than 15–20% of the value of the shares. We should be able to sleep at night if we cap debt at these proportions, knowing we will be able to withstand market movements.

I don't invest using debt, except for the one instance when I first started out investing; however, 2009 seemed like too good an opportunity to miss. In the end, I couldn't make up my mind.

The clearest indication that we were at the low point came from my own inner circle. For the first time my wife queried whether her mother's modest investment in the funds, whose returns helped cover her expenses, might not be better placed in a less volatile fund. This took place in February in our kitchen at home, and I distinctly remember thinking that if even my wife – who had been and is a firm believer in what we do – was wavering, then the end of the crisis could not be far off.

As it happened, the low point of the crisis coincided with our Investor Days. Barcelona on Thursday, 5 March and Madrid on Monday, 9 March – the same day the markets hit rock bottom. We are talking about prices which hadn't been seen since 1996, 13 years earlier. On 9 March, the S&P 500 was trading at 57% below the peak of a year and a half before. The second largest crash in history after 1929.

When we arrived in Barcelona, the international fund's NAV was at nine euros per share, down 62% on a high of 23.6 euros in July 2007 – just 18 months earlier. Never in my worst nightmares did I think a portfolio managed by us would suffer losses of 25–30% in value, let alone 62%… We didn't quite know how our clients were going to react. We had done a good job explaining our approach over the years, and we had redoubled our efforts in 2008, but we were talking about enormous losses.

We gave an extremely exhaustive presentation, going into more detail than ever and disaggregating the portfolio to a level of granularity rarely seen in the market. For example, we spoke of our two biggest investments: BMW, which was being given away at 11 euros (it's now trading at 70 euros) and Ferrovial, trading at three euros (it's now priced at 20 euros).

BMW
Source: Bloomberg.

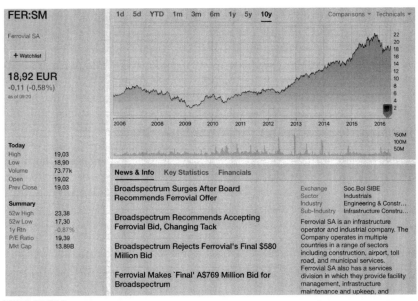

FERROVIAL
Source: Bloomberg.

As always, we made sure to handle all the audience's questions and the response was overwhelming: not only were they understanding and interested, but they applauded at the end of the conference. We were applauded. This might well be the most extraordinary thing to have happened to me in all my years as an investor. People who had seen 60% of their savings wiped out (only temporarily, mind you, as we insisted) applauding the people 'responsible' for these losses. Three days later the applause was repeated in Madrid, and this surprising show of confidence gave us renewed strength to continue fighting the falls.

But the rot stopped that same day, on 9 March. It's worth pausing a moment to talk about the viability of the company and ourselves as managers, something I also gave consideration to at the suggestion of my wife. In 2009 we were managing two billion euros, a massive drop from 6.5 billion in July 2007. We never took on debt and were always backed up by Acciona, meaning that we faced the crisis from a healthy position. We made a quick calculation and believed we could endure additional market falls of 75–80% before the company's future was in jeopardy. In other words, we could go from 6.5 billion euros in assets to 500 million and still maintain the same investment approach and team. This was an additional source of comfort.

Maintaining a break-even or a low earnings threshold, both professionally and personally, is a key trait for being able to survive independently and remain resilient. It was surprising to learn that some of our competitors folded, citing insufficient funds, when they were still managing hundreds of thousands of euros or dollars. In some cases it covered up a semi-fraud; closures can happen because managers are paid success fees and the losses would have prevented them from collecting for a long while. But in other cases the foundations of the company were plain shaky, failing to give consideration to a worst-case scenario and its implications.

The professional resilience of a robust company should also be accompanied by an extremely low threshold of family or personal outgoings, enabling us to overcome a variety of circumstances in our private life. We should always be prepared to be calm in the face of hardship; neither excessive debt nor a lavish lifestyle are compatible with our style of management. Both my wife and I have always been acutely aware of this.

I sincerely believe that the approach to investing and living need to be congruent.

But at the time what really calmed our nerves was the rapid recovery in the markets from 9 March onwards. In March, various stocks which had taken a major kicking – such as Debenhams, Esprinet, Oce, etc. – rebounded by 80–170%. In some of these companies we had increased our positions thanks to the leverage generated from Ciba, and we were particularly satisfied to see that many of the revivals came after the companies published good results. Which is how it should be.

By the second quarter the results were through the roof. 21% for the Spanish portfolio and 43% on the global side. The recovery in the global portfolio was the strongest we'd posted in a quarter, and it was followed by continued increases in the second half of the year. Bestinver's NAV, which touched bottom at nine euros in March, ended the year at 18, a 100% increase on our nadir and up 71% on the start of the year.

THE QUALITY OF COMPANIES

One of the accusations that could be laid at our door is that, despite foreseeing the excesses of the financial system, we didn't set aside enough liquidity to deal with the consequences. However, the reality is that we liked our companies and believed they would stand up to any situation. It's worth reiterating that, although for our taste some sectors might be overvalued or at potential risk, if we believe the portfolio is in good shape then the best approach is to wait until the storm abates.

However, in hindsight it was clear that the quality of companies in our global portfolio was not as good as it ideally should have been in order to withstand a crisis. Our Spanish portfolio was formed of a very good selection of defensive stocks and exporters, embodied by Ferrovial, which represented 9%. But this wasn't true of the global portfolio, where in some cases we were still too focused on price at the expense of quality.

Indeed, the crisis confirmed that high-quality companies at reasonable prices perform better over the long term than companies which are straight cheap. It's a path that takes us from Graham, specialist in companies with very underpriced real assets, to Buffett, focused on higher-quality stock, proxied by the degree of competitive advantage they enjoy.

Many investors have gone down this path, practically all the value investors. The main reason is that it delivers better results over the long term, although there aren't many studies to back up this assertion, making it initially a far from obvious conclusion. Added to this, when we are young and start out investing, we have an excessive desire to do well and make our mark, meaning we tend to favour the cheapest companies, which on face value offer the greatest potential upside. As we mature, after having stepped on a few booby and/or value traps (cheap companies in bad businesses, which languish for years, failing to create value) and our economic situation improves, our tastes tend to shift towards quality, even if you have to pay a bit more for it.

We will discuss the road to quality in more detail later on, but for now I will just mention that my catalyst for going down this route was a small book by Joel Greenblatt, *The Little Book That Beats the Market*,[12] which provides statistical confirmation that quality is worthwhile. After reflecting on our own portfolio – which was of moderate quality – and given our desire for greater resilience in the future, we began to move more deliberately down this path. This meant that in 2009, certain stocks such as Schindler (old friend), Wolters Kluwer (another old friend), and Thales made it (back) into our portfolio, going on to amply reward us. On the flipside, as they began regaining value, we partially or totally offloaded stocks such as Debenhams, Smurfit Kappa, CIR (partially), and Alapis.

The natural implication of making this shift to quality, and our growing confidence in our stock selection, was an increase in the concentration of our global portfolio. By this time, we had around 60–70 stocks in our portfolio, which is where it remained.

2010–2012: EUROPEAN AND SPANISH CRISIS

Surprisingly, the global financial crisis didn't have an immediate impact on European economies, as the initial assumption was that the European financial system was more robust than the American one. But in 2010, with Greece already in the cross-hairs, the market began to fret about Europe, particularly the so-called periphery countries, which included Spain. Aside from Spain, like everyone else we were caught off guard by what had been happening in the periphery, including Portugal.

In Spain, time slipped by with the government engaged in a mindless Keynesian policy, spending money that the country couldn't afford. Meanwhile, the financial system was entering a palliative stage, hitting crisis point in 2012. Up until then, Spanish banks were still managing to hide their problems, extending and pretending bad loans while everyone around them turned a blind eye. It was in nobody's interest to tell the truth, neither the financial system, nor the political class, nor the real-estate sector, nor the people who had taken out loans knowing they wouldn't be able to pay. The Bank of Spain's experts knew what was going on but were silenced by the bank's political leadership.

---

[12]Greenblatt (2006).

It's worth remembering that in Spain the worst atrocities were committed in the cajas, 'not for profit' savings banks controlled by regional political powers. It wasn't greedy capitalists. It was once again the political class protecting their individual interests. Only when they were no longer able to pay the salaries of real-estate workers and bankers were they left with no option but to come clean.

The European crisis began in Greece in the spring of 2010 and exploded once and for all in summer 2011, setting the markets tumbling until summer 2012. Over many years, a number of European countries – chiefly Spain, Greece, Portugal, and Ireland – had lived beyond their means, generating large external imbalances which were covered by significant foreign financial inflows. In Spain and Ireland the investments had focused on the real-estate sector, which contributed next to nothing to increasing productivity and wealth. History was repeating what had happened in Asia a decade earlier.

When it became obvious that this type of growth wasn't sustainable, the external funding dried up and it was revealed that the Emperor was indeed naked. Injections of public spending did nothing more than worsen the problem, slapping a sticking plaster over it until 2012, when there was no other option but to face up to reality, particularly in Spain, the largest of the peripheral economies.

We had been anticipating this would happen for some time. And so, in the three years from 2010 to 2012, our Iberian portfolio went up slightly in value, while the Spanish index retreated another 30%. For the second time in 10 years we had managed to avoid significant losses on Spanish equities (though it was unavoidable in 2008).

Our portfolio of defensive and/or exporter stocks fulfilled its purpose perfectly during this tumultuous period and, eventually, we found ourselves in a new era in which bad news came flooding to the front pages of the newspapers, meeting the necessary conditions for us to invest in Spain. In 2012, 10 years down the road, we began to buy purely 'Spanish' stocks such as Antena 3, Mediaset (Tele 5), and Catalana Occidente, observing that the crisis was beginning to be reflected in the prices, which had fallen well below global and even European markets. However, it wasn't until 2013 that the first Spanish banks returned to our portfolio after 15 years of abstinence – in the form of Bankia and Bankinter. We didn't take part in Bankia's initial flotation in July 2011, but we did get involved in the post-rescue return in 2013. We liked the new governing board, the management team, and the high level of provisioning they had demanded before accepting the challenge of taking the bank forward.

2011 brought about a change of government in Spain. Initially the impact was limited. Despite having an absolute majority in Parliament, the centre-right PP party wasn't bold enough to act decisively. However, the continued deterioration of the situation and outside (mainly German) pressure forced them to be more determined:

- The critical state of the financial sector was recognised with support from European organisations. This created the conditions for the real-estate sector to gradually find a real market price for its assets.
- State spending was frozen. It wasn't dramatically reduced, but at least it was a change of stance compared with the past.
- A labour market reform was introduced to add flexibility to the relationship between employers and employees, enabling companies to better adjust to changing market conditions.

Overall, this brutal crisis, caused by living beyond our means for too long, brought about a certain change of mindset among my countrymen. The priority was no longer finding a cushy position as a local government official in a place close to home; this was no longer possible. You now had to go on the hunt for work wherever it could be found, even in faraway countries.

The result of all this is that I now sincerely believe that Spain has a unique opportunity to capitalise on its resources and make a leap forward in its global positioning. With world-class infrastructure (telecommunications, transport, hospitality, etc.), a privileged geographical location bridging three continents, and a degree of restraint in labour and real-estate costs, it's an attractive proposition for global entrepreneurs with ambitions to create new businesses or build on what they have.

There is no denying that Spain still has its fair share of problems, such as corruption or finding a fit for regional governments within a more viable and austere state structure, but they are not so serious as to detract from the advantages. I don't consider myself a rampant patriot, but I'm fond of my country and would like my countrymen to have a good future. I am making my own small contribution by returning to Spain, creating a company along with a good group of professionals, giving a service to clients who like our way of working, and contributing as best I can to promote my city and country.

Seen from today's vantage point, our biggest error at this point in the crisis was failing to have greater conviction in these purely Spanish stocks. Having waited for so long and got the timing right, we weren't decisive enough, only investing around 10% of the Iberian portfolio. I couldn't convince Álvaro, who had begun to develop a very negative view of the markets, and I didn't want to push him into it.

The European crisis also had some repercussions on the global portfolio, but they were modest. We only suffered significant losses in summer 2011, thereafter gradually recovering them. All of our top picks, to which we added Exor – the holding company for the Agnelli family – performed well, especially our beloved BMW.

2013–2014: OVER AND OUT

In 2013 my wife and I took the decision to spend two years in London. It was purely family oriented. We wanted to have the experience of living outside of Spain and exposing our children to an English-language education. We had spent the previous two summers in China and the United States, and new technology made it possible to work effectively from anywhere in the world. At least as a fund manager.

Plus, London is not just any old place. It's Europe's financial centre (or at least it was before Brexit), and it therefore gave us the opportunity to investigate whether it was worth setting up an office there to complement our work in Madrid.

It all seemed straightforward enough. However, some problems surfaced in Acciona in relation to my move to London. After mulling it over in summer 2013, I decided that in our type of business, which is almost a craft, being a manager must mean being able to manage the company and not just investments. Once the decision was taken, I tried to find a reasonable accommodation within Bestinver and Acciona, I owed them as much for the understanding and unconditional support I had received over 25 years.

We contemplated various options: taking a stake in the control of the company; diluting the decision-making power of the parent by involving a third partner; parting ways on a friendly basis; and some others. The process was extremely slow, as logically the other party wasn't much interested in changing the status quo, and after 15 months without finding any common ground, tiredness and frustration got the better of me and I announced my departure.

Throughout the entire process my goal was to ensure that clients had a smooth transition, giving them the option to make their own choice. But it didn't work out that way: my departure was abruptly announced and I shoulder much of the blame for this. I thought I would be back working again, one way or another, in no time and that my departure wouldn't be a problem, but I was wrong. I consulted on the interpretation of my contract with five legal advisors, four of whom advised me to work and the fifth recommended I wait out the two years indicated by the contract. I was ultimately convinced by the fifth lawyer, Valeriano Hernández-Tavera, who advised me not to compete but instead patiently sit out my two years. And this – for better or worse – is what I did; it fitted my character and strong aversion to confrontation.

The second, lesser error, was thinking that the price to be paid for working would increase if I stayed on from September to December 2014, and this is perhaps what triggered the resignation at that precise moment. If I had known this wasn't the case, I would have announced my intentions in September and stayed on until December, when I would have finally left.

Either way, two months wouldn't have changed the final result much. I guess the biggest problem for some clients was the lack of an alternative option for continuing with me in the short term.

In sum: errors of judgement on my part and silence on the other side, who didn't respond to my final proposals.

In any case, Bestinver inexplicably turned down my offer to collaborate as part of an orderly transition. However, thanks to the combined efforts of Álvaro, Fernando, and Beltrán de la Lastra (my replacement), and the robustness of the portfolio, everyone who heeded my advice – unfortunately given in private, as I didn't want to make public pronouncements – to keep their savings in Bestinver and not make any hasty decisions, secured reasonable results over those two years. Once again, proof that a good portfolio focused on the long term can withstand anything, including the abrupt departure of one of its managers in a bear market.

The key to not repeating one's errors is owning up to them. We are all responsible for our own errors and learning from them. He who doesn't learn from them faces a bigger problem than the error itself. I made some mistakes, which I hope have taught me an abiding lesson.

My first 25 years of professional life thus came to an end. They have been good for the clients – especially those who were with us from the outset and have seen their savings multiply by 30, with their fund increasing from six to 180 in 20 years. Also for the shareholders, who have received ample dividends, and for us, the employees, who were adequately compensated.

I have now swapped a stable, calm, and very profitable position for the irresistible call of total independence. I think it's the right decision for all parties. It certainly is for me.

During these two years I have followed the markets on a daily basis, at a distance, but nonetheless every day. I have travelled to some of the countries I wanted to get to know better, such as India and UAE. I have written this book, which might be useful to some people. And I have spent more time with my family, friends, and acquaintances.

Now I have embarked on a new endeavour which I hope will be as long and as positive as the previous one: Cobas Asset Management. I have no complaints whatsoever about the first 25 years of investing, nor my last two years away from it. I will try not to have any complaints in the next 25 years, as I get back into the saddle once again …

APPENDIX

Bestinver Internacional Portfolio (31/03/2003)

STOCKS	Investment	% Total
State debt (repo)	200	2.32
TOTAL PUR. ASSETS	200	2.32
TOTAL FIXED INCOME	200	2.32
TOTAL DOMESTIC PORTFOLIO	200	2.32
7-Eleven Inc. (SE)	77	0.89
Advanced Micro Devices (AMD)	44	0.51
Aegon NV (AGNNA)	61	0.71
AGF (AGF)	62	0.72
AholdNV (ANLN)	42	0.49
Alico Inc. (ALCO)	30	0.35
Alstom (ALS FP)	35	0.41
Allied Domecq (ALLD LN)	72	0.83
Allied Waste lnd. (AW US)	55	0.64
AMB Aachener & Mun.DEM (AMB29	23	0.27
American Natl.Insurance (ANAT)	55	0.64
American Real (ACP)	21	0.24
Avenus SA (AVE)	141	1.63
Aviva plc (AV/ LN)	39	0.45
Axel Springer Ver. AG (SPR GR)	100	1.16
Azko Nobel (AKZA NA)	55	0.64
B. Privée Edmond Rothschild RLD	119	1.38
Bally Total Fitness (BFT US)	18	0.21
Barry Callebaut AG (BARN)	89	1.03
Batenburg Beheer (BTBN NA)	21	0.24

STOCKS	Investment	% Total
BE Semiconductor Ind. (BESI)	110	1.27
Bell AG Basel CHF (BELN)	51	0.59
Bell Inds. (BI US)	54	0.63
Bellsouth Corp. (BLS US)	0	0.00
Big Food Group (BFP)	19	0.22
Bilfinger Berger AG (GBF)	131	1.52
Boskalis Westminster (BOKC)	76	0.88
Bristol Myers (BMY US)	74	0.86
Bucher lud. Bearer (BUC SW)	101	1.17
Bohrmann (BUHE)	31	0.36
Cable & Wireless GBP (CW)	0	0.00
Cambridge Antibody Tech (GBP)	23	0.27
Cap Gemini (CAP FP)	19	0.22
Circuit City Stores USD (CC)	48	0.56
CNP Assurance (CNP)	28	0.32
Codan DKK (CORAN)	45	0.52
Commerzbank	0	0.00
Cvs Corporation (CSV US)	51	0.59
Chubb plc (CHB LN)	68	0.79
Daichi Pharma (4505 JP)	5	0.06
Dassault Aviation (AM)	109	1.26
Delhaize Le Lion (DELB)	132	1.53
Devro lutemational (DVO)	129	1.50
E. On AG (EOA)	53	0.61
Earthlink Inc. (ELNK US)	92	1.07
Eastman Kodak (EK)	0	0.00
Edel Music (EDL)	58	0.67
Edipress (EDI)	54	0.63
Electronic D. Systems (EDS US)	24	0.28
Elior (ELR FP)	32	0.37
Escada AG (ESC GR)	43	0.50
Etam Developpement (TAM)	64	0.74
Fairchild Corp-CL A (THE) FA US	52	0.60
Fairfax Financial Holdings (FFH)	176	2.04

STOCKS	Investment	% Total
Federated Dept. Stores Inc. (FD)	33	0.38
Fleming Companics Inc. (FLM)	7	0.08
Fraport AG (FRA GE)	121	1.40
Getronics (GTN)	0	0.00
GEI Informatique (GFI FP)	52	0.60
Glaxosmithldine (GSK LN)	80	0.93
Great Atlantic & Pactea (GAP)	12	0.25
Greencore (GNC ID)	55	0.64
Hagemeyer (HAGN NA)	35	0.41
Havas (HAV FP)	54	0.63
Head	103	1.19
Healthsouth Corp. (HLSH US)	6	0.07
Healthsouth Corp. (BRC US)	0	0.00
Heidrick & Struggles (HSII)	44	0.51
Hochtief (HOT)	112	130
Honeywell Ind. (HON)	22	0.25
Hypovereinsbank (HVM)	12	0.14
IDT Corp.-B (IDT US)	283	3.28
IDT Corp.-B (IDT/B)	0	0.00
Imperial Chen Lids (GBP)	22	0.25
ING (INGA)	63	0.73
Ivax Corp. (IVX US)	38	0.44
Karstadt STK (KAR GR)	40	0.46
Kuoni Reisen CaLB (KUNN)	68	0.79
Level 3 Comm. Inc. (LVLT US)	40	0.46
Liberty Media Corp. (L US)	75	0.87
M-Real B OYJ (MRLBV)	44	0.51
Macintosh Retail Group. (RWNT)	46	0.53
Mcdonalds Corp. (MCD US)	40	0.46
Mediclin (MED GR)	34	0.39
Medisana AG (Mali)	29	0.34
Merck KGAA (MRK GR)	0	0.00
Metallwaren PS (METP)	117	1.36
Metro AG (MEO GR)	127	1.47

STOCKS	Investment	% Total
Mitsui Sumitomo Ins. (8752)	68	0.79
NipponKoa Insurance Co. (8754)	140	1.62
Nortel Networks Corp. (NT)	0	0.00
MT Corp. (9432)	96	1.11
Numico (NUTV)	101	1.17
Nutreco Holding (NUT)	113	1.31
Oce (OCEN)	94	1.09
Of1iceMax (OMX)	76	0.88
Okumura Corp. (1833)	86	1.00
OPG (OPG)	65	0.75
Ordina (ORDN)	74	0.86
Pinkroccade NV (PINK)	44	0.51
PlayBoy Enterprises (PLA)	38	0.44
Premier Oil (PMO)	0	0.00
Prudential plc (PRU LN)	15	0.17
R W E	82	0.95
Randstad Holding (RSTD)	41	0.48
Rite Aid Corporation Com. (RAD)	157	1.82
Roularta Media Group (ROU BB)	89	1.03
Royal & Sun GBP (RSA)	25	0.29
Scottish & Newcastle GBP (SCTN)	65	0.75
Schering (SCH GR)	76	0.88
Schering Plough Corp. (SGP)	42	0.49
Silke Pharmaceuticals (SHP LN)	43	0.50
Shofu INC. (7979)	30	0.35
Six Flugs Inc. (PKS)	23	0.27
SMG (SMG)	44	0.51
Sol Im (SOL)	0	0.00
Somerfield (SOF)	26	0.30
Spherion Corp. (SEN)	0	0.00
SSL International plc (SSL)	72	0.83
Stagecoach Holdings plc. (SGC)	37	0.43
Stork (VMFN)	57	0.66
Suez Lyonnais-Eaux (SZE)	36	0.42

STOCKS	Investment	% Total
Swift Energy Co. (SFY)	37	0.43
Syms Corp. (SYM)	15	0.17
Telegraaf Holding (TEAC)	58	0.67
Tommy Billiger Corp. (TOM)	60	0.70
Topps Inc USD	40	0.46
Toys R US (TOY)	46	0.53
Trinity Mirror (TN1)	66	0.76
United Services Group (UNI)	112	1.30
Valuevision Media Inc. (V VTV US)	18	0.21
Vendex KBB (VNDX)	104	1.21
Vivendi Environ (vie fp)	45	0.52
Vopak (VPK)	49	0.57
Wegener (WEGA)	227	2.63
Wessanen (WESS)	49	0.57
Wolters Kluwer Shares-WLSNC-NA	113	1.31
Yum! Brands Inc. (YUM US)	45	0.52
Zurich Fin. Services AG (ZURN)	66	0.76
TOTAL EQUITIES	8,040	93.18
DWS Japan-Fonds Anteile SI.	388	4.50
TOTAL FUND PARTICIP. FUNDS	388	4.50
TOTAL EXTERNAL PORTFOLIO	8,428	97.68
TOTAL PORTFOLIO (thousands of euros)	8,628	100.00

Source: CNMV.

Theory: The Underpinnings of Investment

The Austrian School
of Economics

Although it was 10 years into my career as an investor before I came across the Austrian economists, discovering them was a major turning point. Their ideas on economics have gone on to provide me with an explanation for economic developments which has proven to be surprisingly coherent with my day-to-day experience in the markets and my work as an investor. They have been marvellous companions along the way. I therefore feel it's logical to devote a chapter to them, even if it may seem a little unorthodox in a book ostensibly about value investment.[1]

Being an expert in economics is not an essential prerequisite for daily investment decisions, but it is definitely useful to have a sound conceptual framework to fall back on; a sufficiently nuanced understanding of economics provides us with some orientation. Indeed, nowadays, I find it very difficult to convey even basic investment concepts without having first established a robust economic framework.

Even though there are hundreds of hedge funds attempting to second guess the direction of the economy, most value investors don't think about

---

[1]Not much has been published on the Austrian School and its links to investment. Though recently two books have come my way. The first book I ran into was *The Dao of Capital* by Mark Spitznagel (2013). I found out about Mark in an interview he gave to the *Financial Times* in May 2016. He focuses his analysis on the roundabout concept, which describes the lengthening of the economy's productive process when it is functioning correctly. It's a different take but I have found it a useful excuse to reacquaint myself with Eugene Böhm von Bawerk's contribution to the school, especially some of his key concepts such as time preference. The second book, the *Austrian School for Investors*, by Taghizadegan *et al.* (2015), was brought to my attention by Gabriel Calzada, Dean of the Francisco Marroquín University. It's also a good introduction to the aspects of the school that are of most interest to us here.

it very much, spending practically no time on forecasting. The latter believe that they add their value through selecting companies. We could even go so far as to say that a lack of interest in the economy is a defining feature of a value investor.

And rightly so, because trying to guess what the economy will do next is tantamount to taking a stab in the dark about how millions of people will behave, particularly the ruling political class, which as we know is almost impossible.

That said, experience has shown that understanding how the so-called economy works, which is no more than understanding human behaviour, can be of significant help in the process of investing for the long term. Investment is about trying to predict the behaviour of consumers, entrepreneurs, workers, politicians, and everything that surrounds us. If we understand their driving impulses and what we can expect from them, then we will already be some of the way down the road. The economy and investment are intimately linked. Not because both disciplines deal in numbers, which to a large degree are superfluous, but because at heart they are about understanding human behaviour. This is the ultimate goal of all good economists and investors.

Fortunately, there is a branch of economic theory that is of particular help to us in this endeavour. In the Austrian School we find what the classists called 'the economy and its economists'. I'm not talking about sorcerer's apprentices, but rather down-to-earth, perceptive individuals able to explain an array of human behaviour, particularly in relation to the economy. This economy and its economists will not tell us how much GDP will grow by next year, nor what inflation will do, but it can alert us to what might happen in a country or a particular sector over time based on how different economic actors are currently behaving. A warning of where the dangers might lurk and where it's safe to swim. Ultimately, it will provide us with a set of critical variables to hone in on. The latter almost never coincide with what your run-of-the-mill, neoclassical economists consider to be important.

This chapter will therefore focus on this group of marginalised, outcast, and oft-forgotten Austrian economists, with the aim of demonstrating how understanding human action in the economy can enable us to see the future more clearly and live the present moment with greater peace of mind.

I could have simply limited myself to recommending Ludwig von Mises' superb *Human Action*[2] or Murray N. Rothbard's *History of Economic*

---

[2]von Mises (1995).

Thought,[3] but both run to more than a thousand pages and I don't want to put anybody off. Furthermore, given their significance to my tale, I feel that the Austrian School deserves more than a simple footnote in this book.

What follows is an attempt to provide a brief overview of the school and its main tenets, based on Huerta de Soto, Jesús's excellent primer, *The Austrian School*.[4] I will finish up by discussing possible applications for their ideas to investment.

BRIEF HISTORY OF THE AUSTRIAN SCHOOL

Origins

The Austrian School formally came into existence in the nineteenth century with Carl Menger and the subjectivist revolution brought about by the publication of his *Principles of Economics*.[5] But the basic ideas of the school go back even further and have their historical antecedents in Taoism, as highlighted by Rothbard.

By then, the Roman legal tradition had already been developed on the basis of accumulated customs and the evolutionary development of institutions – a key focus of attention for Friedrich A. Hayek – and its formation and development continued with contributions from successive generations. As Huerta de Soto, Jesús recalls, Cato observed that:

> *In contrast, our Roman republic is not the personal creation of one man, but of many. It has not been founded during the lifetime of any specific individual, but over a number of centuries and generations. For there has never been in the world a man intelligent enough to foresee everything, and even if we could concentrate all brainpower into the head of one man, it would be impossible for him to take everything into account at the same time, without having accumulated the experience which practice provides over the course of a long period in history.*
>
> **(in Jesús Huerta de Soto's *Austrian School*)**

---

[3] Rothbard (2000).
[4] de Soto (2008).
[5] Menger (1985).

The timelessness of these words speaks for itself, and they have been developed over time by numerous thinkers, culminating with Hayek in the twentieth century. After the Romans and following the Thomistic traditions, various Spaniards belonging to the Salamanca School during the Spanish Golden Age made critical contributions to what – centuries later – would become Austrian thought. In fact, Hayek regarded them as the main pioneers of market economy theory. The key thinkers in the Salamanca School were: Diego de Covarrubias, Luis Saraiva de la Calle, Luis de Molina, Juan de Lugo, Juan de Salas, Juan de Mariana, Martín de Azpilcueta, and some others. An array of stars who created and discovered concepts such as the subjective theory of value, the appropriate relationship between prices and costs, the dynamic nature of markets, the resulting impossibility of reaching economic equilibrium, the principle of time preference, and the distortionary nature of inflation. Evidently, the sixteenth- and seventeenth-century members of the Salamanca School had their heads more firmly screwed on than most twenty-first-century economists, including various Nobel Prize winners.

However, following their demise the subjectivist school fell into decline, which was partly the doing of Adam Smith. The renowned father of modern economics made some exceptional contributions, but he distanced himself from the subjectivist tradition, developing an objective labour theory of value and assigning great importance to the natural price equilibrium.

The labour theory of value subsequently formed the basis for Marx's ideas. As Rothbard would later argue, the development of economic thought is far from linear, as is the case in physical sciences, but it instead moves in constant fits and starts.

Nonetheless, some farsighted economists kept the subjectivist flame alive during the eighteenth and nineteenth centuries. In particular, Cantillon, Turgot, and Say in France; and Jaime Balmes in Spain. Say, for example, developed the famous Say's Law, which states that supply creates its own demand; the income from selling our products enables us to demand other products that appeal to us. This simple idea was misconstrued by Keynes a century later when he developed the erroneous concept of insufficient demand, the idea that demand in an economy can be less than supply, requiring artificial stimulation. Unfortunately, this nonsensical notion has stayed with us to this day, continuing to wreak the same damage as it has done over the centuries.

FAMILY TREE OF THE AUSTRIAN SCHOOL

Carl Menger
(1840–1921)
* Founder of the Austrian School
* Formed part of the marginal revolution
* The Method dispute (Methodenstreit)
* Critic of German historicism
* Spontaneous origin of money

Eugen von Böhm-Bawerk
(1851–1914)
* Contributed to initial development of AS
* Contributions to theory of capital and interest
* Critic of Marx's theory of exploitation

Friedrich Von Wieser
(1851–1926)
* Highlighted the informative role of the price system
* Contributed to the theory of imputation

Ludwig von Mises
(1881–1973)
* Systematised Austrian School thinking
* Understood that the economy forms part of praxeology. *Theory and History*
* Developed the theory of the economic calculation problem in socialism
* The first to systematise the Austrian theory of the economic cycle
* Critic of interventionism and all types of socialism

Joseph A. Schumpeter
(1883–1950)
* Entrepreneurship and innovation
* Contributions to the history of economic thought

Gottfried von Haberler
(1900–1995)
* Made contributions to international trade
* Was a critic of the Austrian theory of the economic cycle

Fritz Machlup
(1902–1983)
* Participates in the Privat Seminar with von Mises in Vienna
* Contributed to different fields in methodology, theory, and policy
* Specialist in international monetary systems
* His reading of von Mises' epistemology generated debate inside and outside the AS

Friedrich A. Hayek
(1899–1992)
* While he was initially influenced by Wieser, he was deeply intellectually indebted to von Mises
* Contributed to various fields such as economics, philosophy of science, law, political philosophy, psychology, and the history of ideas
* Notable contributions to monetary and capital theories and the theory of economic cycles
* Rekindled the tradition of spontaneous order developed under the Scottish Enlightenment
* Extended the theory of the economic calculation problem in socialism
* Understood the need for multidisciplinary approach to complex societal phenomena

Ludwig Lachmann
(1906–1990)
* Studied at the LSE with Hayek, where he assimilated his influence
* Particularly stressed the need for subjectivist economics
* Inspired by Hayek's contributions, he developed a theory on the heterogeneity of capital
* Together with G.L.S. Shackle he contributed to the study of subjective expectations

Israel Kirzner
(1930–)
* Completed his doctorate at New York University under the guidance of Ludwig von Mises
* Contributed to the theory of knowledge, entrepreneurship, theory of subjectivity, heterogeneity of capital, and market ethics

Hans Sennholz
(1922–2007)
* Completed his doctorate under the guidance of von Mises
* Specialist in monetary theory and policy
* Defender of the gold standard and critic of the central banking system

George Reisman
(1937–)
* Completed his doctorate under the guidance of von Mises
* Participated in his private seminar in New York
* Also influenced by Ayn Rand and is today defined as an objectivist
* His book *Capitalism* is the most extensive economic treatise to have been written since *Human Action*

Murray N. Rothbard
(1926–1995)
* He did not receive his doctorate with von Mises but was influenced by him
* Delved into the study of monetary theory and economic cycles
* Notable work on the Great Depression
* Defended anarcho-capitalism using economic, legal, political, and ethical arguments

ECONOMIC POINT OF VIEW

Carl Menger

Carl Menger (1840–1921) encapsulated the essence of these historical predecessors, and in his methodological struggles with the German historicists created the foundations of what would become the modern Austrian School. He advocated a priori logical analysis over the study of history and empirical data.

His book *Principles of Economics* constructs an economic theory based on tangible, creative human beings, in contrast to the objective theoretical beings invented by Adam Smith and Marx. His theory culminated in the law of marginal utility, which states that the value of each marginal unit diminishes in accordance with the end objectives and available means.

Another essential contribution is his theory on the origin and development of the social institutions – linguistic, economic, and cultural. He addresses the question: How is it possible that the institutions which are most significant to and best serve the common good have emerged without the intervention of a deliberate common will to create them? His conclusion is that these institutions appear over time as a result of human interactions, and that these interactions are precisely the main purpose of studying economics. Money is one of the main institutions to which he applied his evolutionary analysis.

After Menger came Eugen von Böhm-Bawerk (1851–1914), who expanded the subjective theory to capital – becoming the first to provide a very extensive explanation for the time structure of production – and to the theory of interest.

His interest theory was the first to employ the concept of time preference as the basis for determining the interest rate, broadening beyond mere monetary exchanges.

Finally, and of particular interest to us, he was the first author to reflect on the psychological component hampering 'correct preference' formation, highlighting the excessive weight assigned by human beings to the present, and inconsistencies in elections. He was the forerunner of behavioural finance, which has become such a focus of interest in recent decades.

Hot on their heels came perhaps the most important thinker in the Austrian School: Ludwig von Mises.

Ludwig von Mises

Ludwig von Mises (1881–1973) was born in Lemberg, in the Austro-Hungarian Empire. He became an economist after reading Menger's *Principles of Economics*. And, after attending a seminar by von Böhm-Bawerk in Vienna, he began lecturing there and later in Geneva. When the

Nazis rose to power he was forced to flee to the United States, giving classes at New York University. His contributions were defining.

In his theory of the value of money and, especially, through his regression theorem, he established that today's demand for money is based on yesterday's valuation of money, and yesterday's valuation was based on the previous day's, and so on until the moment of very inception when an original commodity – such as gold – was first used as money.

In his insightful theory of economic cycles, he highlights how cycles originate from the creation of credit without prior savings, through a fractional reserve banking system – not supported by gold – and with the acquiescence of central banks. On this basis, banks grant long-term loans using short-term deposits provided by clients. Since the bank does not maintain all the necessary money in the account to pay the depositor, it conjures money 'out of nothing'. Huerta de Soto, Jesús explains in *Money, Bank Credit and Economic Cycles*[6] that the bank breaks its deposit contract with the client by lending their money to a third party. On this point and others, there are some disagreements between members of the school. There is no uniform viewpoint – just like in any other school of thought.

In his theory on the impossibility of socialism, von Mises starts with the premise that nobody is capable of accumulating perfect knowledge and information on everything that is being created in a dynamic economy at a given point in time. The need for countless assessments of different economic agents' ends and means makes it impossible to adjust the available resources to their desired goals. All of this is beyond the capabilities of a single person or a group of wise men, and attempting to do so only leads to extreme disorder in human actions in the economy. Accordingly, in his entrepreneurship theory, he portrays humans as tangible, free, and creative beings, acting as the protagonists in a dynamic social process.

Von Mises was responsible for creating the Austrian Institute of Economic Research, which, led by Hayek, was the only one to predict the catastrophe that would take place after 1929. He even went so far as to turn down an offer of work in the Austrian Kreditanstalt because of his concerns about their situation.[7]

Meanwhile, one of the leading lights of the neoclassical school, Irving Fisher, was quoted as saying in 1929 – with astonishing naivety – that 'stock prices have reached what looks like a permanently high plateau'.[8]

---

[6] de Soto (2006).

[7] See Skousen (1993). The bank ultimately ended up in insolvency, brought about by the depression.

[8] For more examples of predictions made by Austrian economists, see Taghizadegan *et al.* (2015, chapter 3).

In 1949, von Mises penned his masterpiece: *Human Action*, which is the Austrian School's most important book. It is an inspiring read, and I highly recommend it to anyone who wants to dive into these issues in more detail.

Friedrich A. Hayek

Friedrich A. Hayek (1899–1992) was von Mises' most brilliant student. Hayek was the one responsible for introducing me to the Austrian School. In 2000 I came across his book *The Road to Serfdom*,[9] which had a major impact in the aftermath of the Second World War, despite not being his best work. He definitely won me over with his last book, *The Fatal Conceit*.[10] The book provides a superb overview of his thinking, especially in relation to the creation and development of institutions and the spontaneous order of the market.

Hayek was also born in the Austro-Hungarian Empire, in Vienna. Initially inclined towards holding socialist views, he abandoned them after reading von Mises' *Socialism*.[11] He became a disciple of the former and brilliantly took forward his work. He completed von Mises' explanation of the cycle, emphasising the importance of interest rate manipulation.

Artificial credit creation with low interest rates is the main driver of unchecked economic booms, which inevitably end in painful recessions, severely correcting previous excesses. In applying his theory in 1928 he was able to predict the crisis to come: the Fed tried to offset price falls driven by the enormous increase in productivity in the 1920s through lowering interest rates. The Fed failed to realise that this decline in prices was natural, and thus did not need to be fought, in turn provoking an excess of liquidity in the system. (Something similar happened in 2015, although with less of an increase in productivity.) Surprisingly, when – mainly neo-classical – economists and historians analyse the depression of the 1930s, Hayek is barely mentioned, even though he was engaged in intense intellectual arguments with Keynes, Milton Friedman, and the Chicago School – and, of course, with 'socialists from all parties'.

In his brilliant evolutionary theory on institutions, he reinforced the idea that society is not a system rationally organised by a human mind, but rather a complex process arising from an ongoing natural evolution that cannot be consciously managed. Society has its own dynamic and spontaneous order,

---

[9]Hayek (1994a).
[10]Hayek (1998).
[11]von Mises (2006).

impossible for a single person to improve through conscious management, as nobody has the information available to do so. Furthermore, to do so would involve significant coercion, preventing each individual from freely pursuing their own ends.

Outside of the strictly economic realm, Hayek also engaged in significant research on rights and the nature of laws. In particular, the concept of liberty as freedom from constraints and justice as equality in the eyes of the law. These concepts have often been perverted by individual interest groups.

Murray N. Rothbard

Murray N. Rothbard (1926–1995) was another of the Austrian School's exceptional thinkers, making very important contributions – such as the previously mentioned *History of Economic Thought*, or *America's Great Depression*,[12] which provides a brilliant explanation of the causes of the American depression of the 1930s.

Huerta de Soto, Jesús

Spain also has its own leading light in the Austrian School, in the form of Huerta de Soto, Jesús, who has undertaken important work in developing various areas, as well as doing a great job in explaining the main ideas of the school in his introductory book, *The Austrian School*.[13] Also worth highlighting is his enlightening book *Money, Bank Credit and Economic Cycles*,[14] which is a great aid in understanding these joyous economic cycles.

MAIN TENETS OF THE AUSTRIAN SCHOOL

Huerta de Soto, Jesús sets out the main tenets of the School in his book on the same subject, as well as the main differences to the neoclassical schools, whether Keynesian or Monetarist. The comparison in the table below is both necessary and enlightening. The neoclassical school dominates current economic thinking, despite having proven incapable of helping us to smoothly navigate our collective life.

---

[12]Rothbard (2000a, 2000b).
[13]de Soto (2008).
[14]de Soto (2006).

Points of comparison	Austrian paradigm	Neoclassical paradigm
1. Concept of economics (essential principle):	A theory of human action understood as a dynamic process (praxeology).	A theory of decision: maximisation subject to restrictions (narrow concept of 'rationality').
2. Methodological outlook:	Subjectivism.	Stereotype of methodological individualism (objectivist).
3. Protagonist of social processes:	Creative entrepreneur.	*Homo economicus.*
4. Possibility that actors may err a priori, and nature of entrepreneurial profit:	Actors may conceivably commit pure entrepreneurial errors that they could have avoided had they shown greater entrepreneurial alertness to identify profit opportunities.	Regrettable errors are not regarded as such, since all past decisions are rationalised in terms of costs and benefits. Entrepreneurial profits are viewed as rent on a factor of production.
5. Concept of information:	Knowledge and information are subjective and dispersed, and they change constantly (entrepreneurial creativity). A radical distinction is drawn between scientific knowledge (objective) and practical knowledge (subjective).	Complete, objective, and constant information (in certain or probabilistic terms) on ends and means is assumed. Practical (entrepreneurial) knowledge is not distinguished from scientific knowledge.
6. Reference point:	General process which tends towards coordination. No distinction is made between micro- and macroeconomics – each economic problem is studied in relation to others.	Model of equilibrium (general or partial). Separation between micro- and macroeconomics.
7. Concept of 'competition':	Process of entrepreneurial rivalry.	State or model of 'perfect competition'.

Points of comparison	Austrian paradigm	Neoclassical paradigm
8. Concept of cost:	Subjective (depends on entrepreneurial alertness and the resulting discovery of new, alternative ends).	Objective and constant (such that a third party can know and measure it).
9. Formalism:	Verbal (abstract and formal) logic which introduces subjective time and human creativity.	Mathematical formalism (symbolic language typical of the analysis of atemporal and constant phenomena).
10. Relationship with the empirical world:	Aprioristic deductive reasoning: radical separation and simultaneous coordination between theory (science) and history (art). History cannot validate theories.	Empirical validation of hypotheses (at least rhetorically).
11. Possibilities of specific prediction:	Impossible, since future events depend on entrepreneurial knowledge which has not yet been created. Only qualitative, theoretical pattern predictions about the discoordinating consequences of interventionalism are possible.	Prediction is an objective which is deliberately pursued.
12. Person responsible for making predictions:	The entrepreneur.	The economic analyst (social engineer).
13. Current state of the paradigm:	Remarkable resurgence over the last 25 years (particularly following the crisis of Keynesianism and the collapse of real socialism).	State of crisis and rapid change.
14. Amount of 'human capital' invested:	A minority, though it is increasing.	The majority, though there are signs of dispersal and disintegration.

(continued)

Points of comparison	Austrian paradigm	Neoclassical paradigm
15. Type of 'human capital' invested:	Multidisciplinary theorists and philosophers. Radical libertarians.	Specialists in economic intervention (piecemeal social engineering). An extremely variable degree of commitment to freedom.
16. Most recent contributions:	• Critical analysis of institutional coercion (socialism and interventionism). • Theory of free banking and economic cycles. • Evolutionary theory of (juridical, moral) institutions. • Theory of entrepreneurship. • Critical analysis of 'social justice'.	• Public choice theory. • Economic analysis of the family. • Economic analysis of law. • New classical macroeconomics. • Economics of information. • New Keynesians.
17. Relative position of different authors:	Rothbard, von Mises, Hayek, Kirzner.	Coase, Friedman, Becker, Samuelson, Stiglitz.

As can be seen, there are numerous and very distinctive differences both in terms of methodology and approach. Some of the key differences are as follows.

The Austrian paradigm is based on a 'theory of human action', which is understood to be an ongoing dynamic and creative process. The objectives to be met and the means to achieve them are not given, nor can they be established at the outset as they are continually changing as a result of an ongoing process of action and reaction among economic agents. Mankind is therefore the main actor in a never-ending process, which never reaches equilibrium – von Mises' 'stationary state' – since there will always be other actors whose actions shatter the expected equilibrium, contributing new elements in the process. The main protagonist is the creative entrepreneur who tries to capitalise on market disorder to earn a profit by offering a product or service at the lowest possible cost. This contributes to channelling market processes towards an equilibrium which evidently is never fully attained.

As Huerta de Soto, Jesús puts it:

The fundamental economic problem which the Austrian School seeks to address is very different from the focus of neoclassical analysis: Austrians study the dynamic process of social coordination in which individuals constantly and entrepreneurially generate new information as they seek the ends and means that they consider relevant within the context of each action they are immersed in and, by so doing, they inadvertently set in motion a spontaneous process of coordination.

The protagonist, the creative businessmen or entrepreneur, is the hero in our story, who sacrifices their savings to fulfil a new need, or to take a different approach to resolving an existing need. They take on this risk without knowing if they are making the right decision; it is worth recalling that 90% of companies do not survive past three years. When a successful entrepreneur is criticised for obtaining large profits, it is worth remembering the countless mistakes made by the entrepreneur themselves and others before them, which underpin the success and have helped contribute information.

Crucially, this entrepreneur can make pure errors, resulting from a failure to properly forecast the future in terms of demand and prices, or in terms of costs. Since information is always partial and subjective and constantly being created by economic actors, it is impossible for anyone to have full certainty about what is happening and even less so about what will happen. Therefore, specific forecasts are impossible, given that they depend on knowledge which in most cases has not yet been created. The only thing an entrepreneur can do is make general predictions, which will have a greater or lesser chance of being fulfilled in accordance with the rationale underpinning the a priori analysis, which ultimately is an inward-looking analysis of events, or – in other words – a personal reflection on how reality works on the basis of a small number of axioms which are irrefutable in any situation (for example, you cannot act and not act at the same time).

Although the Austrian economists made some successful forecasts, trying to predict the future is a very common conceit: searching and believing that causal relationships have been found which do not exist, and overlooking the existence of completely unpredictable but recurring phenomena, as Nassim Nicholas Taleb explains.

That is why the Austrians regard 'applying natural sciences methods to social sciences to be a basic error of enormous severity'. In economic science there is no such thing as constant or functional relationships, because we are analysing human behaviour – human actions – with an innate and infinite creative capacity. As Newton put it: 'I can calculate the motion of heavenly bodies, but not the madness of people'. He was referring to the South Sea Company stock market bubble in 1720, which he suffered first-hand.

Isaac Newton

The most famous English scientist, Sir Isaac Newton, lost £20,000 in the '**South Sea Company**' bubble, which in 1720 was his entire life savings. As a result he said:

"I can calculate the motion of heavenly bodies, but not the madness of people".

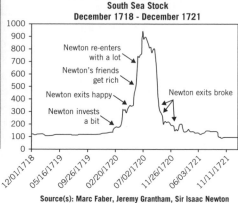

South Sea Stock
December 1718 - December 1721

Source(s): Marc Faber, Jeremy Grantham, Sir Isaac Newton

Source: Grantham, Mayo.

Another point of focus for Austrian theory is 'the concept of cost'. For Austrian economists, costs are subjective, as Huerta de Soto, Jesús explains: 'Cost is the subjective value the actor attaches to those ends they give up when they decide to pursue a certain course of action'. In other words, costs are not objective and given, but are instead discovered through action and, evidently, vary in each moment depending on the circumstances and alternatives. Ultimately, it is an opportunity cost. What do I forgo doing with the resource I am using: material, time, work, etc.?

These are the most important concepts from an investment perspective, but it is worth emphasising that the school has a very extensive body of work, covering practically every field that may be of personal interest to us. I am not completely in agreement with all the ideas that have been developed – for example, Rothbard's curious theory regarding the legitimacy of blackmail, which states that with available information we can act as we see fit, and with blackmail we give a last opportunity to the person being blackmailed – but on balance I think the Austrian School's ideas explain a large part of the reality of our existence.

APPLICATIONS TO INVESTMENT

What we have discussed so far might seem like an irrelevant theoretical confab, far removed from the world of investment. Nothing could be further from the truth. Admittedly, it won't tell us much about where stock prices will be next month or year, nor which emerging sector will take off in the years to come, nor what GDP growth is going to be like in one country or another. But it does help provide some perspective on the economic backdrop, a bird's eye view of sorts, and therefore perhaps a somewhat better understanding of what is happening: for example, which countries are taking the right steps or which sectors may be receiving too much capital, and therefore which countries stand to reap rewards in the future and which sectors are likely to encounter difficulties generating decent medium-term returns.

What follows are some of the Austrian School's main ideas, which I find to be particularly applicable to the investment process.

1. Markets work, by definition. The markets are formed of millions of people interacting with each other, made up of entrepreneurs with different goals and means, which only they can fully grasp. Meddling in these interactions artificially distorts the market, creating different results which are inferior to those intended by the people involved. It is possible that intervention may achieve better outcomes in the short term for the individuals responsible for it, but the overall results are worse for society as a whole since they are not freely chosen by them.

The accepted mainstream economic wisdom is that the market fails on a regular basis – imperfect competition, externalities, public goods, etc. – and this needs to be corrected. However, it's not clear how the market is erring when people are freely pursuing their own objectives, successfully or otherwise. In general, correct definition of property rights resolves such 'failures'. But even if we accept that market failures exist, how do we know that the solution is going to be better than the original error? In fact, any solution is ultimately going to come from people who similarly have their own errors to overcome. The discussion can go on for ever.

My experience is that the more intervention there is, the most disorder there will be. This can reach the level of chaos in state-managed economies, as was the case in the Soviet Union. This is further exacerbated by the fact that intervention is normally accompanied by arbitrary legal action: justice is not the same for everyone.

Real-world application: the greater the intervention, the less economic growth and legal security there will be, leading to greater reluctance to invest in the economy. A surprising example is Brazil. I have always been puzzled as to why Brazil, despite its great development potential, has been blighted by high interest rates as a result of persistent inflation. I discovered the problem for myself in my only trip there in 2010: the economy is subject to excessive levels of intervention, controlled by a hotchpotch of pressure groups. Companies demand tariff protection and they are granted it; workers demand protections which cannot be sustained by their productivity and they also get their own way. Furthermore, the politicians are unable to reach an agreement on dismantling the bloated government bureaucracy (the automobile company Fiat employs 1,000 people just to present multiple tax declarations). This excessive intervention leads to countless bottlenecks, resulting in inequality and imbalances, with certain social groups obtaining excessive income, while others languish amid high inflation and stagnant growth. The new government seemingly wants to put an end to public spending growth, and reform labour laws and the tax mess; time will tell whether they are successful.[15]

China is the opposite case. Despite supposedly being a socialist economic system, government intervention – as already noted – is largely absent from a broad spectrum of the economy, unleashing such fierce competition that the economy has been able to grow rapidly without inflation.

Intervention in the money markets warrants special attention. We will discuss the harmful consequences of such intervention, which progressively dilutes the value of money, in more detail later on. Indeed, the extent to which there is monetary intervention is potentially a useful predictor of long-term exchange rates. While it is impossible to say anything meaningful about the short term, a high degree of intervention is a probable signal of long-term currency depreciation to come.

2. Markets are never in equilibrium. Markets are locked in a constant and never-ending process, and there will always be an entrepreneur attempting to exploit new knowledge or temporary disorder to offer a product at an attractive price and reasonable cost. The presence of alert entrepreneurs makes it very difficult, and sometimes impossible, for a company to sustain exceptional profits over a long period of time. There will always be

---

[15] As I am reviewing the English version of this book, the Brazilian government is on the verge of collapse due to corruption issues.

somebody attempting to copy a good idea which generates high returns on capital employed.

As such, there are very few companies able to maintain a durable competitive advantage, and such advantages tend only to be time-limited, because knowledge developments inevitably provoke unpredictable changes. The flipside is that this also implies that nothing lasts for ever. Sectors in crisis with an excess of capital will sooner or later experience capital outflows, improving the situation for those left behind.

Accordingly, nearly all sectors end up reverting towards a reasonable return on capital, which is neither high nor low – between 5% and 10%, although in recent years it has been above the historical average. This rewards risk-taking and investors' willingness to forego their time preference.

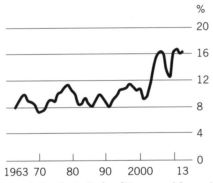

Source: Bureau of Economic Analysis; Federal Reserve; *Measuring and Managing the Value of Companies* (6th edn), McKinsey Corporate Performance, August 2015.

Real-world application: investors need to be conscious of excess or insufficient returns in a specific sector, patiently waiting for the situation to change. The clearest example are cyclical companies whose business is subject to ups and downs in supply and demand, with knock-on effects on returns. In any case, the goal is to find companies who obtain high returns because of competitive advantages, but in doing so it is vital to understand where these returns come from and whether they can be sustained over time.

These first two ideas – the idea that markets work and that they are always in the process of seeking equilibrium – and their corresponding applications, may seem self-evident. However, it would seem to be less clear to mainstream schools of thought or analysts talking up their own sectors. In reality, both principles must not only be recalled, but also emphasised.

3. **Economic growth is fundamentally based on increases in productivity resulting from division of labour, financed by savings.** The 'extended order', as Hayek refers to it, is what facilitates this division of labour, enabling us to organise ourselves and develop trust beyond the limited confines of our family or clans. An increase in savings and productivity is facilitated by a favourable institutional framework, where stability predominates.[16] The legal framework is therefore essential to ensuring that the consequences of our behaviour are predictable: the rule of law must be real and effective.

Real-world application: after having carefully analysed the type of growth being experienced by one country or a group of countries, it is crucial to determine whether such growth is solid – based on savings and productivity – or unstable – built on credit and plunder.

Until 2009, Chinese growth was supported by strong increases in productivity, overseeing the inclusion of millions of people into the market and with very high savings rates. This happened because of an increasing roll-back of intervention in the market and a degree of legal stability. There were exceptions in strategic sectors, though this is hardly uncommon in the rest of the world. Since 2010, the increase in leverage, reflecting insufficiently developed capital markets, has raised doubts about China's growth model, although my perception is that entrepreneurial creativity will outweigh relative debt excesses in the future.

The polar opposite has happened in Spain. In the first decade of the twenty-first century growth was fuelled by massive indebtedness. When it became clear that this unbalanced growth was unsustainable, there was a sudden blowback from failed projects, which brought about a sharp adjustment in labour and land costs. This correction helped realign factors of production with their underlying productivity, putting growth on a healthier and more sustainable footing, with a progressive reduction in debt levels.

I was particularly sceptical about the alarms that were being raised about China prior to 2009, because I understood that China's development was

---

[16]The causes of the significant development seen over the last 300 years have been attributed to institutions, ideas, individuals, the development of energy capabilities, or luck. See Smith (1982), Landes (1999), Acemoglu and Robinson (2012), McCloskey (2016). McCloskey makes a convincing case that the great advance from 1700 to 1800 had its origins in egalitarian ideas, as it became acceptable and conceivable for everyone to be successful in their commercial ventures. The freedom and dignity of common people came to the fore for the first time as a result of what she refers to as the four Rs: reform, revolution, revolt, and reading.

taking place because of a deepening of the markets, and we invested in companies able to capitalise on this, such as BMW, Schindler, and others. I have become more wary since 2010, but I still remain reasonably upbeat.

By contrast, in Spain, after having refrained from investing in sectors closely linked to the economy for various years, in 2012 we started investing again after noting a healthier pattern of growth.

4. Time is an essential aspect of the Austrian explanation of the productive process, which is about making an immediate sacrifice for the development of greater future productive capacity and an increase in productivity. Production is not instantaneous and this process needs to take place over various phases, ranging from the use of essential materials – land, gas, etc. – to the products consumed at the end of the chain.

Real-world application: our investment process should look beyond the immediate satisfaction of our consumption – and subsequent investment needs. We should save and sacrifice immediate returns when beginning to invest. We will only reap the rewards if we can see beyond the initial moment of investment.

The parallels between a healthy long-term productive and investment process are evident and aesthetically glaring.

Sacrifice is a crucial element of the process, but as we will see in Chapter 9, it runs contrary to our nature; we are not wired that way. A deep understanding of the functioning of the economy – how humans behave – will help with this approach, especially when the investment community is typically extremely myopic.

5. A particular type of intervention in the money market is especially important: currency manipulation through the control of interest rates by central banks. This generates significant distortions in the credit market, investment excesses, and financial bubbles, which result in the creation or exacerbation of economic cycles, which can become especially pronounced and elongated. Central bankers do not possess exceptional knowledge enabling them to accurately determine monetary conditions or set the right interest rate; their only advantage is having access to relevant information 15 days before other operators. And not only this, but they are tied by political and personal bonds, which undermine their independence when it comes to taking decisions. It is very difficult to escape consensus or conventional thinking when one's professional career is on the line.

In truth, an interest rate based on the decisions made by all market actors would be a better reflection of the needs at any given time, as implicitly acknowledged by Alan Greenspan, the most famous central banker in recent decades: 'I said that I was still worried why share prices were too high, but that the Fed would not be able to second guess the movements of "hundreds of well-informed investors". By contrast, the Fed took a position aimed at protecting the economy from the eventual crash'.

Here Greenspan is not referring to bond investors, who determine the price of money, but to equity investors. However, there is no way to distinguish one group's knowledge from another. Thus, following his reasoning, it is also not logical to 'second guess' the movements of 'hundreds of well-informed fixed-income investors' and thus try to control interest rates – as the Fed does.

Real-world application: investors should steer clear of economies whose growth is based on credit creation under the auspices of low interest rates established by central banks. This was how we avoided permanent capital losses during the 2006–2007 financial bubble. We had practically no exposure to the real-estate and financial sectors.

Perhaps the most instructive example of the impact of intervention on an economy in the twentieth century is the different policy approaches employed by authorities in the United States during the 1921–1922 crisis and the 1929–1945 depression. In the former, the market was allowed to freely adjust, eliminating bad investment and the crisis was overcome within months. However, in the 1930s, after having maintained an excessively lax monetary policy at the end of the 1920s, a second major error was made – as explained by Hayek at the time: free price formation was not permitted – the essential market adjustment mechanism. Wages were frozen while product prices were in freefall. The result was a build-up of losses across a multitude of companies and an inevitable flurry of insolvencies. It was only after the Second World War that the controls introduced by Herbert Hoover and Franklin D. Roosevelt were dismantled and an impressive post-war economic boom ensued.[17]

In 2016, at the bidding of their political masters, central banks continue to aggressively manipulate rates. Thankfully, the hangover from the previous crisis means that this money creation is not clearly flowing out of the financial system into the rest of the economy; but this could change at any moment, leading to a significant loss of currency value and consequent hyperinflation.

6. **The economy's natural state is deflationary, when there is no artificial boosting of the amount of money in circulation.** Productivity

---

[17]See Rothbard (2000b) and Grant (2014) (both useful for understanding the crisis of the 1920s and 1930s), and Higgs (2006) on the end of the depression following the Second World War.

increases enable more goods to be produced for the same amount of money. This is positive for the consumer, who benefits from a continued reduction in prices relative to wages, as has been the case for computers or telephones.

The strongest growth in the American economy's history took place from the end of the civil war up to the completion of the nineteenth century. These 30 glorious years were characterised by pronounced deflation. Admittedly, there have also been two well-known deflationary processes which have been accompanied by continued recessions, as we have seen in the United States in the 1930s and in Japan during the last 25 years. Nonetheless, in Japan, per capita growth has been positive and similar to that of other developed economies; the essential problem there is the lack of population growth. The causes of the Great Depression in America have already been discussed and can be found in the successive interventions which prevented the price of production factors from adjusting to their underlying productivity.

Recently, there have been instances of deflation and strong growth in Spain, Ireland, and the Baltic States. Spain, for example, has just seen three years of deflation, from 2013 to 2015, which has been accompanied by economic growth of 2%.

In truth, deflation is not a cause of stagnation but rather a symptom and part of the solution to the problem. In Spain, it was clear that labour and real-estate costs had risen beyond fair value and the economy did not recover until they returned to market levels. 25 years ago Japan was the most expensive country in the world, and it's highly plausible that this was part of the problem that had to be addressed, along with excessive intervention in large sections of the economy, the lack of meritocracy, and the demographic problem.

It's common to read and hear about the dangers of deflation, but these tend to be more invented than real: they don't create a liquidity trap, nor mass unemployment, nor a fall in output.[18]

So why is there so much fuss about deflation? These warnings are mainly sounded by governments, who are generally indebted[19] and stand to lose

---

[18] See Bagus (2006).

[19] As can be seen in the chart, global public debt has grown very rapidly in the last 15 years, made worse by having insufficient assets to offset it, as happens to households and companies.

from deflation. The weight of debt increases with deflation. The amount of debt remains constant, but money gains value because it can buy more things and, accordingly, more effort is needed to pay back the debt. By contrast, inflation makes debt repayment easier. So which will the state and its associates prefer – inflation or deflation? The answer is obvious.

Global Public Debt at 66% of Average Debt/GDP (2015) & Rising... +9% annually during 8 years vs. +2% GDP growth for the 50 largest economies

Page 85: Global Debt by Type (in billions of $, constant exchange rate 2014)

Annualised rate of annual growth

	2000–2007	2000–Q2:15
Households	8.5	3.0
Corporate	5.7	6.4
Public	5.9	8.7
Financial	9.6	3.7

$208 — $41 Households, $59 Corporate, $59 Public, $49 Financial
$138 — $33, $59, ...
$84 — $19, $25, $21, $20
$138 — $37, $32, $37
Q4:00, Q4:07, Q2:15

Total debt as % GDP: 250, 274, 299   GDP growth 4.1 2.2

Source: McKinsey Global Institute (3/16) IMF.

Real-world application: the most likely outcome in an economy subject to state intervention is high inflation. The government is judge and jury and unsurprisingly rules in its own interest. It is therefore best to be prepared by investing in real assets: public or private shares, houses or commodities. Always. We will discuss this in more detail in the next chapter.

7. The absence of a currency linked to gold – or a similar commodity free from political decision – means that the currency will permanently depreciate in relation to real assets. This has always been the case and will continue that way. Government pressure for currency depreciation is unrelenting.[20]

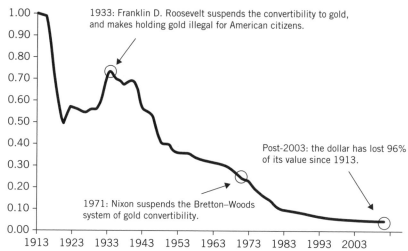

Purchasing power of $1 since establishment of Federal Reserve in 1913
Source: BLS IPC Data.

Real-world application: once again, it is best to only invest in real assets, aside from occasional liquidity needs. I repeat, always. We will also go into this issue in the next chapter.

8. **Product prices – which depend on consumers' willingness to pay – determine costs and not the reverse, as many people think.** It's surprising how widespread this misconception is. For example, the *Financial Times*' 'Lex' column, the most prestigious global financial column, has made the same error on more than one occasion.

The Bernstein analyst, Paul Gait, has analysed the issue for mining companies, observing that the correlation between costs and prices in the previous period is very high. The price ended up determining costs over the next two years.

---

[20]This is perfectly explained in Rothbard (2010).

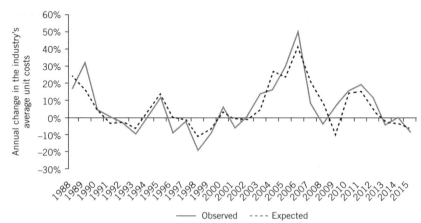

Observed changes in the costs of industrial mining according to price changes in the previous two years

Source: estimates and analysis by Wood Mackenzie, AME, Bloomberg LP, and Bernstein.

Thermal coal and oil are clear examples of two commodities where recent falls in costs followed prior declines in prices.

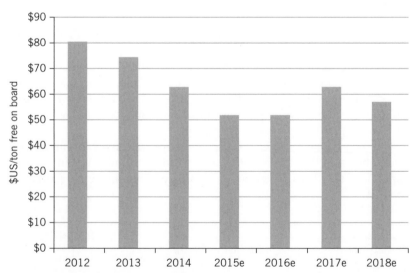

Average cost of coal mines in Australia

Source: Wood Mackenzie, Morgan Stanley Research.

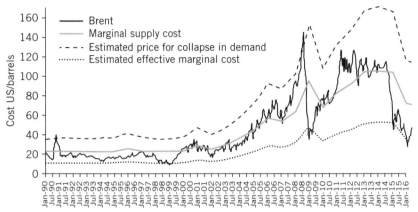

The marginal cost of output for the top 50 Upstream (prospecting and production) fell by 30% to $US73/barrel in 2015, driven by deflation in industry costs
Source: Bernstein analysis and estimates.

Real-world application: marginal costs – associated with the final and most expensive producer – are constantly changing in line with the scale of demand. If the demand for oil is 80 million barrels a day and barrel number 80 million costs 100 dollars to produce, then the market price will be 100 dollars and everyone who is able, will produce at a cost below 100 dollars. If the demand falls to 50 million barrels, the marginal price will also fall, and so, if the marginal producer who produces barrel number 50 million does so at a price of 40 dollars/barrel, the market price will be 40 dollars and it will only be produced by those who do so below 40 dollars. If the demand falls to 0 barrels, the cost will be 0 dollars and nobody will produce. It seems obvious, but not to everyone.

Investors should not forget the order: first demand is calculated, then the costs necessary to meet that demand.

9. Production costs are subjective, meaning that any production structure is liable to vary depending on the circumstances. Cost is equal to my best alternative. Since these alternatives are variable and subjective, the cost is also variable and subjective.

Real-world application: do not take costs as given. This is a common error when looking at commodity or cyclical companies, or companies with novel products. Costs continually vary in accordance with changing market conditions or technological developments. A lot of engineers have found themselves out of work following the decline in oil prices in 2014 and 2015, reducing their options and meaning that they are willing to work for less money, reducing mining costs. The same effect has come from the development of shale oil and gas in the United States, which is an alternative technology that has facilitated a reduction in the costs of producing a marginal barrel.

10. **Economic models are – to all intents and purposes – useless.** Attempting to model unpredictable human behaviour and probable, but unknown, future events is impossible. The best we can manage are limited general predictions.

Real-world application: avoid falling into the trap of thinking that we can precisely forecast what will happen. This is particularly true for economic forecasts, which are subject to changes that are not only probable, but certain and impossible to predict. More general predictions can be useful, but they should always focus on long-term underlying patterns. If in doubt, resort to the trusty calculator which does only the most basic of operations, avoiding the temptation to get sucked into excessive complexity.

This is not an exhaustive list of ideas and applications, but it covers some of the most useful ones from an investment perspective. Overall, there is no direct or close link between cause and effect, but rather a combination of concepts which enable us to disentangle this path with more confidence.

CONCLUSION: SUBJECTIVISM AND OBJECTIVE PRICE

It might seem like a contradiction to be continually talking about the subjectivist methodology applied by Austrian economists – which puts mankind's activity at the centre and where nothing is objective, due to man's continually changing activity – while at the same time discussing my 'objective/target' price for the companies I invest in based on my valuations.

In reality, what we are doing when we invest is trying to predict the direction entrepreneurs (understood in the widest sense to include all of us) will take in the future, thereby bringing about a change in current subjective valuations. We are interested in discovering the future 'objective' value, which is no more than the sum of countless subjective valuations made by these entrepreneurs. It is a purely entrepreneurial endeavour: attempting to predict where a new market need will arise, who could meet it, and at what cost. Once this has been estimated, the aim is to see whether securities markets will allow us to capitalise on incorrect price formation resulting from entrepreneurial errors by other agents. Once again, it is a purely entrepreneurial endeavour.

In conclusion, my experience is that the long-term outlook that all investors should adopt is perfectly complemented by the Austrian School of economics, with its sound logical framework and similar long-term perspective. Understanding the general functioning of economic institutions serves as a compass which gives us knowledge, providing us with the necessary peace of mind to be able to navigate troubled waters without fearing that we will run aground.

CHAPTER 5

Investment

Now that we have a conceptual economic framework to employ, we can turn specifically to investment. In doing so, the key point I want to highlight is the vital role of saving. Saving, unsurprisingly, is key to investment and the ultimate source of future wealth. Without savings, there can be no healthy investment or general well-being.

SAVING AND INVESTMENT

Each individual accumulates savings at a different rate, requiring a varying degree of sacrifice in terms of income that is not consumed. Saving finances technological development and wealth creation, and is responsible for the continual improvement in the standards of living that we enjoy today.

Although some misled people warn of a supposed one-off savings glut, an excess of savings is never bad news; it always contributes to financing projects which improve the productive structure. If an excess of savings results in very low returns and savings cannot be put to good use over a reasonable period of time, they will end up being consumed in products and services.

Personal propensity to save depends on a large number of factors: income, age, consumption or investment opportunities, concerns about the future or an inheritance... No two people have the same propensity to save, nor does this propensity remain stable over time.

In reality, saving, for a lot of people, is a – fortuitous – problem to be resolved. The key questions we ask ourselves are: What to do with them? How to preserve them? How to grow them? Will I be able to retire?

It is surprising how little time we spend addressing these questions. When we buy a house we spend months researching and weighing up the pros and cons. This is logical; frequently it is the biggest investment decision of our lives. The same thing is true when we buy a car or decide where to go on holiday. We weigh up the different options, leaning towards one or another after an exhaustive analysis of the advantages and disadvantages.

However, when it comes to deciding whether it is advisable to buy Telefónica shares, or determining which mutual fund is most suitable for our savings, it is surprising that we take this decision in a matter of minutes. We often do so after listening to the somewhat self-interested advice of those around us, without receiving truly qualified guidance, and without dedicating the time to study and reflect on a decision of this magnitude.

As fund managers, we have earned the trust of thousands of clients. This is a meaningful figure – bearing in mind that we don't do any marketing – but it is also ridiculous. In Spain there are nearly 10 million shareholders in mutual funds. How is it possible that a product which has offered clients such clear value – a 15% annualised return over 20 years – is not more popular? I am not complaining, instead simply pointing out that it is surprising and particularly serious given that these days the Internet places all the necessary information at our fingertips.

Deciding how to invest our savings should always be a slow and deliberate process – assessing alternative options according to our individual needs and the characteristics of the alternatives. Like nearly everything in life, knowing ourselves is the first step to making the right decision, which does not necessarily involve going after the best possible return. Later on I will try to describe the problems associated with having a personality that is not well suited to investment, but for the time being I will focus on something less ambitious: providing a simple explanation of the different investment possibilities for our savings.

REAL OR MONETARY INVESTMENT

When looking at investment alternatives, I will avoid a typical description of the multitude of asset types. Instead, I will focus on simple classification to narrow things down and go straight to the heart of the problem: investment in real assets or investment in monetary assets. Strangely enough, I recently discovered that von Böhm-Bawerk distinguished between goods and promises, which comes down to real and monetary assets. I mainly consider shares as investment in real assets, although I also analyse other assets that are more easily replicable, or commodities.[1]

This classification between real and monetary assets is not that common, but it helps to significantly sharpen the investment landscape.

---

[1]Whether legal rights and relationships are economic goods (von Böhm-Bawerk, 1962, pp. 25–138). Found in Merino (2015).

Investment in Real Assets

Real assets reflect ownership of underlying assets, albeit with greater or lesser immediacy. Such assets create income for the specific service they provide to society. This includes shares, real-estate properties (homes, hotels, offices, etc.), commodities (gold, oil, copper, etc.), art (in the broadest sense, including any type of collection), and, generally, any product or service which is valued and demanded by human beings: tables, chairs, income rights for a sports personality or artist, etc.

Real assets also encompass all the capabilities and qualities that we might develop ourselves: education, skills, relationships, etc.

The essential characteristics of real assets are: 'ownership of the thing', which can be direct or indirect (shares, for example, are representations of property), total or partial (we can own the whole asset or a minimal percentage); and 'variability in the income generated by the assets'. The degree of income variability will depend, firstly, on society's interest in the product, which will change over time and will be immediately reflected in the price that society is prepared to pay for the good. And, secondly, the producer's capacity to offer the product at a reasonable cost, because not everyone is in a position to supply efficiently.

As the photos below show, real assets come in many shapes and forms, covering a very significant part of the assets owned by the majority of people. This is especially true for people on low incomes, who limit their savings to immediate material goods: houses, furniture, cars, etc.

The main upshot of owning an asset which fulfils a service demanded by society is that it will sustain its purchasing power reasonably well in any economic environment, so long as society retains an interest in it. Returns on real assets will vary according to numerous factors, but their ability to retain purchasing power reasonably well is irrefutable and crucial.

However, within the category of real assets it is worth quickly distinguishing between unique assets or assets with a distinct competitive advantage, and assets that are easily replicated or substituted. There is no clear cut-off between both types of assets; instead, there is a continuous line, with unique assets at one extreme with a very high capacity to generate exceptional income. Actions in listed companies protected by very high barriers to entry are an example: say, Coca-Cola in the twentieth century and Facebook in the twenty-first.

Examples of real assets are shopping centres, education, industrial plants, farms, houses, thermal power plants, and roads.

Commodities, especially gold, are at the other extreme. They are subject to technological improvements that have resulted in continuous reductions in mining costs and, accordingly, their price. However, in recent years, mining costs have become dearer as a result of sudden and spectacular growth in China. This has offset the impact of technological advances, but it is unlikely to be a long-lasting effect.

Different real assets – shares with less competitive advantages, real-estate assets, and other assets – are located along this line according to their relative quality.

Monetary Investment

Monetary investment grants the investor a promise to pay a fixed income in a specific currency. Normally this promise is backed up by income flows generated by the issuer, albeit with certain limitations.

In this case, the investor does not own the entity that has issued the payment promise, they only own a promise governed by a contract in a specified currency.

Bank deposits and debt issues by government and companies are examples of this type of investment.

It is true that non-payment in the case of private debt issues could allow the investor to have access to ownership as a last resort, thus recovering at least part of the investment. But the same is not true for public debt. In the words of the outstanding and oft-overlooked Harry Scherman: 'This type of [public] promise does not represent, in most cases, any type of tangible wealth'. Public debt offers no type of guarantee, other than the word of the issuer. We will never be able to access the government's assets; they have more tanks than any investor. (Elliot Associates recently tried to recover part of their investment in Argentinian government bonds, going after some of the country's assets around the globe, such as the Argentinian navy training vessel. This search was not very successful, but the change of government resulted in an eventual agreement.)

However, the problem here is not so much obvious non-payment, which for private debt is protected by underlying assets, but a less obvious form of non-payment. Specifically, the loss of value of the promise to pay as a result of the loss in value of the currency in which the contract is denominated or referenced. This problem is less obvious and as such much more dangerous for the saver, because it can be hidden or supressed over many years behind a façade of apparent stability. As investors we receive interest each month or year without fluctuations or surprises, until one day the crisis can no longer be contained and it suddenly explodes.

Furthermore, all types of promises to pay, both private and public, can be affected – not just exceptional defaults.

In reality, the two types of assets described – real and monetary – are not comparable because they are different in nature. On the one side, we are talking about payment rights deriving from ownership of an asset which interests the public (real assets), while on the other we are talking about a promise to pay backed up by paper money (monetary assets).

The only reason that financial markets typically compare shares and bonds – the clearest embodiments of both asset types – is for ease. Appendix A at the end of this chapter explains how these ideas impact on the key concept of the discount rate.

WHICH TYPE OF ASSET IS MORE ATTRACTIVE, OFFERING HIGHER RETURNS OVER THE LONG RUN?

The key question is: Which type of asset is more attractive as a long-term investment? Which offers more returns? Which is less risky?

The response should begin with an upfront reasoning based on Austrian logic: the number one objective of any investor should be to maintain the purchasing power of their savings. This is a priority and a fundamental basic principle. The idea of gaining purchasing power is subsequent to at least sustaining the starting position.

Real assets fulfil this role, by definition they maintain purchasing power; we can adapt them to any economic environment. The relative attractiveness of these assets will depend on their quality, represented by their degree of distinctiveness. As we will see, the most attractive assets are listed shares (and unique talents).

By contrast, there is no room in a long-term perspective for investing in monetary assets held hostage to the currency in which they are denominated. As a result of the abandonment of the gold standard or any other type of similar currency anchor, currencies are subject to continual depreciation, induced by monetary inflation. The latter is a result of the issue of more paper money than would correspond to output growth (in reality, output does not need more money when it expands, any quantity of money is optimal to support output. We have already noted that the natural state for an economy is deflationary).

As such, a priori, it would appear that real assets provide a greater probability of maintaining the purchasing power of our savings.

On the basis of this a priori self-evident premise, the next step is to see whether it has been confirmed over time.

HISTORIC EVIDENCE

Despite the difficulties of comparing such different assets, we are going to look at historical evidence. We will then dive into the theoretical explanations for the results. As we underlined in Chapter 4, without a logical foundation, empirical analysis has no value.

The evidence can be found in a multitude of studies on the long-term returns of different assets. Listed shares and public debt are the assets that have received the most thorough analysis, but we can also investigate the performance of other real assets.

Starting with Jeremy Siegel's well-known study, American equities have obtained long-term real (after inflation) annual returns of 6.6%. Purchasing power has gone up by 6.6% every year. These are data for the last 200 years, and are surprisingly consistent over time. So much so that seen from this perspective, major crises – such as 1929 – look like small bumps on the road.

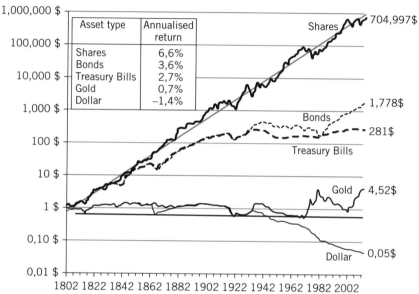

Total real return on US equities, bonds, Treasury bills, gold, and the dollar, 1802–2012
Source: Siegel (2014).

Economic growth is ultimately the basis for generating equity returns, since they mirror the behaviour of economies. In the long run, countries with sound and healthy structures, which save, invest, and do not excessively indebt themselves – in other words, countries where they do things right – grow, create employment, and have a strong financial system, enabling new projects to be taken on and providing liquidity to those who finance these projects with their savings. These ingredients create a developed capital market, which, over the long term, reflects the positive performance of the economy, allowing good returns to be obtained by not just initial investors in business projects, but also investors providing liquidity to these projects through share purchases of listed companies at a later stage in their development.

The global economy has grown by 3% each year over the last 100 years. This has been enough to allow for healthy and attractive capital markets for saving and investment. While some authors disagree, the increase in the value of long-term equities reflects a stable economic environment, which allows for this creation of real wealth.[2]

Other assets have performed much less strongly over time than equities: government bonds have obtained a return of 3.6%; Treasury bills, 2.7%; and gold, 0.7%. The abandonment of the gold standard and the subsequent increase in inflation have led to a decline in returns on fixed income over the last 80 years compared with the previous period, putting more recent returns below this 3.6%. Meanwhile, gold has performed better since the end of the 1960s, when the last currency anchor to the gold standard was removed.

Although a difference of 2–3% per year may seem small, over the long term the effect is astonishing. Just compare the differences in accumulated assets in each case: one dollar of shares in 1802 converts to 704,997 dollars in 2012, in real terms. In other words, purchasing power has increased 700,000 times! Meanwhile, this same dollar, invested in bonds, would have translated into 1,778 dollars. Certainly a reasonable return, but clearly less than what is on offer from equities.

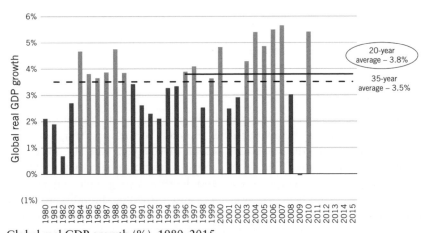

Global real GDP growth (%), 1980–2015
Source: IMF WEO, 4/16. Stephen Roach, 'A World Turned Inside Out', Yale Jackson Institute for Global Affairs, 5/16.

---

[2]Ritter (2005).

A dollar of gold, typically used for refuge, would have converted into 4.52 dollars, barely maintaining its purchasing power, meanwhile leaving the dollar under the mattress would have led to a devastating loss of purchasing power, with paper money losing 95% of its value: that dollar would have converted into five cents of purchasing power.

Equity outperformance has taken place in all the countries under study, as can be seen in the following chart:

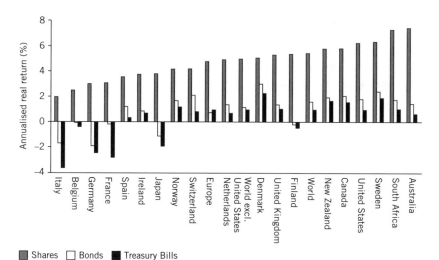

■ Shares □ Bonds ■ Treasury Bills

Real annual return in equities vs. bonds and Treasury bills internationally, 1900–2010
Source: based on Dimson *et al.* (2011).

The analysis for other countries has been performed for a shorter period: 1900–2000, but with no less resounding results. All countries exhibit greater returns from equities compared with fixed income. Including countries that have gone through wars and calamitous financial situations, such as Germany and Japan. My own country, Spain, posts a real annual return of 3.6% for equities. Also a long way above fixed income.

This analysis used countries accounting for 89% of the market in 1990, meaning that the sample is very representative. Moreover, in countries registering lower equity returns – such as Germany, Italy, France, and Belgium – bonds performed even worse, with negative real returns.

Finally, in the worst-case scenario, such as a Soviet-style revolutionary confiscation of assets, the investment is a lost cause regardless of the asset. Therefore, there is no greater risk associated with equities.

In conclusion, despite the difficulties involved in forecasting, we can calmly assert that over the long term, owning a diversified portfolio of shares will produce a greater return and a larger increase in the purchasing power of our savings than any other alternative investment, especially in comparison with monetary assets. Later on we will develop a logical explanation for this, which will tie in with the explanation related to economic growth.

We can also confirm that other real assets have performed more poorly than equities. We have seen what happened with gold, and if we analyse other assets such as real estate (see Appendix B at the end of this chapter), oil or metals, we will find that they maintain their purchasing power, but fall a long way short of the return on equities.

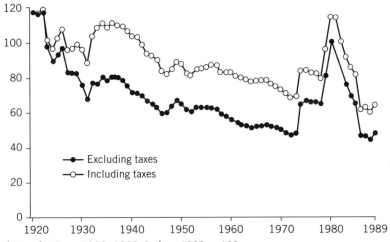

Real petrol prices, 1920–1989. Index: 1982 = 100
Source: Simon (1998).

This is because these assets are easily replicated or substituted. The increase in productivity from technological developments and better management methods systematically lowers production costs and, as a consequence, thanks to competition, consumer prices. This is why they are barely able to maintain their purchasing power: each year they have to fight against a 1% or 2% price reduction due to improvements in production.

Real copper prices, 1801–1990. Index: 1982 = 100
Source: Simon (1998).

These 'other' real assets can endure long periods of lower returns than monetary assets, but they have a notable advantage over the latter: their defensive character. Not all investors attach the same importance to peace of mind, but I think it is essential. Maintaining the purchasing power of savings during times of high drama is crucial for an investor. That is why I am willing to sacrifice some return in exchange for the certainty of sustaining long-term purchasing power. We will also see a little later why real assets defend themselves better in these dramatic moments.

VOLATILITY (NOT RISK)

Curiously, the positive difference in return from equities is known as a 'risk premium'. Implicit in this language is the idea that greater return implies taking on more risk. As we will see, this could not be further from the truth.

Equities are subject to greater short-term volatility, but not over the long term. The longer the timeframe we analyse, the more this volatility progressively diminishes.

In the chart below we can see that for periods of up to five years, the maximum positive return on equities is the highest among all assets, but so too are the losses. This fits with our vision of the variability of shares. But this is no longer the case for periods of 10 years: the worst 10-year period for an equity investor saw an annual real loss of 4.1%, compared with 5.4% for bonds.

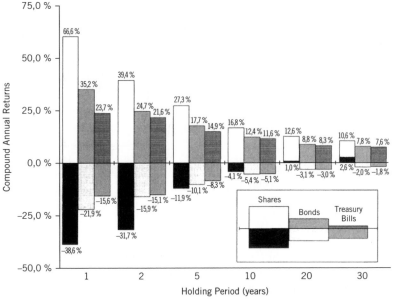

Maximum and minimum annual returns on equities, bonds, and Treasury bills over holding periods of one, two, five, 10, 20, and 30 years, 1802–2012
Source: Siegel (2014).

The better performance of equities becomes even more accentuated over longer periods: there is no period over a 20-year tenure where equities lose purchasing power; the worst period saw a return of 1% above inflation. The same thing happens over 30 years: the worst period generated a real return of 2.6%. By contrast, the worst 20- and 30-year periods for bonds are very negative.

If we employ the usual calculation of volatility as the standard deviation of returns, we obtain similar results, as would be expected.

From all this we reach the surprising conclusion that for all long-term investors, equities not only offer greater returns, but do so taking on less volatility. This might not appear intuitive to the reader, which is why it is necessary to analyse the rationale in a degree of detail.

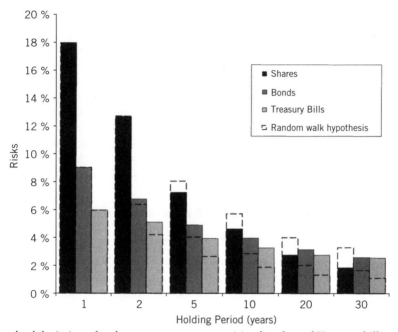

Standard deviation of real average returns on equities, bonds, and Treasury bills over various holding periods. Historical data and random walk hypothesis
Source: Siegel (2015).

WHAT IS RISK?

Before we get started, it is worth clarifying that volatility is not the best measure of risk. The risk of an investment is the possibility of a permanent loss of purchasing power as the result of making an error of judgement.

We have seen that the possibility of this happening in a diversified long-term portfolio of equities is very limited. Investing in an index or in an index fund, we can reduce the possible errors involved in the specific selection of stocks.

Volatility measures the intensity of changes in asset prices, which may or may not be related to what is going on with the underlying asset. In fact, volatility is the long-term investor's best friend, enabling them to find opportunities that would not otherwise have existed. Greater short-term volatility means that more investment opportunities will arise and increased long-term returns with less risk. For example, if the market collapses and equities fall by 50%, we will be buying cheaper assets and taking on less risk. The underlying rationale is that the fall is not justified by good reasons (and there is mean reversion), but is instead a consequence of erratic human behaviour, something that we will turn to later.

By contrast, with monetary assets this risk, or the potential for a permanent loss of purchasing power, is very real and could be very significant. This has been the case on countless occasions over the course of history, where we have seen continual state defaults and currency depreciations. In some cases, losses have reached 100%, such as in Germany in 1921–1923.

As we have pointed out, when an investment in equities has been completely wiped out due to a revolution or a similarly dramatic situation, the same has happened to investments in monetary assets. In other words, in the worst case we are equally badly protected with both types of assets.

WHY DO EQUITIES OFFER BOTH GREATER RETURNS AND LESS LONG-TERM RISK?

This surprising result, which contrasts with what we read daily in the economic press and the typical recommendations of financial advisors, has a relatively simple explanation if we consider the basic nature of the two types of assets.

In real assets, and specifically in shares, we are co-owners of assets which are overseen by other owners, who normally – though we cannot say always, because on occasions corporate governance is not up to scratch – take the same long-term perspective, which is key to the company's future success. The environment is important, and if there is an economic or financial crisis which depreciates the currency, the company will be affected. However, the capacity to adapt and the company's long-term vision will enable it to continue with the business under new circumstances, dealing with currency or legislative changes: it will switch to selling its products in reals, pesos, or drachma, or at a higher price if there is hyperinflation, but ultimately if the product is good and people need it, the company will continue selling it under the new circumstances and will continue generating surpluses in the form of profit.

The cause of this currency depreciation is the increase in the amount of money in circulation, which also leads to an increase in the price of assets in this reference currency. These are two sides of the same coin: inflation and currency depreciation. When an asset which offers a service to society – an office, a house, a sausage, or a mobile phone factory – faces an inflationary situation, the company will adjust the price of its products and the remuneration of the factors of production in line with the new state of play. If prices increase by 5%, it will increase its prices and costs by 5% and therefore the relative situation does not change. If prices increase by 50%, the same thing will happen, and equally if they increase by 1,000% per day. Obviously, these would be far from ideal operating conditions, but the company can adapt and at least survive. Accordingly, the owners will also maintain their relative position and even improve relative to holders of fixed-income assets, whose prices cannot adapt to the new situation.

Taking a stake in an asset though shares or, in other words, being a co-owner of a company which produces a tangible, concrete, and real good – which is valued and demanded by other economic agents – is what enables us to protect ourselves against the main investment risk: the depreciation of the currency in which it is denominated.

By contrast, when holding monetary assets we depend entirely on the value of the currency, which is always subject to political vicissitudes. There are both time preference and principal–agent problems. While as investors we are thinking in the long term, in the future, politicians think about 'their future', a future which is almost always too short and bracketed by the next elections. With re-election at the forefront of their minds, politicians will tend to delay necessary but difficult and impossible decisions for as long as possible, leading to an accumulation of unresolved problems, which sooner or later will lead to structural imbalances, loss of confidence in the economy, and inflationary depreciation of the currency. For us, this means the immediate loss of value of our monetary investment.

The principal–agent problem arises due to the misalignment of interests between investors in monetary assets and politicians and/or their advisors or intellectual inspirers. The latter can make errors, due to the always unforeseeable consequences of their actions, but these errors tend only to emerge in the medium and long run, meaning they do not suffer a significant risk in the short term. Later on they will try to explain them away by 'unforeseen' external factors or due to previous poor decision-making, but the error will remain.

There are some monetary assets with defence mechanisms against currency depreciation, such as inflation-linked bonds. But at times of high inflation the government in question will repudiate this type of debt precisely because it is the most onerous of them all. A government in crisis will not pay interest rates of 30% if inflation were to be close to these levels.

To conclude, an alternative way to visualise this can be seen in Jeremy Siegel's charts, set out on the following page. These charts show that during short periods (a year, for example), equities are the best asset, despite having a lower return in high-inflation periods; over longer periods (30 years), equities perform steadily and very positively, close to their average historical return. The same is not true for Treasury bonds and bills, which suffer enormously under high inflation.

Consider an example: we are offered the choice between a stake in the future earnings of Cristiano Ronaldo or Lionel Messi. Let's say 10% of their future earnings over the next 10 years (assume the offer arrives when both are at the peak of their careers) or a bond issued by them payable over 10 years in euros. We will not dwell on analysing the potential return on both offers – this will depend on the future of the players. However, the option linked to earnings will face greater volatility – as there could be injuries or game changes – but it will typically offer a greater return.

The problem with the bond is that it faces an additional risk of currency depreciation. Imagine that there is a financial crisis and the reference currency loses value. Either our players change teams or currency. They will do whatever it takes to continue maximising their capacity to generate earnings in this new economic context: they will earn in dollars or yuan, or they will go to the Japanese league; they will adapt. And we will continue receiving our 10%, albeit with some changes in purchasing power, in one sense or another, depending on whether football becomes more or less appealing to society during the crisis.

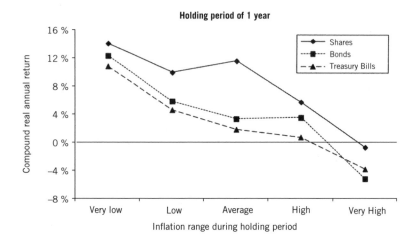

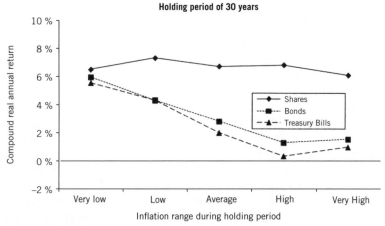

Holding periods and inflation, 1871–2012
Source: Siegel (2014).

Meanwhile, investors holding Ronaldo or Messi bonds, which for a while have lived comfortably with the apparent lesser volatility of their bond, when faced with the shock, will now receive payment in a euro which is of less value. They will have suffered a loss of purchasing power in the same proportion as the depreciation of the currency (less what they have earned in interest).

In general, in these extreme situations the impact passed on to the bond through loss of currency value exceeds what the owner of a share might lose in profits from not having completely adjusted to the new circumstances. Such extreme situations come unannounced, but they always put in an appearance. Therefore, provided that we are willing to accept more short-term volatility, as shareholders with a stake in profits we will be avoiding future financial disasters that sooner or later will take place, and which dramatically affect monetary assets.

Argentina

Speaking of Lionel Messi, let's also talk about Argentina, a country which was the seventh global power at the start of the twentieth century. In 2000, after various years of pegging its currency to the American dollar, economic imbalances resulted in the umpteenth suspension of payments by the country and the imposition of the so-called 'corralito', preventing dollar deposits from being taken out of bank accounts. The peso–dollar exchange rate, which had been maintained until then at one, immediately fell by half, meaning two pesos were needed to buy a dollar.

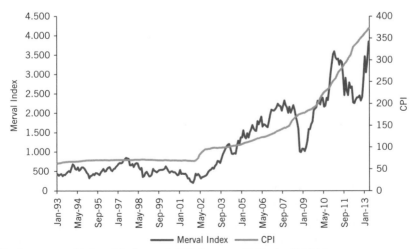

Performance of Merval Index and CPI: January 1993–April 2013
Source: Guerra (2012), based on BCBA, INDEC, and IPEC-Santa Fe databases.

This was a really extreme and dramatic predicament, which led to falls in the price of public debt and shares. But it didn't last long. A few months after the payments suspension, equities embarked on a meteoric rise, enabling investors to recover the losses inflicted by the currency depreciation.

As can be seen, the adjustment of equities to inflation is almost perfect. However, the public debt story is very different.

Today, over 15 years later, Argentinian public debt has lost 70% of its value, while the Merval, the Argentinian stock exchange, has multiplied in value by 20 – compensating the loss in value of the Argentinian peso, which is now at 1/15 against the dollar.

Argentinian bond. Performance 2000-2008
Source: Bloomberg.

Argentina is just one of countless examples that have taken place over the course of history, but the mechanism is similar in nearly all of them. For example, on 20 June 2016, in the *Financial Times*, there were two news items on two countries, Venezuela and Egypt, where one can see the problem evolving practically in real time. In 2016, according to the IMF, inflation in Venezuela reached 480% per annum and in Egypt a flood of house purchases are being made in the face of generalised distrust in the country's leaders.

It is clear that in less developed countries, where distrust of governments is much higher, the attraction of real assets has always been clear to savers.

MORE ON THE POLITICAL PROBLEM

We have seen how the problem with fixed income is inflation, which destroys the purchasing power of money. Why is there inflation? We will follow Murray N. Rothbard, who addresses this question in his book *What Has*

Government Done To Our Money?[3] I have already spoken of this brief but outstanding account of the origin and evolution of money, and how government intervention impacts on this evolution: 'If government can find ways to engage in counterfeiting – the creation of new money out of thin air – it can quickly produce its own money without taking the trouble to sell services or mine gold. It can then appropriate resources slyly and almost unnoticed, without rousing the hostility touched off by taxation'.

Purchasing power is destroyed by currency depreciation, which – to re-emphasise – is a result of the increase in the money supply in circulation. It is a problem of supply and demand: the more money there is in circulation, the less value it has in relation to other goods. And why increase the money in circulation?

This is where the political class comes into play. After having exhausted the possibilities of increasing taxes, given that there is always a limit that the public is unwilling to cross, and after having also reached a limit on public debt issue, investors too run out of patience ('The limit is the point at which promises to pay stop being credible') – the political class then has to find other funding mechanisms. And the most suitable mechanism for their interests is to issue paper money – especially after the abolition of the gold standard, which supported currency issue with something tangible, robust, and real – currently under the control of the central banks, administered by the political class.

Little by little, the springs that forestalled currency depreciation have been dismantled, ending up with today's current paper money, which is useless at holding its value over the long term.

In addition to the significant depreciation problem, there is another serious issue: the new paper money in circulation is not neutral. To begin with, it favours those who are closest to the government, who will be up to speed with looming political manoeuvring. It also complicates future decisions, since it creates an instability that was prophesied by Lenin in his famous words: 'The simplest way to exterminate the very spirit of capitalism is therefore to flood the country with notes of a high face-value without financial guarantees of any sort'.[4] But what is more, it impoverishes the saver who lends and invests, and improves the situation of the debtor, which is frequently the state. This explains the natural and remorseless tendency of governments to depreciate currencies via inflation.

In fact, as Carmen Reinhart and Ken Rogoff have explained,[5] nearly all states at one time or another have reneged on their promises to pay (be it via currency debasement, default, or issue of more paper).

---

[3] Rothbard (2010).
[4] White and Schuler (2009).
[5] Reinhart and Rogoff (2011).

As it happens, Spain, during its golden Imperial Age in the sixteenth century, when it was the great economic power of its time, suspended payments six times. One of the direst cases, as we have already highlighted, was Germany during the 1920s, but we could list dozens of similar situations. Once again, the elimination of the gold standard has facilitated a system of monetary inflation as a form of non-payment.

But why do states do these things? Firstly, they do them because they can. A large number of states have been created through violence, and all have a monopoly on force. This combines with two previously mentioned factors which are inherent to the state: the principal–agent or representation problem, derived from the logic of political action, and the time preference problem, resulting from electoral cycles.

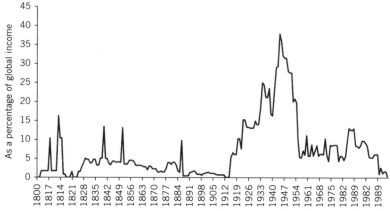

Percentage of countries in default
Source: Reinhart and Rogoff (2011).

The political class which controls the state structure has different interests from investors. Marcus Olson[6] explains that the best-organised groups ensure that political power moves in the direction they intend. Well-organised business organisations, civil servant groups, and workers in trade unions achieve their objectives more quickly and effectively than companies that are unattached to lobbies, or isolated workers, or unemployed people.

Logically, these groups are led by people motivated by very human incentives (the public choice school has explained this extensively). Like all of us, these people have their interests, objectives, careers, tactics, jealousies, plans, etc. We are talking about individuals who do not normally expose

---

[6]Olson (2000).

their own capital and, therefore, do not take risks in their decisions. If they are right, they will take responsibility for them and if not, they will disown them, but everyone will give their own account of what has happened and propose additional measures to correct the problem.

As Hans Herman Hoppe illustrates,[7] the time preference problem derives from electoral cycles, which prevent long-term decisions – with limited electoral visibility – from being taken. What politician will confront elections promising public austerity? It is not common, although there are some honourable exceptions in advanced and mature societies like Germany where this is almost always the case and, more recently, in the United Kingdom.

The question is: How to put aside money in good times for leaner periods? This is what any sensible head of household does. By contrast, for political leaders wanting to continue governing, it will almost never be the best approach, because 30–40% of voters who grant them the capacity to govern (usually representing around 25% of the population) will call the shots. Within this decisive group, the best organised will shepherd the rest.

I am not talking about replacing democracy with other forms of governance, even though major countries such as China have managed to deliver extraordinary improvements in living standards with a non-democratic regime. Instead, the goal is to highlight the flaws in order to make progress. Either way, as von Mises used to say, democracy will always be the best way to get rid of inept leaders.

However, there is no need to be overly reverent to democracy either, as happens when certain people speak of the tyranny of markets over the democratic majority. There is no better expression of popular will than people's actions in daily life: decisions on work, buying and selling, leisure, health, etc. These decisions involve a lot of time and effort, something we cannot be sure applies when it comes to casting their vote in elections. Ultimately, the only people who really weigh up their votes are those who have a high degree of civic awareness and few prejudices, something difficult to marry up.

Surprisingly, some people think the opposite: they consider the person who votes every time to be extremely sensible and knowledgeable, but – somehow – in the periods between elections they seem to think this same person becomes a useless being who has to be helped to make decisions on the products and services they should buy. This distorted vision of reality usually originates with interested parties (politicians prone to intervention and 'intellectuals' with little audience), since it is clear that the tyranny of the market is all of us taking much more considered decisions than how we decide to vote.

---

[7]Hoppe (2011).

Finally, financial markets move for infinite reasons: economic developments, political decisions, unexpected shocks, technological innovations, etc. All of them have different impacts and we cannot and should not seek to analyse them in depth, due to the difficulty of establishing appropriate relations between cause and effect. We have focused on the heart of the matter. The – to some degree measurable – impact of some decisions, mainly political, on the two main types of assets. We measure this impact through currency depreciation, which has a very serious effect on one of these assets: monetary assets.

CONCLUSION

The conclusion of this chapter is that both logical and empirical results lead us to the same outcome. We should invest our savings with people who have a similar perspective and time horizon to us. This is the only sensible thing to do. And as the optimal thing for investment is always to take a long-term outlook or horizon, which is the only perspective that allows us to make minimal predictions, we should steer clear of monetary assets influenced by a political class that has an unavoidably short-term point of view.

We should therefore invest in real assets, particularly equities, which fulfil the specific needs of the population and are managed by people or business leaders with a long-term perspective and optimal capacity to adjust to changes in the environment. (Later on we will see that it is essential that they be people or business leaders in the most radical sense: entrepreneurs. It is surprising to see how executives are often confused with business leaders or entrepreneurs, which reaches the point of absurdity when awards such as 'Entrepreneur of the Year' are given to executives.)

In addition to equities, other real assets will also protect us against currency depreciation processes, which tend to be more frequent since the disappearance of the gold standard. However, as they are easily replicable, these assets do not reach the same level of return as equities. Some investors with an 'Austrian' background lean towards gold or treasury at times of political uncertainty or excessive currency manipulation, as occurred in 2016. It is worth reiterating that there is no sense in maintaining liquidity in an asset (treasury) subject to a brutal loss of value, precisely as a result of this currency manipulation. It is patently incoherent and can only be forgiven if this treasury is supported by gold or another reliable reserve.

Neither is the argument convincing that some monetary assets offer liquidity. This function can be perfectly met by other real assets, such as some well-capitalised equities at reasonable prices. We can always find shares with these characteristics, and the excuse that their prices will fall in a crisis holds no water, given that, firstly, these crises are always temporary and our horizon should be long term, and secondly, we should invest resources that are not immediately needed.

Investing in gold is more coherent, but time has shown that equities – property deeds for companies that produce real goods and services demanded by society – perform exceptionally over the long term, with returns that are substantially better than other assets, taking on less long-term volatility and less short- and long-term risk.

The conclusion is unequivocal: the bulk of our savings should be invested long term and in equities. We only need hold positions in monetary assets to cover occasional cash needs.[8]

APPENDIX A

Discount Rate

As a direct consequence of the subjective nature of our investment alternatives and the practical impossibility of recommending investment in monetary assets, it is worth clarifying and setting out my approach to an essential concept in the investment world: discount rates.[9]

The discount rate is the rate at which possible investments have to be discounted. It reflects the notion that it is not the same thing to receive income from our investments, or the principal itself, in year one as opposed to year five. Another way of thinking about it is as the opportunity cost. Investing in one thing means not investing in another, and discounting is effectively comparing one with the other.

In standard financial practice these flows of money are discounted at the risk-free rate plus a risk premium.

The risk-free rate is normally the interest rate on the bond issued by the government where the investment is taking place, which historically varies between 2% and 10%: a wide range, which reflects the historic strength

---

[8] In addition to short-term liquidity purposes, the only other exception that has any sense is the need to match assets with similar liabilities, so that they therefore depreciate simultaneously. Insurance companies hold liabilities, mathematical reserves, which they can match appropriately – at least some of them – with monetary assets. If the currency depreciates, both liabilities and assets will be similarly affected. The one who suffers is the insured party, who will see that the insured promises to pay are insufficient to cover the expected or unexpected situation. However, from the company's perspective they will have acted 'correctly', by matching assets and liabilities. Once again it is an agency problem: in the strict sense the company is fulfilling its obligations, but it is not giving a true solution to the client.

[9] For a more technical explanation of the ideas developed in this section, see Olbrich *et al.* (2015).

of the government issuer and, particularly, its repayment capacity in a non-depreciated currency in which the debt is issued.

The risk premium, as indicated by its name, is the additional premium required of an asset to invest in it. The incorrect assumption here is that the asset is more risky than the government bond. Historically, this premium has stood at around 3%.

CAPM theorists (in Chapter 6 we will engage in a more detailed discussion of the Capital Asset Pricing Model) incorrectly believe that the risk premium is a market parameter, instead of being personal to each investor. They therefore think that this premium can be calculated.

Finally, this risk premium is weighted by the volatility of the share price in the market: Beta. The market has a Beta of one. Less volatile shares have a Beta of less than one, while more volatile stocks are above one.

$$\text{Current value of investment} = Io + \sum_{t=1}^{N} \frac{\text{cash flow}}{(1+i)^t}$$

i is therefore the rate at which income flows are discounted.

This is standard practice, but I don't see any logic to it. Personally, I never use this discount rate and in the professional world I have only resorted to it on very rare occasions when the market pricing of 'risk' assets is very high. Even if we were to assume it made sense to equate risk and volatility – despite this being illogical, as we have already discussed – each investor has their own disposition towards assumable risk. 'Market risk' does not exist.

Just as when we analyse a company's future profits and all investors have a different opinion, it seems logical that each investor will discount at their preferred rate, using the 'risk premium' and Beta they consider appropriate. In Chapter 6 we will critique the CAPM more extensively.

Therefore, as investors, each of us should discount according to our preferences and alternatives, and after reading this chapter we now know that we should only invest in real assets and our alternative is other real assets. As we have seen, there is empirical evidence that investment in equities offers greater returns and involves taking on less risk than fixed income, especially since currencies are no longer backed by the gold standard. In situations of serious crisis there is a natural tendency for the currency to lose value; it is the easiest way out for a political class facing elections. And in this situation the crucial advantage of real assets is their capacity to adapt to a currency depreciation, or even new currencies.

Equities are a mere reflection of this ownership, making them an optimal way to protect against inflation in moments of serious monetary crisis.

The Discount Rate: My Own Version

Since real – supposedly risky – assets are the best way to preserve our purchasing power, and given that non-real assets are an unacceptable alternative, how do I discount my investment in assets?

I reiterate: with other real assets.

$$\text{Current value of investment} = Io + \sum_{t=1}^{N} \frac{\text{cash flow}}{(1 + ia)^t}$$

ia representing the return on my real investment alternative.

As a matter of fact, my best alternative investment has always been the funds I have directly managed, initially by myself and later on as part of a team. This is obvious, but worth highlighting as it is not that common in the financial market. If I devote myself to investing money and I have a diversified portfolio of good assets, how could this not be my best alternative? How could I ask potential clients to invest with me if it wasn't the case?

I have to compare any possible alternative investment – whether they be, for example, new business projects (generally friends and acquaintances), gold, or houses – with my preferred alternative: my funds. So far I have not had any doubt, which is why I have nearly all my family assets invested in them.

Ultimately, it is about discounting or comparing any investment option with the best possible alternative. And, for me, my best alternative is investing in the funds I manage. If I expect to obtain a return of 8% with my fund, I would not consider investing in any project where I don't expect at least an 8–10% return, assuming the same level of security.

Furthermore, the fund has an additional advantage: it does not require extra attention, it doesn't need time. This element must be included in the required additional return. It is obviously a very personal decision. A property or investment project is highly time-consuming, and we should demand an extra return from them precisely for this reason.

If I didn't manage funds, my second best alternative would be fundamental mutual funds (semi-passives: we will discuss these in more detail in Chapter 6), or equity funds managed by people I trust. Finally, I would consider other types of real assets: real estate, commodities, or entrepreneurial projects. But these are less attractive to me, either because they are very replicable assets, lacking the ability to set their own price (real estate and commodities), or they are actually very risky (entrepreneurial projects).

I have spoken about what applies for me, but this approach should be adapted to an investor's personal situation. Typically, the average investor (who has not read this or Jeremy Siegel's book) is more comfortable investing in property. Intuitively it is easier to wrap your head around. So any possible investment should be compared with – or discounted against – the investor's best alternative, which might well be a particular property. Only if they find a better alternative, such as a good fund manager, passive index, stock, entrepreneurial project, etc. should they take money out of their base investment.

On a professional level, the attitude is much the same when deciding between different stocks. The decision to invest in a particular stock should be discounted or compared with investing in other stocks.

And not with fixed income. Only in very specific situations can this stance be softened and a degree of flexibility introduced. There are some motives for occasional flexibility.

One could be because other market actors don't have such a radical outlook and this means that at points in time, when equities are expensive, it makes sense to temporarily hold more liquidity. The market normally prices between a P/E ratio of 10 and 20, with a historical average of 15. If the market is pricing at a P/E of close to 20, it is worth having liquidity. It is difficult to sustain a P/E of 20 or above for a very long period of time, because the biggest factor weighing down equities starts to come into play: the impact of price volatility on the perception of assets. This means that investors have tended not to be willing to pay above a P/E of 15 for prolonged periods of time.

This is an empirical reality, but not necessarily logical. Some day this perception might change and the historic average could increase to 20, at this point the long-term return on equity and fixed-income assets would be brought practically into line.

The second, more practical reason, is the added flexibility very liquid assets provide for managing redemptions or the emergence of sudden investment alternatives. This is less important because – as previously mentioned – this can be resolved by having a portfolio of large, liquid stocks which fulfil the same function.

In sum, we should discount using our best alternative. For me this alternative will never be a monetary asset based on paper money, but rather the mutual fund that I manage.

APPENDIX B

How to Invest Over a Lifetime

Circumstances change over time and it does not make sense to apply the same rules to differing personal situations. At some points we are not willing to accept volatility, while at other times losses are more tolerable. Across the OECD as a whole the majority of savings are invested in the real estate sector, 74%, while investment in equities and funds is minute, less than five percent.

We have already seen that this distribution does not have much long-term economic rationale, while acknowledging the emotional logic. I am going to propose an alternative investment over time.

Composition of Net Wealth in Spain (OECD)

	SPAIN	OECD	USA
Non-financial assets	**80.7%**	**74.1%**	**48.5%**
Primary residence	53.9%	51.2%	31.5%
Other real-estate property	23.7%	17.4%	12.8%
Vehicles	2.6%	3.2%	3.4%
Other non-financial assets	0.4%	4.5%	0.8%
Financial assets	**19.3%**	**25.9%**	**51.5%**
Deposits	5.3%	7.6%	7.0%
Bonds and other fixed-income securities	0.2%	0.9%	2.0%
Mutual funds	0.8%	2.0%	7.6%
Net equity in unincorporated partnerships	9.0%	6.7%	4.5%
Shares	0.9%	2.3%	5.7%
Unlisted shares and other own funds	0.8%	2.1%	14.2%
Other financial assets distinct from pension funds	0.7%	0.9%	1.1%
Life insurance and individual and voluntary pensions	1.6%	4.2%	9.4%
Liabilities	**10.1%**	**14.1%**	**18.7%**
Loans – primary residence	6.1%	8.4%	13.0%
Other real-estate loans	2.6%	2.0%	2.9%
Other loans	1.4%	2.4%	2.8%

Source: Moncada and Rallo (2016).

First Steps

One's main asset is in fact oneself. Our priority should be to improve our skills and become an attractive proposition to those around us. This normally implies a monetary sacrifice or time investment, which is possibly the most rewarding of them all.

Once we have exhausted our opportunities for prsonal development, we can consider how to approach the investor process.

When we are young, students or workers, we should start by investing all of our meagre savings in shares, or mutual funds which invest in equities.[10]

---

[10]For simplicity, in this appendix we refer only to equities, but in the next chapter we will go into more detail on the different investment options in terms of funds and shares.

At this stage in life we can afford to take on greater volatility, making it logical to try to obtain the best return possible and try to start constructing a small amount of capital. If we suffer losses, there will be time to recover them.

Peter Lynch said that our first investment should be a house, our home, and this can make a lot of sense if we form a family – with all the responsibilities that entails. But if this takes some time to happen, as is the case these days in nearly all developed societies, equities are a more attractive initial proposition.

The real-estate sector is very much entrenched in our lives; until recently we didn't know about other forms of investment. Our forefathers did not have access to the infinite possibilities currently on offer, and they felt secure with their own property. But houses – as can be seen in the next chart – sustain little more than the purchasing power of our savings. The well-known market and real-estate analyst, Robert Shiller, presents similar results.

Nominal and real houses prices in the United States, 1950–2012
Source: Siegel (2015).

It is worth remembering that houses are a commodity. They are easily replicable goods, which tend not to age well. We have remarked on how technological development enables productivity to increase by 1–2% each year, meaning that the price of materials and production tends to decline in real terms by the same amount.

Obviously, this is not true for the other major component in the sector: land. But the planet, excluding some special spots such as Monaco or Hong Kong, currently provides us with all the land necessary to multiply the number of global inhabitants. In any case, this multiplication is not going to happen; population growth is set to decline dramatically by the middle of the century. As such, it seems unlikely that the value of land will experience major growth either.

However, the decline in prices is partially offset by the fact that with increased wealth, we are demanding better building materials.

In addition to being an easily replicable commodity with limited real increases in value, there are also maintenance costs to consider, which we know can be very high; transactions costs, which vary by country but are far from negligible; and management costs, which can become very uncomfortable or expensive for the owner.

There are some specific exceptions in the centre of large cities, due to space restrictions. But these are also replicable over time, and their overall performance cannot change all that much from the rest of the real-estate sector. Even a city centre can change with time. For example, in Madrid the centre of gravity has shifted northward, with a consequent loss in value of certain buildings in the old 'centre'.

We can conclude that houses are like gold: they avoid the worst, but add little compared with equities.

Either way, the major problem at this point in life is having the capacity to save – either because of a paltry income or a lack of self-control over consumption.

Stabilisation

When we settle down, and create a family, two things can happen.

(1) We do not have any savings available. In which case – despite what we have already said – buying a house is the number one option, because a monthly mortgage payment forces us to save. Somebody who does not have any savings when they form a family, after several years of working, needs moral support to save and the obligation to pay back a loan serves this purpose. It is not the most optimal investment, but it compensates personality traits or the simple lack of resources which prevents us from doing the right thing: investing in shares. A mortgage mitigates the tendency to spend and not save, and makes up for a possible aversion to the visible volatility of equities, despite their great attraction.

Furthermore, some young people can't save because their salaries are very low, or because they have taken on debt to pay for their studies. In the case of the latter, after paying down the debt, if they have the capacity to save they should invest in shares, since they might have the right personality for it.

(2) We have now accumulated a small amount of capital. The choice is then between buying a house or renting. If the right course has been followed, we will have invested in equities for some years and have acquired some experience and confidence. The most natural thing would be to continue down this path, renting a property until we have sufficient assets in shares and it becomes potentially interesting to start diversifying.

It might be the case that our partner is more adverse to volatility and is not as comfortable investing in shares. This would be the time to think about buying a house. The decision should be based on the relative valuation of the two things at the specific point in time (sometimes one market is clearly more attractive than another) and one's individual degree of aversion to volatility.

Normally, the stock market pre-empts the real-estate market, meaning that it is common to be able to buy a house by selling shares. In my case, I always invested in shares up until 1998, when we bought our house. Equities had performed exceptionally in the previous years, and the price of houses had remained very static over five years, making it an optimal time in relative terms. Either way, shares have the presumption of innocence; only in very specific moments is it better to invest in houses. Equities are the right path most of the time.

Volatility is a problem that should not concern the reader of this book. I think I have made clear the enormous opportunity cost involved with monetary assets or relatively undistinctive real assets, such as houses, so my recommendation is to dive into the explanations set out here and try to overcome any aversion to volatility. It may help to review the reference list included in this and other books.

Maturity

Life goes on and it may become harder to save. General advice from this point on becomes less useful, as personal circumstances dominate. As a general concept, if money is not required for something specific or in the short term, equities remain the main option.

With the passage of time, and as we close in on retirement, we can think about holding more liquidity to cover expenses over the next two or three years. But this will depend on the total capital available and our aversion to volatility. If our accumulated capital is significant, this liquidity is unnecessary; even a significant market crash will not change our way of life. If it is not very elevated, it is worth having a part of our savings in fixed income to reduce the short-term volatility of income flows needed in daily life.

We always refer to volatility rather than risk, because as we know they are not the same thing. When we invest in equities we take on more short-term volatility but less risk over all time horizons.

If we follow this simple advice, we will have a comfortable retirement with reasonable savings and, above all, the habit of stoically accepting market movements, even taking an interest, knowing that we can take advantage of them.

Order of Preference

I conclude with a list of the order of preference of the different generic assets.

1. Listed shares (in Chapter 6 we will distinguish between different equity funds and equities themselves). The advantage over non-listed equities is that they are more susceptible to aberrations resulting from panic and euphoria. When somebody sells their company on the private market they are fully aware of its future potential. The same is not true for public stock, where investors are either unwilling to stray from the pack or lack sufficient knowledge.[11] Enduring movements derived from these aberrations will enable us to capitalise more from listed stocks.
2. Other real assets. The choice should be made between them according to each asset's current position in the cycle and our knowledge and experience of each of them. The latter reason is why houses are often the best option, although any real asset serves the purpose of preserving our purchasing power well enough, protecting us from extreme crises.
3. Monetary assets – only for short-term liquidity needs. Despite a reasonable performance since 1800, following the abandonment of the gold standard the real return has declined significantly and they are subject to unacceptable political risk.

This is a simple scheme, but it could be useful for steering us along the right path.

---

[11]It is worth repeating here that investing in our education offers very high returns, meaning that we should exhaust this option before thinking about equities.

[You might think I am saying all this because I invest in equities for a living, making this a rather self-interested recommendation. This would be getting it the wrong way round. I invest in equities because, after analysing all the possibilities, I believe that it is the best way to sustain the purchasing power of my savings and that is what I am explaining. If it were better to invest in other assets, I would do so and I would recommend others to do the same thing.]

CHAPTER 6

Passive and/or Active Management

We have made up our mind that investing our savings in equities is the way to go, safe in the knowledge that they offer the best relationship between risk and return. Now we have to tackle the next step in the investment process: deciding how we gain exposure to stocks.

The markets offer a range of options, creating confusion which can only be penetrated on a sporadic basis. But there is no reason to be pessimistic, because the problem can be simplified. If we focus on what's available, we can see that there are four options on offer for investing in equities:

1. Passive management (via Index Funds [IF] or Exchange-Traded Funds [ETF]).
2. Active management:
   - fundamental index funds
   - active managers
   - direct investment in shares.

Mutual funds cover three of the four options for investing in equities, but despite this, in my home country of Spain, 60% of people don't even know what a mutual fund is. So, for the sake of clarity, a mutual fund is a collective investment undertaking which brings together funds from different investors to invest in a variety of financial instruments. The responsibility for the latter is normally delegated to a fund manager. There are thousands of funds available across the world, catering to all types of investors.

Professional money management is currently at something of a cross-roads. Investors are tired of paying high fees for products offering little value-added – only 7% of funds beat the indexes in the United States and the United Kingdom – while the availability of information makes it possible to carry out a more detailed analysis of the different alternatives on offer.

Accordingly, over the last 15 years passive management – investment in an index in return for paying low fees – has expanded to represent 35% of global assets, reaching nearly 40% in the United States. This type of management was almost non-existent at the turn of the century.[1]

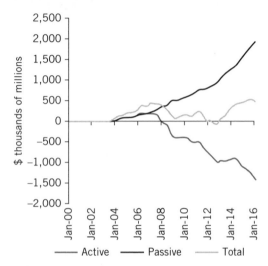

Global cumulative flow in active and passive equity funds

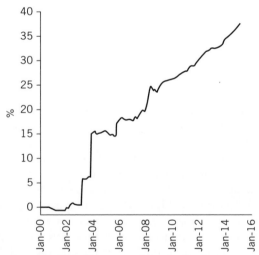

Percentage of passive global funds over total equity funds
Source: EPFR Global, ICI, Bernstein.

---

[1]Fraser-Jenkins *et al.* (2015).

This trend, which is taking place in other sectors – Walmart, low-cost airlines, etc. – seems unstoppable. The development of a new type of passive fundamental index – which I will refer to as semi-passive – could push up these proportions much further still. Even the regulators and other public bodies are reviewing the costs associated with active management, penalising high costs and forcing them lower. The evolution of Vanguard's costs, the pioneer in passive management, are a good illustration of this. This is very welcome news, since a large number of so-called value-added managers don't, in fact, add any.

Vanguard

Average fees %

Assets under management

Source: Vanguard.

However, sooner or later this type of growth will hit a ceiling. There will come a point when the inefficiencies arising from an essentially 'brainless' method of investing will create excessive distortions in the market, attracting new capital to active management. Eventually, passive management will find its appropriate place in the market.

PASSIVE MANAGEMENT

Passive management means investing in funds which replicate an index. In recent times, there has been a particular surge in interest in a specific type of index fund, exchange-traded funds (ETFs). Both types of funds are similar, although ETFs trade on regulated markets and can be bought and sold over the course of a day, like shares, whereas normal index funds are assigned a net asset value at the end of every session.

Generally, passive index funds are created in proportion to the sizes of the companies that make up the index, with some exceptions – such as the Dow Jones, which is based on share prices. So Apple or General Electric will have a greater weight than a small company – in proportion to their relative size.

The main advantage of index funds is that they lower management costs, with fees of below 25 basis points (0.25%), while over the long term sustaining and improving the purchasing power of savings. Indeed, the results discussed in Chapter 5 comparing equities with other assets are based on the performance of the US stock exchange indexes.

However, deciding to invest passively is in itself an active decision. Firstly, it assumes that the market is efficient and thus a good alternative for people who don't want to go to much effort and, secondly, a choice still has to be made among the myriad of possible indexes. There are a lot of indexes out there, meaning careful deliberation is needed, though products based on the American S&P 500, the IBEX 35 in Spain, or the MSCI for a global portfolio readily tick the boxes of being low cost and pretty automated. Either way, it is not a complete cop-out from having to think a little.

However, for an investor with a long-term perspective, the main virtue of ETFs – being able to invest over the course of the day – is not critical. Indeed, it carries with it the added uncertainty that providing such liquidity could lead to valuation problems, in turn complicating future developments. Some assets lack the necessary liquidity to be able to provide near-instantaneous valuations, which has led some ETF experts to warn of potential problems in future large-scale crises.

The pioneer and biggest player in the passive world is the Vanguard Group, which also benefits from having a mutual company structure, meaning that profits are invested in reducing fees. Its founder and forefather is John Bogle, a fervent proponent of passive management. He has written various books, the most famous of which is probably *Common Sense on Mutual Funds*.[2]

Bogle's advice focuses on extolling the virtues of passive management:

- Select low-cost funds.
- Choose expensive advisors wisely.
- Analyse the fund's performance in detail and use the results of the analysis appropriately. It is important to understand what happened.
- Be sceptical about guru investors.
- Etc.

---

[2]Bogle (2009).

In other words: a lot of common sense, bearing in mind that it is extremely hard to beat the market, since the market is all of us and not everybody can be better than average.

In sum, passive management is a suitable approach for investors who are convinced of the case for investing in a certain type of asset (there are also funds for bonds and other assets) and are aware of the difficulties involved in beating the market while bearing moderate costs.

ACTIVE MANAGEMENT

As we explained in Chapter 4, the market always trends towards efficiency but almost never gets there, since information is not only changing but being created every second. Everybody is creating relevant new information for those around them through their everyday decisions. Not everybody is aware of this new information, sometimes we aren't even aware of it ourselves.

Some economists have attempted to prove that the market is efficient and that it captures all available information, rendering any attempt to obtain above-market returns pointless. But such static efficiency is impossible. Even if it were possible, it wouldn't give us relevant information, since it would not reflect the dynamic nature of information: no market can hold information that is only known to the person creating it, and even this person may be barely conscious of it.

(This section continues with some concepts which may be difficult to understand for the uninitiated, so the reader has the option to jump directly to the final two concluding paragraphs, which contain a revealing quote from Warren Buffett.)

The most well-known model for applying efficient markets to the valuation of financial market assets is the Capital Asset Pricing Model (CAPM). It has its origins in Harry Markowitz's so-called modern portfolio theory, which maintains that the best alternative investment is the market index. The latter can only be beaten if we take on leverage, which at the same time implies greater volatility. My summary of the theory is going to be brief, because from analysing the starting hypotheses it rapidly becomes clear that there is little point devoting much time to it. The hypotheses are that:

1. Individuals cannot affect prices; they have known and homogenous expectations for expected return, volatility, and correlations. (After having determined that the essence of human action is in the subjective intentions of individuals, it should already be clear that the premises underpinning this assumption are absurd – enough said).

2. All individuals plan to invest over the same time horizon, of one year (words fail me …).
3. The return on assets corresponds to a bell-shaped normal distribution, the statistically most frequent, where the majority of observations lie in the centre. Returns are explained by mathematical expectation and volatility by standard deviation. (It has already been proven that there are a myriad of exceptions to the normal distribution;[3] to add salt to the wounds, a basic error is made in confusing volatility with risk.)
4. Individuals can lend and borrow unlimited amounts of a risk-free asset. The asset market is perfect; individuals can buy any fraction of an asset. (Once again, unrealistic assumptions, risk is confused with volatility and the view of financial markets is extremely rose-tinted.)
5. Information is free and available to all. (Yet again I'm flabbergasted, literally speechless …).

With such unrealistic assumptions, it is hardly surprising that the CAPM doesn't get us very far. The main conclusions, according to Pablo Fernández,[4] are that all investors:

1. Will always combine a risk-free asset with the market portfolio.
2. Will have the same portfolio of risky assets: the market portfolio.
3. Will agree on the expected return and expected variance of the market portfolio and of every asset.
4. Will agree on the market risk premium and on the Beta of every asset.
5. Will agree that the market portfolio (on a chart of expected return–variance) is on the minimum variance frontier and is efficient.
6. Will expect returns on their assets according to the stocks' Betas.

As Fernández observes, the CAPM is an absurd model because it is based on absurd hypotheses. Obviously, these conclusions are not fulfilled in real life.

The underlying problem is the impossibility of modelling human behaviour, with its ever-changing ends and means, which sometimes the actors themselves don't comprehend. And it is especially unrealistic when applied using a static analysis and nonsensical assumptions. Furthermore,

---

[3] Taleb (2012).
[4] Fernández (2015).

the model is extremely dangerous, because it can appear as though it is helping to mitigate investment risks, increasing exposure to assets to levels above where they would normally be if the model were not being used. It provides a false sense of security, which – together with massive recourse to debt – led to the Long-Term Capital Management hedge fund debacle in 1998, which had an extremely negative long-term impact on the markets.

The biggest empirical blow to the model comes from a study by Fama and French.[5] They show that for the period 1963–1990, the correlation between the return on stocks and their Betas was very small, while the relationships between return and size and results and price-to-book value were much more significant.

Main Findings of the French and Fama article

Company size	Average Beta	Annual Average Return	Company Beta	Average Beta	Annual Average Return	Company Price/ Book Value	Average Beta	Annual Average Return
1 (biggest)	0.93	10.7%	1 (high)	1.68	15.1%	1 (high)	1.35	5.9%
2	1.02	11.4%	2	1.52	16.0%	2	1.32	10.4%
3	1.08	13.2%	3	1.41	14.8%	3	1.30	11.6%
4	1.16	12.8%	4	1.32	14.8%	4	1.28	12.5%
5	1.22	14.0%	5	1.26	15.6%	5	1.27	14.0%
6	1.24	15.5%	6	1.19	15.6%	6	1.27	15.6%
7	1.33	15.0%	7	1.13	15.7%	7	1.27	17.3%
8	1.34	14.9%	8	1.04	15.1%	8	1.27	18.0%
9	1.39	15.5%	9	0.92	15.8%	9	1.29	19.1%
10 (smallest)	1.44	18.2%	10 (low)	0.80	14.4%	10 (low)	1.34	22.6%

French and Fama conclude that: 'Our tests do not support the most basic prediction of the CAPM Sharpe–Lintner–Black model, that average stock returns are positively related to their market Betas'.

---

[5] Fama and French (1992).

If you haven't followed much of the above, don't worry. As Buffett says: 'Half of the attendees at the Berkshire Hathaway annual general meeting don't know what Beta is, the other half couldn't care less'.

The main conclusion here is that financial markets are not as efficient as some people make out, providing a window of opportunity to those who believe they can obtain better returns.

We will see how.

Fundamental Index Funds: Passive or Semi-passive Management Using Criteria

The first step towards active management is not particularly active. In reality, it is semi-passive – as we shall see.

The passive funds or ETF indexes discussed in the previous section are based on underlying indexes – S&P 500, IBEX 35, MSCI World Index, etc. – whose component parts are determined according to their size. In other words, large companies have a proportionately greater weight than smaller companies, in accordance with their relative size. This creates a perverse effect – when a business flounders, its price falls and it is ultimately expelled from the index – and in a passive index we accompany it throughout this downward journey to expulsion. Normally, this business is then substituted for one that has grown a lot and therefore has increased its capitalisation, something we have not taken part in. Put simply, we end up buying stocks that have already risen and selling them once they have fallen. Completely the wrong way round.

Therefore, if passive management doesn't convince us and we want to do something more in the belief that the market may not always be efficient and that we can do better, then the next option is a variation on index or exchange-traded funds: passive funds which have a predefined strategy able to beat the index. This is also known as factor investing or investing with fundamental index funds (FIFs). This could include funds that invest in companies with a low P/E ratio or a high dividend yield.

These FIFs make sense if they are able to obtain a better return than the market or the passive capitalisation indexes. And this can arise because of mean reversion, which is one of the least understand phenomena in human behavioural analysis. We will discuss this in more detail in Chapter 9.

Various authors have demonstrated that share prices experience mean reversion: after a bad spell, they improve and outperform the market and vice-versa, bubbles deflate. Stocks which trade with low multiples perform better than average, while high-multiple stocks perform worse, both trending towards the mean.[6]

James P. O'Shaughnessy has extensively and clearly analysed a multitude of investment strategies over the last 50 years, enabling us to verify which have been the most successful in dealing with mean reversion.

As can be seen from the table on the next page, lots of strategies beat the market on a regular basis. Over the period from 1964 to 2009, a strategy including all American stock obtained an 11.2% annual return. A pretty attractive return, but various alternative approaches could have fared better through building portfolios focused on a series of criteria:

- Low P/E ratio.
- Low EV/EBITDA (EBITDA is essentially an estimate of operating profit and EV is the enterprise value, the sum of debt plus stock market capitalisation).
- Low price/sales ratio.
- High dividend yield.
- Etc.

For example, a strategy which includes the group of shares with the lowest EV/EBITDA ratio would have obtained an annual return of 16.58% (by contrast, stocks with the highest ratio would have posted a measly 5.33% return).

He also considers various combinations of strategies, which deliver even better results. For example, he includes the following criteria in what he calls the 'Value Factor Three' strategy:

1. Price/book value.
2. P/E ratio.
3. Price/sales.
4. EBITDA/EV.
5. Price/cash flow.
6. Share buyback.

The Value Factor Three strategy, which employs the best combination of these factors – low P/E ratio, low price/sales, etc. – would have obtained an annual return of 17.39%.

---

[6]Siegel (2014), Vishny *et al.* (1994), as well as various Fama and French articles.

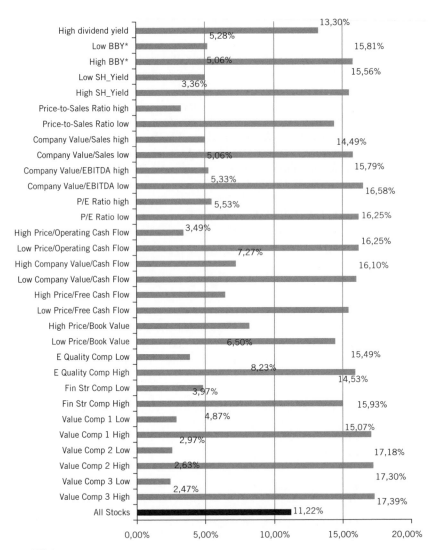

*All shares

Average rates of compound annual return over 46 years up to 31 December 2009; results of applying different strategies across an array of investment products Source: O'Shaughnessy (2012).

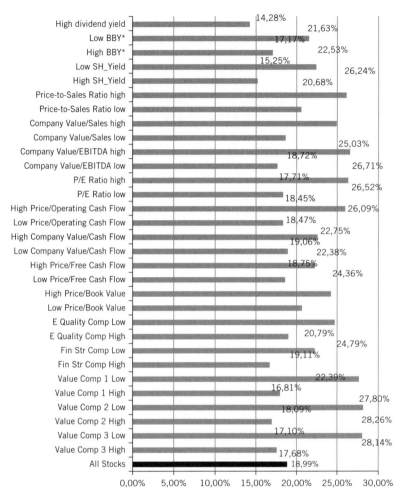

*All shares

Standard deviation of the returns on different strategies across the investment universe (higher implies greater risk)
Source: O'Shaughnessy (2012).

Thus it would appear that it is in fact possible to improve on the results of capitalisation indexes using indexes of different criteria.

And surprisingly, if we add the concept of 'price momentum' to these 'value'-based strategies, the results are even better: among all value stocks, the best performers over the last six months post a higher return during the following year. Some of the strategies calculated on this basis would have obtained a 23% annual return.

The fund managers at the hedge fund AQR have reached the same conclusion: value plus price momentum is the way to go.[7]

The logic behind 'price momentum' is that if you buy a stock which is already starting to rise then the opportunity cost is lower, reducing the time spent waiting for the rest of the market to wake up to the opportunity. This waiting time is the biggest problem for value investors, because we have a natural impulse to buy too soon and sell too early. In any case, for somebody accustomed to buying shares when they are on the way down, it feels counterintuitive to buy what is rising, making it a challenge to apply this 'price momentum' strategy.

O'Shaughnessy[8] provides a detailed ranking of strategies, alongside the associated risks. It could be argued that such studies – which analyse the past – are a case of 'data mining', but in reality there is a logic to these results, underpinned by the concept of mean reversion.

The bigger challenge is choosing among the endless options. Even so, choosing one of these approaches makes a lot of sense, given that they can significantly outperform the indexes by between 5% and 10% a year. In reality, all active managers – especially us value investors – are constantly shuffling between the most attractive strategies. We are all on the lookout for cheap companies, using a variety of criteria to analyse them. When we post good results, they come from repeatedly applying these strategies, albeit sometimes intuitively or unwittingly.

Semi-passive or fundamental strategies, like passive approaches, save on management costs, but also help guard against character flaws that can prevent us from taking the right decisions. The more automatic the decision, the easier it will be. The downside is that when markets are performing poorly and the strategy itself is not working – and this can happen for lengthy periods of time – there is no shoulder to cry on. We are out in the wilderness on our own with no one to reassure us. This can be tough.

Obviously, there are not enough funds to cater for every possible form of semi-passive management, but the main alternatives are covered. In this regard, it's worth highlighting Dimensional Funds, which work directly with academics – especially Fama and French – to offer strategies that could obtain above-market returns. Not only have they developed some of the value strategies discussed here, but they also offer other types. AQR invest along these lines. Wisdom Tree is another asset manager specialised in this type of management, although the heavyweights, Blackrock and the like, also now offer semi-passive options.

---

[7] Asness *et al.* (2015).
[8] O'Shaughnessy (2012), pp. 597 ff.

Active Managers

The next step is to consider whether an active manager can do any better than these high-performing strategies. The answer is far from obvious, as can be seen in O'Shaughnessy:

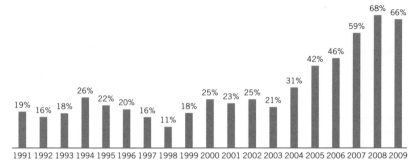

Percentage of all equity funds with track records of more than 10 years of outperforming the S&P 500 in the 10 years up to 31 December each year
Source: O'Shaughnessy (2012).

Over the years, only 30% of American asset managers have managed to beat the indexes. Furthermore, according to the S&P Dow Jones Indices, in the last 10 years, 80% of European funds (France, Spain, Denmark, Switzerland, and Holland) failed to outperform the indexes. The success rate is even worse in Spain.[9] (There are several studies on this topic, with different results, but always with a minority of managers beating the indexes.)

But the problem runs deeper still. Although some active managers have obtained good results, there is scant chance that they will continue to do so in the future. Research by two Morningstar analysts, Alex Bryan and James Li,[10] shows that we have the same probability of outperforming the market in the future by investing with the worst-performing investors as we do with those who have the best track record (although for a horizon of less than a year, a certain persistence remains due to the 'price momentum' of certain stocks). Indeed, the CNMV – Spain's securities market regulator – requires all funds to provide a mandatory warning that past performance is no guarantee of future results.

Furthermore, if there are semi-passive strategies with proven track records of beating the indexes, why would we need an active manager?

---

[9]For Europe, see 'FTfm', *Financial Times*, 21 March 2016; for Spain, see Fernández *et al.* (2016).
[10]Bryan and Li (2016).

Truth be told, there isn't much need. If we don't know anyone whose approach or results inspire us with confidence, it's clearly better to stay within the confines of passive or semi-passive management.

That said, I could certainly recommend some managers whose approach I find convincing and who have the results to substantiate it. I could also refer to a 1970s study by Buffett on his investment friends, who posted exceptional results by taking the right approach.[11]

The Superinvestors of Graham-and-Doddsville

	No. years	Index performance	Investor performance
Walter Jl. Schloss	28 1/4	8.4%	16.1%
Tweedy, Browne Inc.	15 3/4	7.0%	16.0%
Buffett Partnership, Ltd	13	7.4%	23.8%
Sequoia Fund. Inc.	14	10.0%	17.2%
Charles Munger	14	5.0%	13.7%
Pacific Partners, Ltd	19	7.8%	23.6%
Perlmeter Investments	18	7.0%	19.0%

Source: Buffett (1984).

But nothing guarantees that future returns will replicate former glories, as the regulators rightly require us to point out to clients.

However, we can sustain an argument that most investors who have obtained excellent results did so by applying the previously mentioned value criteria. Furthermore, despite the cost of fees and the lack of certainty on results, there are still some reasons for investing with active managers:

1. Some managers capitalise on market inefficiency and may continue doing so in the future. It's undeniable. Look no further than Buffett.
2. We may not know how to choose or even find the right semi-passive or fundamental fund for us.[12] With a good asset manager we delegate the choice of strategy to them to apply: low P/E ratio, high dividend yield, low price/book value, etc. The best active managers are constantly shuffling between multiple strategies to find attractive stocks (whether consciously or otherwise), and this is exactly why they obtain good results. We could go so far as to say that some active managers are closet selectors of semi-passive strategies.

---

[11]Buffett (1984).

[12]By way of illustration, see *Barron's* complicated panel of ETF recommendations, 7 May. Choosing quickly becomes a very active decision (see the appendix at the end of this chapter).

It's true that it comes at a price, as they charge high fees, but sometimes it is worthwhile paying (bear in mind that unless we do the work ourselves, the person helping us find the right semi-passive fund will also charge).

3. The right strategy can vary from year to year, meaning that the portfolio needs ongoing adjustment. This is part of the job of being an active manager, but it's not easy for a private investor to do.

4. We are talking about our life savings and being in close contact with a fund manager that we trust can be a tremendous reassurance. Especially a manager who has a clear and consistent strategy, delivers good results, and to whom we can 'put a face'. It is not easy to mentally prepare oneself for a passive and anonymous strategy, even if that may be the best approach for our future well-being. While a degree of automatism helps protect us from our own character flaws, it is also true that good advice from our asset manager can help during times of doubt or market difficulties, which are very frequent occurrences.

The 'emotional side of finance' suggests that we need help to overcome anxiety brought on by investment. Meir Statman also points to other factors, such as status-seeking or the desire to have the ear of a recognised authority, which can drive us to seek out 'prestigious' investors.[13]

5. Another psychological benefit is the illusion of control or of having been responsible for success. If we choose an asset manager who is sufficiently responsive, we can have the sense of controlling decisions, as if we were the ones calling the shots. It's the closest thing possible to taking the decision to invest in a particular stock.

Berkshire Performance vs. S&P 500

Year	Percentage Annual Change		
	In Book Value per Berkshire Share	In Book Value per Berkshire Share	In Book Value per Berkshire Share
1965	23.8	49.5	10.0
1966	20.3	(3.4)	(11.7)
1967	11.0	13.3	30.9
1968	19.0	77.8	11.0
1969	16.2	19.4	(8.4)
1970	12.0	(4.6)	3.9

---

[13]Tuckett and Taffler (2012).

Year	Percentage Annual Change		
	In Book Value per Berkshire Share	In Market Value per Berkshire Share	In S&P 500 with Dividends Included
1971	16.4	80.5	14.6
1972	21.7	8.1	18.9
1973	4.7	(2.5)	(14.8)
1974	5.5	(48.7)	(26.4)
1975	21.9	2.5	37.2
1976	59.3	129.3	23.6
1977	31.9	46.8	(7.4)
1978	24.0	14.5	6.4
1979	35.7	102.5	18.2
1980	19.3	32.8	32.3
1981	31.4	31.8	(5.0)
1982	40.0	38.4	21.4
1983	32.3	69.0	22.4
1984	13.6	(2.7)	6.1
1985	48.2	93.7	31.6
1986	26.1	14.2	18.6
1987	19.5	4.6	5.1
1988	20.1	59.3	16.6
1989	44.4	84.6	31.7
1990	7.4	(23.1)	(3.1)
1991	39.6	35.6	30.5
1992	20.3	29.8	7.6
1993	14.3	38.9	10.1
1994	13.9	25.0	1.3
1995	43.1	57.4	37.6
1996	31.8	6.2	23.0
1997	34.1	34.9	33.4
1998	48.3	52.2	28.6
1999	0.5	(19.9)	21.0
2000	6.5	26.6	(9.1)

Year	Percentage Annual Change		
	In Book Value per Berkshire Share	In Market Value per Berkshire Share	In S&P 500 with Dividends Included
2001	(6.2)	6.5	(11.9)
2002	10.0	(3.8)	(22.1)
2003	21.0	15.8	28.7
2004	10.5	4.3	10.9
2005	6.4	0.8	4.9
2006	18.4	24.1	15.8
2007	11.0	28.7	5.5
2008	(9.6)	(31.8)	(37.0)
2009	19.8	2.7	26.5
2010	13.0	21.4	15.1
2011	4.6	(4.7)	2.1
2012	14.4	16.8	16.0
2013	18.2	32.7	32.4
2014	8.3	27.0	13.7
2015	6.4	(12.5)	1.4
Compound annual return 1965-2015	19.2%	20.8%	9.7%
Total return	798,981%	1,598,284%	11,355%

Source: Berkshire Hathaway Annual Report, 2015.

None of these motives are conclusive; we haven't resolved the problem and some readers will doubtless remain unconvinced. But there are reasons for considering investing through an active manager, so long as we trust them. If we come across somebody or a particular team whose track record is reassuring to us, then it may make sense to invest. If not, we can stick to passive strategies and we won't be putting our foot in it.

But it is worth emphasising that the search cannot be superficial. It is vital to have an in-depth understanding of the manager or team: their approach to business, investment, and, of course, their outlook on life. I find it a real struggle to recommend other managers, as I don't have the time to carry out a rigorous appraisal, but when I do so it is after getting to know them in as much detail as possible. If we are able to meet the asset manager in person, so much the better.

And having a good track record is not enough; it's crucial to know how it was constructed. All of us are subject to the whims of luck, and it's important to determine the role played by underlying logic in the results.

It's no easy task, but there are good active managers out there in the financial markets. At times the market becomes entranced by undeniable irrationality, and investors who are able to make the most of it will obtain very positive results.

Direct Investment in Shares

The last option is investing directly in stocks, analysing and buying the most attractive options. And why not? I know some superb private investors who have a long-term approach, enjoying the total freedom from only being accountable to themselves. Nowadays we have the tools to be able to perform our own analysis and execute our investments in stocks. The only thing that's needed is time and desire.

The best way for these potential investors to obtain good results is by focusing on stocks identified from the previously mentioned strategies; doing so consistently, without wavering. It's difficult, but not impossible. One starting point is to search for and analyse the stocks selected by investors with a respectable track record, who have spent a lot of time thinking about them. Part of the work in selecting stocks has already been done for us. From then on it's a question of developing one's own criteria and sticking to them consistently.

The next chapters are aimed at such audacious investors, but they may also be useful to anyone seeking an active management fund. We will get into the detail of how to overcome the problem. It can be done!

A final word before we go wild and start buying. Taxes are the main problem with direct investing. The tax burden on individual investors from buying shares directly is greater than when investing in a fund. This is at least the case in Europe, where investors in regulated funds generally pay next to no taxes – for capital gains or dividends associated with shares – so long as they maintain their savings in these funds. This helps to significantly delay any possible tax bill. Furthermore, in Spain, transfers between funds are tax-exempt, meaning that if we keep our savings within the funds loop we may end up never paying those taxes.

That is why I personally refrain from investing directly in equities. Obviously it's a big help managing my own mutual funds, since I can invest my savings in the funds we manage.

CONCLUSION

There are a lot of different ways to gain exposure to equities, which are the best asset to invest in. It's no easy task choosing between them, and the best option may well be a combination of them all: indexes, whether passive or fundamental, some active managers who appeal to us, and a few personal stock picks to keep us 'on our toes'.

There is no magic formula for determining the exact proportion. For me there's no option but to invest 100% of my savings directly in equities – investing in my funds is equivalent to buying direct. However, I would recommend readers to start their analysis with index funds, gradually building up confidence to move towards more active alternatives as they get a better grip on the markets.

The right proportion for each reader will depend on their individual circumstances and, especially, the time they are willing to dedicate to the decision. The more effort we put in, the further we move away from passivity – almost by definition. But regardless of the ultimate mix, we can be sure that choosing to invest in equities will put us on the right path to maintain the purchasing power of our savings.

However, it's worth reiterating that there's no room to be frivolous by buying stocks without giving sufficient thought to it. This is a recipe for losing money. If we want to invest, each decision demands the same amount of time as if we were buying a car, a house, or deciding on a doctor for a complicated illness. If we are not prepared to make the time commitment, it's better to seek a good professional who can recommend us passive, semi-passive, or active management, ensuring we also select the right advisor.

APPENDIX

There follows an example from *Barron's*, illustrating the extent to which choosing between 'passive' products can end up becoming an 'active' business: The Pros' Picks.

Our Experts Share How They are Investing in Today's Confounding Market

ETF/Ticker	Recent Price	Market Valuation (billions)	Comment
JOHN FORLINES' PICKS			
iShares International High-Yield Bund/HVXU	$48.27	$0.2	Owns primarily junk bonds issued by European companies, but also has some Canadian and UK-based bonds
iShares U.S. Preferred Stock ETF/PFF	$38.88	$15.2	Preferred shares are largely issued by financial companies; the ETF yields 5.6%
iShares MSCIEAFE Minimum Volatility/EFAV	$66.73	$6.7	An international stock index that weeds out the market's most volatile stocks

ETF/Ticker	Recent Price	Market Valuation (billions)	Comment
iShares MSCI USA Minimum Volatility/USMV	44.08	12.5	Same as above in strategy. This ETF has been one of the most popular this year in terms of attracting new money
iShares MSCI Canada/EWC	24.15	2.7	A single-country ETF comprised mainly of financial and energy companies; should rise if oil prices rally further
iShares MSCI Australia/EWA	19.51	1.6	Australia is a commodity producer that exports heavily to China; this ETF is a way to avoid the risks of owning Chinese stocks directly
DAVID CLEARY'S PICKS			
iShares Global Materials/MXI	$49.29	$0.2	Includes materials-sector companies around the globe, such as miners and chemical companies
iShares Latin America 40/ILF	25.37	0.7	Regional ETF that loads up on Brazil and Mexico; another diversified play on recovering commodity prices
PowerShares Fundamental High-Yield Corporate Bond Portfolio/PHB	18.15	0.8	An index-tracking fund that screens for debt issued by companies, based on cash flow and other measures, and excludes those with the lowest credit ratings
VanEck Vectors Fallen Angel High-Yield Bond/ANGL	26.77	0.2	Aims to squeeze yields from bonds issued by companies that have been recently downgraded
FRITZ FOLT'S PICKS			
iShares Gold Trust/IAU	$12.34	$8.0	Large ETF that tracks the price of gold bullion; has a lower expense ratio than the SPDR Gold Shares (GLD)
VanEck Vectors Gold Miners/GDX	24.18	6.9	A basket of well-known miners including Barrick Gold and Newmont Mining, which tend to rise and fall faster than gold prices

ETF/Ticker	Recent Price	Market Valuation (billions)	Comment
iShares MSCI Brazil Capped/EWZ	27.64	3.3	The largest Brazil-themed ETF on the market, it trades in high volumes
EGShares India Infrastructure/INXX	10.30	0.04	An index tracker focused on a small group of Indian industrial and materials companies
PowerShares QQQ/QQQ	105.02	34.3	One of the oldest ETFs, it tracks the Nasdaq-100, synonymous with growth and tech stocks
Vanguard Small-Cap Value/VBR	102.48	6.4	A low-cost index of small US stocks with relatively lower valuations
WILL MCGOUGH'S PICKS			
iShares Core MSCI Emerging Markets/IEMG	$40.12	$10.6	A low-cost emerging market index that includes small caps and counts South Korea as an 'emerging' country
SPDR MSCI Emerging Markets Quality Mix/QEMM	47.94	0.1	A low-cost, broad emerging-market ETF that blends stocks with profitability, low volatility, and value
iShares Core High Dividend/HDV	78.75	5.1	Dividend-themed, it aims to capture stocks with fundamentals that support better dividend and earnings potential than its peers
iShares Core MSCI EAFE/IEFA	53.20	11.1	Owns share of European, Australian, and Japanese stocks, but excludes US and Canadian stocks

Source: *Barron's*, 7 May 2016.

CHAPTER 7

Investing in Stocks (I): Foundations and Principles

We know that we have to invest in real assets and that shares are the best option. We also know that we can invest in shares through index funds, semi-passive or fundamental funds, and actively managed funds. And finally, there's also the option of investing directly in stocks.

It's a risky business trying to systematically outperform the indexes; history says as much. Yet some of us are either sufficiently arrogant, deluded, or audacious to take on the challenge. After all, we all think we are better drivers than the rest.

This part of the book is aimed at those daring enthusiasts or professionals prepared to take on the indexes at their own game. Flying in the face of history and current trends as they remorselessly shift towards passive management.

Investing in stocks is not easy. You have to buy what nobody else wants and sell what everyone else is trying to buy. It's a fight against our very nature. An endeavour that can be hugely rewarding in the long term, if things work out, but that will test our wits on a daily basis. But we are not powerless, as I will try to explain. Indeed, it is an art to which some of us have dedicated our professional life and where I may add most value.

FOUNDATIONS AND EXPERIENCE

Graham

Although they might not know it, nearly all value investors started out life investing like Benjamin Graham, Columbia University professor and 'creator' of value investing. Until Graham arrived on the scene, stock market investment amounted to little more than blundering around with speculative gambles. Thanks to Graham's teaching, based on an extensive analysis of the forces at work in the markets, it has now become a serious and demanding craft.

His biggest contribution came in the form of two now classic books: *Security Analysis* and *The Intelligent Investor*.[1] In the first book, he provided a detailed analysis of the tools needed for scrutinising a company and investing properly; in the second, he describes the investment process, developing concepts which have gone on to be crucial for many of us.

Perhaps the most important of them all is the idea of the margin of safety. It's a simple but crucial concept: we should maximise our safety by investing in shares whose intrinsic value is significantly above their market price. A 50% discount is preferable to 30%. This margin of safety affords us protection against inevitable valuation errors.

Specifically, his main recommendation for maximising the margin of safety is to buy shares in companies whose price is below the company's liquidation value, excluding fixed assets. In other words: the value of the company's current assets (stock, account receivables, and treasury), less all liabilities, should be above its market price.

It is a very demanding condition, which made sense 80 years ago. The stock market had been decimated by the Great Depression and many companies were cheap enough to fulfil this criterion. For Graham it was of little concern what the company did, it just needed to be cheap.

The legendary Warren Buffett started out investing by following in his maestro's footsteps, and most good investors started the same way. I guess when you are starting out you want to rapidly prove yourself and you trawl the markets for anything cheap, without pausing to think, convinced that this path will enable you to make money as quickly as possible.

However, experience ultimately teaches us that many of these cheap stocks are to be found in challenging sectors or subject to major competitiveness challenges, and in the long term can remain eternal duds. Time is not on our side with such stocks, since the returns on capital are low and the potential upside is slow to materialise and uncertain. The balance sheet isn't everything.

Philip Fisher/Joel Greenblatt

I have oversimplified Graham, who also took account of other factors, such as growth or stable results, although he didn't put as much emphasis on them. Either way, from this point on, most investors began to pay attention

---

[1]Graham (1988, 2009).

to other drivers, such as growth or business quality, assigning increasing weight to them over time.

Phil Fisher played a pivotal role in the transformation undergone by many investors. It was under the influence of his partner, Charlie Munger, that Buffett first became attracted to Fisher's philosophy. Fisher was another successful long-term investor, who wrote at least two superb books: *Common Stocks and Uncommon Profits* and *Conservative Investors Sleep Well*.[2] He put his money on investing in long-term growth stocks, with very robust competitive advantages that were capable of being sustained and increased over time. The price paid for them was not as important, since if the company performed well, it would be able to sustain a high multiple. This idea is less intuitive and therefore harder to digest than simply buying something cheap; it means paying seemingly expensive prices for something that will only yield results after a period of time.

This is ultimately the road that Buffett has gone down. Thus, most value investors are also indirectly indebted to Fisher to some degree or another. For us, the shift towards quality was a slow one, perhaps too slow, all the while trying to pay as little as possible for it.

Up until that point I had maintained a certain unshakeable bias towards investing in cheap assets, whose quality was not always proven. It was a mix that had produced good results and it was a challenge to change my ways.

Every investor develops at their own pace. The trigger to ultimately revolutionise my approach once and for all was Joel Gleenblatt, who convinced me that we had to make a decisive shift towards quality, without looking back.

I came across Greenblatt's short book, *The Little Book That Beats the Market*,[3] in a bookshop in New York in December 2008 by accident, without searching for it and almost reluctantly. I had heard of him in a book given to me by Mohnish Pabrai: *The Dhandoo Investor*.[4] Mohnish is an excellent investor, who we had got to know the year before at Ciccio Azzollini's always interesting and enjoyable investment conference, organised each July in Trani, southern Italy.

Mohnish is also something of a maverick; every year he gives his friends and acquaintances a book. Giving books as presents can be a double-edged sword, you are asking the recipient to devote some of their time to something that may or may not interest them. I generally don't like being given books, because I always have interesting books lined up to read and I have the

---

[2] Fisher (1996a,b).
[3] Greenblatt (2006).
[4] Pabrai (2007).

vice – for better or worse – of reading every book that is given to me, almost without fail. As I don't have endless time for reading, these books can end up becoming a poisoned chalice.

However, you gradually discover that books which are dropped into your lap have the major benefit of shaking you out of your comfort zone, which tends to be limited to what you already know and authors whose opinions you share. Mohnish's books open up new worlds, from Atul Gawande's recent book *Being Mortal*,[5] which gives an excellent insight into care for terminal illnesses, to Pavithra K. Mehta and Suchira Shenoy's *Infinite Vision*,[6] on Aravind, the Indian organisation specialised in low-cost treatment of eye diseases. The topics are diverse and take you into lives and situations that you didn't even know existed, let alone believed could interest you.

The end of 2008 was an apt moment to ring the changes. Although we were convinced that we had taken the right approach to preparing for the crisis, investing at reasonable prices, there was scope to keep improving. It is crucial to have one's own set of sound principles (preferably the right ones!), but they need to be flexible enough to adapt to potential refinements along the way. It's not an easy balance: robust but not stubborn; flexible but not indecisive; it's all perfectly possible in theory, but very hard to implement in practice.

Getting back to Greenblatt. What he does in his invaluable book is give empirical proof that quality shares bought at a good price will always outperform other stocks. To do so, he classifies each stock according to two criteria: quality, measured by ROCE (return on capital employed) and price, measured by the inverse P/E ratio (price to earnings, the price that we pay for each unit of earnings), the free cash flow yield.

He uses a numerical classification for both return and price: 1, 2, 3, 4,…, with 1 being the stock with the highest ROCE under the return criteria and 1 the highest free cash flow under the price criteria. He then adds the points obtained by each share in both rankings to produce a definitive classification, which he calls the 'magic formula'. It's simple but effective: the companies with the lowest sum of both factors deliver the best long-term returns. Furthermore, the same is true throughout the ranking; companies situated in the lowest 10% post a better return than the second 10%, the second decile outperforms the third, and so on until the last 10%.

Mark Spitznagel reaches similar conclusions by analysing companies with a high ROCE and low price. In contrast to Greenblatt, he proxies low price through the relationship between stock market capitalisation and

---

[5] Gawande (2014).
[6] Mehta and Shenoy (2011).

capital employed net of cash or debt. As can be seen in the chart on the following page, the stocks with the best combination of both – which he refers to as Sigfrieds – obtain exceptional long-term results.

This is because these companies are facing short-run P&L problems, which are resolved over the medium term. His approach delivers better results than Greenblatt, which he attributes to Greenblatt's use of price/free cash flow, which means that the formula is excessively growth sensitive.

Magic Formula Results

	Magic Formula (%)	Market Average (%)	S&P 500 (%)
1988	27.1	24.8	16.6
1989	44.6	18.0	31.7
1990	1.7	(16.1)	(3.1)
1991	70.6	45.6	30.5
1992	32.4	11.4	7.6
1993	17.2	15.9	10.1
1994	22.0	(4.5)	1.3
1995	34.0	29.1	37.6
1996	17.3	14.9	23.0
1997	40.4	16.8	33.4
1998	25.5	(2.0)	28.6
1999	53.0	36.1	21.0
2000	7.9	(16.8)	(9.1)
2001	69.6	11.5	(11.9)
2002	(4.0)	(24.2)	(22.1)
2003	79.9	68.8	28.7
2004	19.3	17.8	10.9
	30.8	**12.3**	**12.4**

Note: The return on the 'market average' is an index with weights that are identical to an investment universe of 3,500 stocks. Each share in the index contributes an identical amount to the return. The S&P 500 is an index with market weights of the 500 largest stocks. The largest stocks (those with the largest stock market capitalisation) are assigned a higher weight than smaller stocks.
Source: Greenblatt (2006).

Spitznagel is the only investor I know who applies strictly 'Austrian' criteria to investment.

The exceptional results obtained by both Greenblatt and Spitznagel are surprising, but logical: good companies bought at reasonable prices should obtain better returns on the markets. As ever, the problem with applying these approaches is that the formulas deliver over the long term, but they can also underperform for relatively long periods, for example three years. This makes it tough for both professional and enthusiast investors to keep faith when things aren't working.

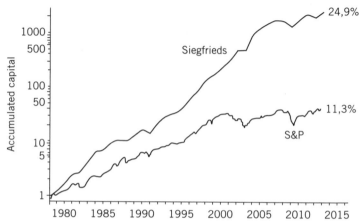

Siegfrieds vs. 'Average Johanns' of the S&P
Source: Spitznagel (2013).

However, Greenblatt's simple experiment persuaded me, and it inspired me to make the definitive leap to quality. We had already been tentatively moving in that direction, but without the necessary conviction and consistency. We needed to go all in.

Those readers who don't want to continue can stop here and apply the formulas, either through a fund which uses them or by themselves. Various funds take this approach and it's essentially another very appealing form of semi-passive management.

The more adventurous can keep reading.

WARREN BUFFETT

Warren Buffett deserves a mention apart. He is the best investor ever. Period. His track record and personal modesty have won the hearts and minds of countless followers. I am personally hugely indebted to him. As a young person starting out investing, having somebody to look up to is as important as having intellectual ability or capacity for hard work.

Finding out about him and his approach from the outset made life a lot easier for me. He helped me discover and crystallise vital concepts and he has been a pillar of support during bouts of 'investor solitude'.

A lot of Buffett's wisdom can be found in the Berkshire Hathaway Annual Reports. They are a good way to become better acquainted with him. The best thing is to go to the horse's mouth, though various authors have also put together useful collections of his thinking.[7]

Buffett has achieved a 20.8% annual return over the course of more than 50 years as an investor. This compares with the 9.7% obtained by the benchmark S&P 500 index.[8] These results are exceptional, but equally important – as ever – is what lies behind these astonishing numbers. He has a real treasure trove of personal and corporate wisdom which warrants greater attention.

When investors or friends ask me about anything to do with investment, I try to respond to the best of my abilities, but I almost always end up having to acknowledge that 'Buffett's already said it'. He has voiced an opinion on nearly everything and is almost always on the mark. As Jack Walsh, former CEO of General Electric, remarked: 'He is the smartest guy in any room'. We are all aware of how useful his wisdom on investment can be; however, it's a surprise to me that his ideas on business management are not better known, since taking them on board is the best MBA around.

It's worth remembering that he has invested in hundreds of companies, participated in numerous management boards, and dealt with countless company chairmen, senior executives, politicians, etc. All of this means he has reached conclusions which are well worth reviewing.

Buffett's investment approach is already well known, but it's worth recapping. He invests in a stock as if he were buying the whole business. The company must be an attractive economic proposition to meet his investment criteria. It's of secondary consequence to him whether it trades on a public market; if the market were closed for the next 10 years, he would still go ahead with the decision to buy. His ideal holding period is for ever (he has always been endowed with patient

(continued)

---

[7]The most comprehensive are by Lawrence A. Cunningham and Carol J. Loomis, which have been useful in putting together this brief summary of his ideas.
[8]Berkshire Hathaway Annual Report, 2015.

capital, but the crucial thing is that he doesn't consider himself to be an economic or stock market analyst, or even a stock picker; he is a business analyst). One of his favourite notions is that investors should be able to invest solely in 10 company stocks over their lifetime; doing so would mean their decisions would be much more deliberate if this were to be the case, settling only for the best.

Buffett also resuscitates Ben Graham's imagined character: Mr Market, our partner in different businesses, who comes knocking on our door every day, offering to buy or sell a stake in one of his businesses. We have to accept the propositions that interest us and graciously turn down the rest. There is no obligation to accept anything, since Mr Market isn't always rational and sometimes he comes to us with absurd propositions. He is emotionally unstable and whimsical, inclined to bouts of euphoria and anxiety. His offers can be surprising, even when business conditions have barely changed and it's vital not to get swept up in his mood swings. You should exploit Mr Market, not let him lead you.

Ironically, and quite rightly, Buffett doesn't find any meaning to the expression *value investing*. As if there could be any other way to invest? How can you not invest without looking for value in an investment? Nor does he distinguish between growth and value stocks. It is all about buying a flow of earnings at an acceptable price; the pace of earnings growth is a second-order issue.

Like nearly all serious investors, he prefers buying on secondary markets over taking part in an IPO (initial public offering). IPOs happen at the time and price of the seller's choosing, normally to their advantage. Information is more symmetric in the normal, secondary market.

He invests in stable businesses, such as Coca-Cola and Gillette (now Procter & Gamble), avoiding companies where there are risks of major disruption to market conditions, such as tech firms.

In studying the investments we have made in both subsidiary companies and common stocks, you will see that we favor businesses and industries unlikely to experience major change. The reason for that is simple: making either type of purchase, we are searching for operations that we believe are virtually certain to possess enormous competitive strength 10 or 20 years from now. A fast-changing industry environment may offer the chance for huge wins, but it precludes the certainty we seek.

I should emphasize that, as citizens, Charlie and I welcome change: fresh ideas, new products, innovative processes and the like cause our country's standard of living to rise, and that's clearly good. As investors, however, our reaction to a fermenting industry is much like our attitude toward space exploration: we applaud the endeavor but prefer to skip the ride.[9]

The risk of change forms part of his famous circle of competence: every investor must know the size of their circle and stay within it. It isn't easy, given our natural tendency to bite off more than we can chew. At the beginning we have to try to gradually and very prudently expand our circle until we reach a point where it is established and thereafter fully respect it.

He seldom invests in the banking sector. The sector's inherent indebtedness (with little capital, banks can balloon to have balance sheets 15–20 times larger) dangerously magnifies any error. I am also extremely cautious about the financial sector, which also includes insurance companies. I only invest in Spanish institutions where my knowledge of their management and internal operations affords me some peace of mind.

Naturally, he doesn't believe in the theory that the market is always efficient. In general it is efficient, but not always, and this small difference is crucial, enabling us to capitalise on it. Furthermore, risk is not about Beta nor market share price volatility. We could go so far as to say that volatility is in fact the ally of the long-term investor.

Buffett defines risk as the possible loss of long-term purchasing power and to avoid this happening he advocates analysing:

1. The business's long-term characteristics.
2. Managers' ability to optimise the business and to effectively reinvest earned profit as well as remunerate shareholders.
3. The purchase price.
4. Inflation and tax levels.

(continued)

---

[9]Berkshire Hathaway Annual Report, 1996.

These four factors are what determine risk, not share price volatility.

He has often illustrated this by citing his own experience with the initial purchase of Berkshire. It was the worst investment he ever made, because it was a business lacking a competitive advantage and destined to shut down.

Over time, he shifted from buying cheap businesses towards focusing on quality businesses; in other words, companies with high returns on capital employed, a criterion which he has stood by over the last few decades.

He has also frequently acknowledged that good managers will inevitably run into bad businesses. Noting, ironically, that the bad business will keep its reputation while the good investor will lose theirs.

He has written and spoken extensively on corporate governance, and is a firm critic – for example – of bad practices in setting incentives for executives. The remunerations committees of management boards base their decisions on recommendations from self-interested advisors, who provide their advice based on how other companies pay. This leads to a wage spiral which reaches obscene levels, completely out of touch with the executives' actual performance. Breaking this dynamic is not easy, because the very same executives appoint the directors. One of the biggest errors is failing to take account of capital employed or retained earnings in objective-based variable remuneration. As one of several possible solutions, he advocates always taking account of the cost of capital when setting incentives.

In general, it is difficult for the management board to take independent decisions, since at the end of the day the Chairman proposes the directors, and they know it. Cronyism in the boardroom does not make for an environment conducive to taking decisions, which may not be to the Chairman's liking. Suffice to say that in Spain, I can't think of a single successful case of activism and we can be sure there has been a fair amount of bad management. Buffett believes that directors should own a significant number of shares in the company but earn very little for being directors, meaning that they can't live off the position itself.

As an investor, I have always placed more confidence on companies which have reference or majority shareholders, whose assets are on the line. That said, there should be appropriate separation between shareholders and management, since family members are not always best suited to managing. In

Europe, and particularly in Spain, I have very little faith in ownerless companies, as the interests of executives are seldom ever aligned with the shareholders.

It is especially remarkable how little importance Buffett assigns to growth plans. It is far more important to him that the company sets out the right strategy, since growth will follow in due course. Many short-term growth targets get in the way of taking the right long-term decisions. As such, he is well known for his willingness to ride out patchy results, considering this to be part and parcel of business.

He also has a very clear stance on mergers and acquisitions: it is important to avoid the urge to grow for growth's sake; the focus should be on acquisitions that make sense and not overpaying. It is important to avoid watering down a quality business with inferior acquisitions. How many times have we seen companies offload a division or subsidiary, only to go on to feel the need to buy something else to retain their size. One of the most dramatic examples of this I have seen was Portugal Telecom, which – after selling its Brazilian subsidiary, Vivo, at a great price – decided against returning the money to the shareholders, instead going on to buy an inferior Brazilian company, which nearly brought down the whole PT operation.

(continued)

Buffett also makes a distinction on another important aspect of corporate governance – company donations. The main problem here is that executives' and shareholders' interests are not aligned. And it is the executives who decide, according to their interests and the social pressures on them. In my funds I make sure to clearly define that the main goal of the fund is obtaining the best return possible while meeting the letter of the law. I find it uncomfortable imposing my conscience on clients; which is why it is preferable that the returns achieved by the funds enable each of us to act in accordance with our own conscience.

When discussing both investment and company management, Buffett frequently cites the institutional imperative trap which he and others have fallen through. This refers to the natural tendency for investors and managers to act like sheep, copying what our competitors or peers are doing. It's a core part of human nature and as a species, it has served us well. But for investors and managers it yields mediocre results.

Another incredible sign of Buffett's lucidity is the type of shareholder he has courted for Berkshire Hathaway. He doesn't want his shares to be liquid. He doesn't want shareholders to buy and sell his stock. He wants long-term partners who will maintain their positions indefinitely.

> *Our goal is to attract long-term owners who, at the time of purchase, have no timetable or price target for sale but plan instead to stay with us indefinitely. We don't understand the CEO who wants lots of stock activity, for that can be achieved only if many of his owners are constantly exiting. At what other organization – school, club, church, etc. – do leaders cheer when members leave? (However, if there were a broker whose livelihood depended upon the membership turnover in such organizations, you could be sure that there would be at least one proponent of activity, as in: 'There hasn't been much going on in Christianity for a while; maybe we should switch to Buddhism next week'.)*[10]

---

[10]Berkshire Hathaway Annual Report, 1988.

Even when wrapped up in his trademark good humour, he consistently talks up the virtues of having a stable shareholder base. I have always lusted after the same thing: investors who are on the same page as me and who plan to remain by my side. I don't want short-term speculators. Don't get me wrong. Speculators are not bad per se – far from it, they have a crucial role in providing liquidity in the markets – but I would rather keep other company. Short-term redemption fees are intended to send a clear message: think carefully about where you are investing to avoid rapidly repenting.

That said, and while it is obvious that long-term investing should be done with money that's not needed in the short term, unexpected needs can always crop up, requiring us to dip into our savings. Not everything is foreseeable.

Buffett has very clear ideas on share repurchases and subsequent cancellations. Buybacks clearly make sense when there are no better alternative investment options and the share is trading below the intrinsic or target business value. The problem is that executives would rather increase company size via misplaced acquisitions, leading to *diworsification*, diversifying to deteriorate, as Peter Lynch has wittily anointed it. Buffett believes that it only makes sense to use own shares to buy companies when you get more in return, which doesn't usually happen.

My modest activism in the past has always been limited to politely requesting that the investment process should have in mind when repurchasing shares. I invest in stocks because I think they are trading at discount on their intrinsic value. If that wasn't the case – by definition – I wouldn't have invested in them. So it makes sense to buyback and cancel.

It is also worth highlighting some of Buffett's key thoughts on valuation. He defines business quality by the return on capital employed, calculated before goodwill. This is something that I have fully adopted, with the corresponding implication that better returns are synonymous with a better-quality business.

This is how I approach measuring the intrinsic quality of the business, I then analyse the quantity and quality of goodwill in order to assess the management's capacity to make reasonable purchases; in other words, to allocate profit to different uses. It's worth remembering that when one company buys another at above book value, it generates

(*continued*)

goodwill which later has to be amortised. This is not necessarily a bad thing, but once again you have to watch out for managers willing to overpay simply to gain mass.

Any chinks in his armour?

It's virtually impossible to disagree with Buffett on his general investment ideas. For the time being I don't have any discrepancies with him, although lately he has had to pay more dearly for companies – given the size that Berkshire has reached. I always have more rotation in my portfolios, but this is because Europe-domiciled funds pay minimal tax for selling stock, giving us more opportunity to capitalise on market volatility.

That said, I do think Warren steps outside his circle of competence by placing his trust in politicians. Despite the education received from his father and his own comments on the damaging effects of inflation, he seems to think that politicians – with their sometimes perverted incentives – are capable of handling difficult tasks like managing the economy. He recognises his own inability to predict economic cycles, but seems to believe that other people are better equipped for dealing with them. Especially people whose time horizon is not consistent with such management. I think there's a fundamental contradiction in this viewpoint.

So it's on economic theory where I glimpse a minor shortcoming in his world view. It's arguably not essential for investing well, but as discussed in Chapter 4, having a sound economic framework can be an extremely useful orientation in our work as investors. For example, I don't consider Keynes to be a great economist, as Warren does – although in the second half of his life, after losing quite a lot of money in the Great Depression, he did become a sensible investor. His concept of a lack of aggregate demand is particularly prejudicial, and is as outdated as it is incorrect, since his theory assumes that factor prices (salaries) have no downward flexibility. (Try telling that to people who have seen wage cuts of 10–30% in recent years.)[11] I'll say no more, since as Hayek explained,[12] at the end of his days Keynes lost faith in his own theory, but it was too late by then; interventionists of all stripes had already adopted him as their intellectual poster child.

---

[11]For a spot-on critique in Spanish, see Rallo (2011).
[12]Hayek (1994).

Warren also believes that the authorities did the right thing in 2008 by intervening in the markets after the collapse of Lehman Brothers. However, we already know the difficulties that arise in attempting to apply physical science methods to social science: we aren't able to analyse human behaviour by using statistical tools. Such situations are unique and unrepeatable and, in this particular case, we can't know what would have happened without intervention. I suspect that we might have been better off, but we will never know. I guess he doesn't either.

Buffett Alpha and Omega

In sum, it's not just Buffett's ideas on investment which are exceptionally valuable. His personal approach to managing his holdings in a vast number of companies, with a clear delegation of responsibilities, is an example to all empire builders with feet of clay, unable to sustain themselves over the long term. I am convinced this won't happen to him.

SETTLING ON QUALITY

With Greenblatt as a catalyst, the pieces began to fall into place and from then on we stuck to quality companies. There is no scientific way of finding the perfect combination of price and quality. Should we pay dearly for high quality? And anything for moderate quality? Obviously, paying little for quality would be ideal, but practically impossible. Uncovering real gems at an attractive price.

I think over time we ended up finding the right balance at Bestinver. Through applying Greenblatt's criteria, by September 2014, our portfolio had an average ROCE (the companies forming the portfolio) of over 40%, with a free cash flow yield of over 10%. A good set of businesses at an attractive price.

In order to reach this point we progressively sold off stocks that didn't meet the new philosophy and bought only those meeting the quality requirements. It was slow work, requiring us to sell off cheap companies and fight against out attachment to them, but we were convinced that it was the right way to go and we went all in.

However, searching for quality is not about blindly following formulas. While these are a good starting point, they remove the essential human element which is of such importance to those of us who work in this field.

It is not enough to find a high ROCE and low P/E ratio. I have to understand where the profits are coming from and, above all, where they are headed. This is the essence of my work and what I spend most of my time doing. The possible purchase price can be readily found in the daily newspaper or in real time on Bloomberg, but analysing a specific sector and the company's competitive position is what enables us to determine the intrinsic value, which is neither as obvious nor as easy to identify. In fact, it's the great enigma of investment. However, there is a way to begin deciphering it.

COMPETITIVE ADVANTAGES

Few companies can sustain exceptional profits over the long run. The market works, and it goes after such businesses from all angles, usually getting what it wants. The key point is to distinguish between businesses able to withstand the passage of time – even if it's only 25 years – from those which are enjoying a more typical short-term profitability spike.

There are a lot of ways to perform this type of competitive analysis, which MBAs go into in some depth. Some of the clearest and most interesting explanations come from Bruce Greenwald, professor at Columbia University and Pat Dorsey, from Morningstar, who also focuses his analysis from a similar perspective.

Greenwald develops Michael Porter's classic work, which looked at the intensity of competition according to various factors: rivalry among competitors, the existence of substitutes and barriers to entry, and the negotiating power of suppliers and customers. Porter was the first to explain the interaction between companies and the outside world, but Greenwald simplifies the analysis, singling out barriers to entry as being the critical factor. 'One of them [factors] is clearly much more important than the others. It is so dominant that leaders seeking to develop and pursue winning strategies should begin by ignoring the others and focus only on it. That factor is barriers to entry – the force that underlies Porter's "Potential Entrants"'.[13]

A high ROCE and stable market share are both a consequence and a necessary signal of barriers to entry. A low ROCE of around 6–8% is consistent with barrier-free markets, where any competitor can enter and obtain a position, with repeated fluctuations in the market shares of the different actors.

---

[13] Greenwald and Kahn (2005).

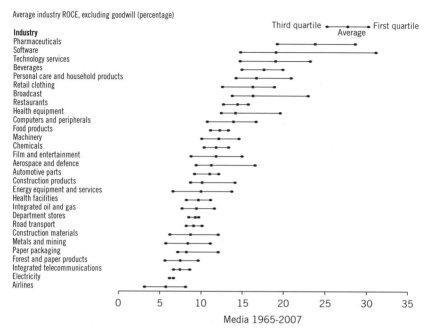

Average industry ROCE, excluding goodwill (percentage)

Industry characteristics determine the sustainability (duration) of the return
Source: Compustat. McKinsey Corporate Performance Centre analysis.

Once a company has been identified as having high profitability in a stable market, the next step is to identify the underlying reasons why there are barriers to entry allowing an exceptional profit to be earned. It's almost impossible for high profits to be maintained over the very long term, but barriers to entry can keep the wolves at bay for a period of time.

If we know and clearly understand these barriers to entry, then we will be able to predict when they might disappear and put in jeopardy the company's advantage and profits. This helps us keep errors to a minimum and enables us to take a stake in this exceptional profit.

Barriers to entry can appear in different forms.

(1) *Through having a cost advantage.* This can arise in various ways. The first is due to the characteristics of production. For example, a mine with access to raw materials: Saudi Arabia and its oil; or the final consumer: quarries or cement plans are small natural monopolies.

The second way cost advantages can arise is from process advantages, both patentable and otherwise. Some companies continually improve their processes, enabling them to maintain an advantage over time. But these are weaker forms of barrier.

Thirdly, the biggest players will be able to enjoy cost advantages over long periods whenever size or scale is essential to watering down fixed costs. These costs can come from manufacturing, advertising, or distribution (an extensive distribution network is very hard to replicate). But it's important to realise that size in itself is not as important as size relative to other competitors; and it's the distance to them, together with the presence of high fixed costs, which constitutes this advantage.

(2) *Through the existence of switching costs.* Companies can get away with charging above-market prices when the client finds it onerous or uncomfortable to change and buy the product or service from a competitor. This might be because they have grown accustomed to it and don't want to change. This is typical of some consumer products, such as Coca-Cola or tobacco.

It might also arise because it involves a cost which doesn't compensate the effort expended, be it in time or possible new risks. This also typically applies to certain products which are essential, but only have a relatively low value in terms of the final product, such as the lubricants manufactured by specialists like Fuchs Petrolub. The cost of shutting down a machine due to a lubrication defect is enormous, especially in relation to the cost of the lubricant. Another example is software which is highly embedded into a company's operations. This is an advantage enjoyed by one of our old favourites, Wolters Kluwer.

Switching costs can also be enhanced by difficulties in finding alternatives. While the Internet has made life a lot easier, it's not always straightforward to make comparisons between products due to differing specifications or a lack of transparency.

(3) *Intangible assets*, through the existence of true brand distinction, enabling a mark-up to be charged on the competition. This happens when you compare Apple with Sony: the latter is well known but lacks the same pull factor, or Coca-Cola compared with other cola brands or tap water.

Patents are also a form of intangible asset (such as pharmaceuticals) or licences (for telephony), which temporarily authorise legal monopolies. Patents suffer the risk of being contested, while licences can be revoked by the granting authority.

(4) *Through 'network effects'.* The more people use a product, the more valuable it is to the client. This makes it harder for new competitors to emerge, who will need to build up this network. An example is Facebook or credit card payment companies, such as Visa, etc.

Companies in such sectors can obtain exceptional profits, with the added benefit of not necessarily requiring excellent management. Nearly anyone can manage such companies in the short run, while in the long run the goal is to continue building on these advantages.

By contrast, for a company which finds itself in a more challenging sector, facing fierce competition, management competence can be the deciding factor. In these cases, a good manager can make all the difference, putting in train ongoing improvement processes which keep the company ahead of its competitors.

Greenwald[14] provides a very good summary of the analysis that needs to be carried out, which he divides into three stages:

1. Developing an industry map.
2. Determining whether the market is protected by barriers to entry.
3. Identifying the sources of these barriers.

Using this approach we can build a full picture of the competitive advantages enjoyed by the company we are analysing.

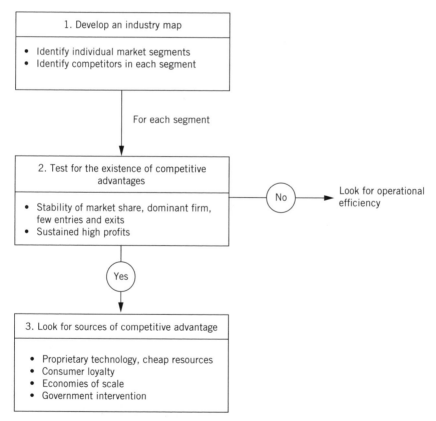

Analysing competitive advantages in three steps

---

[14]Greenwald and Kahn (2005).

What about when there are no advantages or barriers to entry?

Sometimes we may be deceived into thinking that there are barriers, which do not stand up to deeper scrutiny. This can lead to significant errors, meaning it's important to be very cautious:

- A differentiation in itself does not automatically lead to exceptional profits. It is important that it also includes some of the previously mentioned factors; being different from the rest is not enough.
- Sector or company growth is not synonymous with high profitability, but rather a potential sign of problems to come. Growth will attract capital, capping profitability at moderate levels. We know that the market works and, if there are no legal restrictions on competition, that it will manifest itself in one way or another, despite companies' best attempts to aggressively defend their patch.

Another second negative implication of growth is that it can reduce the relative importance of fixed costs, lowering this barrier to entry and stimulating competition.

- It's not enough to have a good new product. It should be the start of something sustainable over time. Hot iPad apps or high-grossing films are examples of 'perishable' products. The advantage will last longer if a franchise can be created around the product, which reduces the risk of the second or third part being a flop, such as Superman 2, 3, … Otherwise, the lack of continuity will mean that it is little more than a flash in the pan.
- Nor is advanced technology the be-all and end-all, since unless it creates unbreachable barriers, it will tend to favour users, but not shareholders. It is worth emphasising that both good products and good technology will be immediately copied by the competition. If a new type of restaurant proves successful, it will be surrounded by imitators within the space of a few months.
- Size in itself is no guarantee of profitability, and can even be counterproductive. Context and, particularly, relative size are crucial to determining its relevance.

Finally, executives' management ability is not a competitive advantage per se, although it's clearly preferable for the management to support the company's development, rather than getting in its way, as can sometimes happen. This is the 'halo effect' explained by Phil Rosenzweig: it's easy to identify good managers based on past results, but the difficult job is predicting which of these managers will continue being successful in the future (the same is also true for mutual fund managers).

THE POSSIBILITY OF REINVESTING

If some of these companies in attractive sectors also offer a certain amount of growth, facilitating reinvestment of capital, then we are looking at a gem, with the added benefit of being coherent with our long-term investment philosophy.

If a company can reinvest with a 20% return on investment over the next 20 years and we are able to buy the stock at a reasonable price, then the return on our investment will be close to this annual 20% over 20 years.

However, bear in mind that the potential for companies with high returns on capital to reinvest a lot of capital are limited, since they tend not to be very capital intensive.

Furthermore, the market will probably be correctly pricing such gems which are capable of obtaining high returns over time, meaning we must wait for the right moment to acquire them at a reasonable price, because they are rarely going to come cheap. We will go into this in the next chapter.

CHAPTER 8

Investing in Stocks (II): Opportunities, Valuation, Management

FINDING THE RIGHT OPPORTUNITY

Finding outstanding companies at a reasonable price is no easy job, but with time and patience the gems will gradually begin to surface.

Typically, we are looking for temporary problems which lower their share price to accessible levels. For example, an unfavourable currency movement which temporarily disrupts exports (for example, BMW or Thales were affected by a strong euro). Or digital migration, which can camouflage underlying business growth (Wolters Kluwer). This is a helpful starting point, but there will always be an element of doubt as to whether the fall is justified or not. And this can only be resolved after a major effort to get to the bottom of any issues raised in the analysis.

Our job is to sniff out these companies while minimising the risk of error, meaning it's important to find ways to reach them without calling into question their quality or sustainability. There are various ways of going about this, but initially we should look to work on familiar terrain, within our circle of competence. We may be in a position where we have developed better knowledge than the average investor; for example, if we have a passion for, say, technology or professional experience, such as working as an energy-saving engineer. We should try to capitalise as much as possible on any such advantages. Perhaps we are familiar with a company with a strong position in a new niche, or which enjoys impenetrable barriers to entry. Something which few people know about.

We shouldn't be alarmed by our supposed lack of experience, having such knowledge will help reduce the chances of failure. Just as an entrepreneur can improve their odds of success by starting out in a familiar field or sector, so can an investor. By contrast, an entrepreneur who creates a company without prior experience is much less likely to be successful, and the same applies to the uninformed investor. Creating a company, taking part in a private project, or investing in listed shares ultimately boil down to the same thing, and knowing the market is the key factor in determining whether the endeavour will be a success or not.

Thus, our first port of call should always be to work in familiar terrain, using implements that are known to us. However, if few ideas spring to mind or we really aren't experts in any area, then we should be on the lookout for other circumstances. The following are some examples of situations, generally relating more to technical market conditions than companies themselves. They are a good starting point and have given me much success in the past, though there's no guarantee that will be the case in the future.

Without dismissing other routes, the following conditions have helped me to find value in listed companies.

(1) *Shareholding structure.* By this I mean family companies or companies which have a single reference shareholder controlling the management. In Europe, they represent 25% of all listed companies. According to a 2015 Credit Suisse Research Institute Report,[1] returns on family companies outperformed the market by 4.5% from 2006 to April 2015. Not a long time period, but it nonetheless confirms my own direct experience.

Family companies generating above-market results (adjusted by sector, as a percentage)
Source: Credit Suisse (2005).

These companies tend to have relatively underdeveloped public or investor relations departments, and generally pay less attention to the

---

[1]Credit Suisse (2015).

market, which penalises them for it. They are still listed companies, enjoying the liquidity and increased transparency this entails, but they remain somewhat aloof from the market.

In contrast to companies where the managers don't have a share in the capital, family companies' interests are generally aligned with other shareholders, enabling them to exert appropriate control over external executives. I worked in one for over 25 years and I can attest to the fact that I had to sweat for every euro of my wage packet. It also means they tend to reduce errors in allocating capital, since they have more of a long-term outlook.

That said, it is best to steer clear of companies where unqualified family members meddle in the management. This tends to weaken the company and generates conflicts of interest. In fact, historic returns decline as management passes from one generation to the next, from founder to second and third generation.[2]

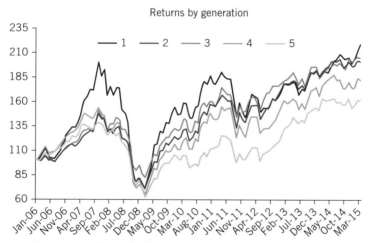

Returns by generation

Return on shares according to holding generation
Source: Credit Suisse (2005).

Another advantage of family companies is that they tend to approach accounting in a way that accurately reflects the company's underlying situation. They generally prefer conservative balance sheets, with little debt and a lot of cash. The market doesn't like this very much, but it's ideal for our purposes. Modern finance theory advocates 'optimising' the balance sheet, taking on the maximum amount of debt possible. We should prefer a less optimal approach. The primary objective of any company or venture

---

[2]Credit Suisse (2015, p. 10).

is survival; after that we can talk about profits. Stable financial foundations are essential for this.

In Europe, family support is even more important still, since it's much harder to get rid of incompetent management than in the United States. As already mentioned, I can't recall a single case of activism in Spain where dissenting shareholders have successfully forced through a change.

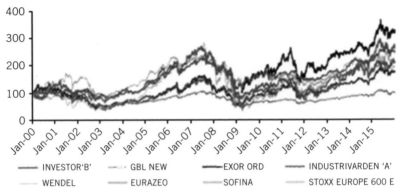

Price of stock in financial holding companies and EuroStoxx 600 since 2000
Source: Bosset (2015).

Even though some family companies have ended up in insolvency – Pescanova, Abengoa, Parmalat and the like – and despite the potential for bickering or mysterious transactions with other family companies (problems that crop up from time to time), I need good reasons to invest in a company when there is no family or manager with a significant holding. The alignment of incentives is crucial.

(2) *Organisation of assets.* Holding companies or conglomerates invest in unrelated businesses, which can sometimes lack coherence, and can deter investors. Very few of them trade at their intrinsic value, not even Berkshire Hathaway – the clearest example of a conglomerate. Accordingly, they don't reflect the sum of their investments.

As can be seen in the table above,[3] such companies perform well in the stock market, and sooner or later end up trading at the value of their investments or even above. It might be necessary to hold on for quite a while until the trading discount is eliminated, and sometimes they only trade at their intrinsic value for a short while, but these are opportunities to capitalise on.

Conglomerates are generally pro-cyclical,[4] performing better in bull markets and vice-versa. Some conglomerates have outstanding businesses

---

[3] Bosset (2015).
[4] Bosset (2015, p. 12).

buried among the fodder, and investing in the parent is usually a good way to access them at an enticing discount.

(3) *Geography.* Attractive distortions can also arise when a business is located in a different country from its headquarters or the market where it trades. Companies which are listed in Europe, but have an important part of their business in the United States – like Ahold or Wolters Kluwer – are an example of this. Such companies appear to lack a clear shareholder base or obvious natural owner. Ahold doesn't appear in Wall Street reports on American supermarkets, while the European reports fail to adequately price its American activity, which accounts for 50% of earnings. This leads to significant discounts relative to Kroger and other North American supermarket chains.

(4) *Small companies.* It stands to reason that the investment community pays less attention to small companies, providing us with the opportunity to uncover some great little gems. The main problem is a lack of liquidity, which can also apply to family companies, conglomerates, preference shares, etc. I already mentioned in Chapter 3 that illiquidity is a false problem and one of the easiest inefficiencies for patient investors to prey on. This can sometimes entail spending various years – or continually – patiently buying a stock to build up a position without affecting its price, or likewise various years unwinding it. Either way, small companies have historically delivered very positive results.[5]

In Spain, such companies have always been a key element of my portfolios: CAF, Elecnor, etc. A very long and varied list, which goes beyond Spain. These days it's less the case, since I have become accustomed to studying larger companies, but that's not an argument for disregarding them, especially in smaller portfolios.

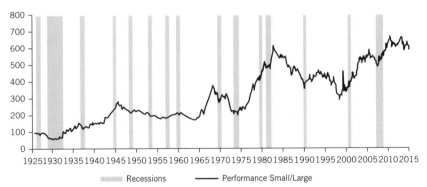

Performance of small caps vs. large caps
Source: Laidler *et al.* (2016).

---

[5]Laidler *et al.* (2016).

(5) *Cyclical companies.* This is probably the easiest and least risky way to find opportunities. Economic cycles need to be tolerated with enormous patience, but it's a reassurance to know that a falling share price is solely a cyclical effect and not due to some unknown competitiveness factor. Cycles always turn around. This means opportunities here are simple to analyse, as we already know what's driving the movements.

The biggest error we can make with the cycle is trying to predict the exact point of inflection, which is a total waste of our time. Instead, we should focus our efforts on stoically enduring the fall. We are never going to know exactly when the low point will come; we will always end up jumping the gun. The crucial thing is to keep buying throughout the fall, since the best results are obtained from the last investments that are made.

However, it's important to be very alert to two factors when looking at these types of companies: the company needs to be an efficient producer and able to operate under low prices; and it shouldn't be holding much debt. Failure to meet these two conditions can put our investment at risk, as the company may not make it out to the other side of the cycle.

The clearest example of a cyclical investment I have returned to time and again is the Spanish company Acerinox, which ticks both boxes, being an efficient producer and operating with little debt.

(6) *Share types.* I have come across discounts in European and Asian preference shares. These types of shares forego voting rights in return for the right to a bigger part of the dividends than common stock. Since we are normally investing in family businesses, losing the voting right shouldn't be a big deal, and the discounts on common stock can sometimes amount to 30–40%.

Supposedly, they are more illiquid, but some preference shares, such as BMW's, have a daily trading volume of around 5,000,000 euros, quite a lot more than various medium-size companies which don't trade at a discount. This is a clear market inefficiency. BMW and Exor are examples of investments I have made along these lines, as well as some Korean companies.

These types of preference shares are different from the American version, which is more like a bond.

(7) *Long-term projects.* Investors lack patience and the stock market isn't always the best place for such projects, leading to incorrect price formation and a possible investment opportunity. Patience is undoubtedly an investor's biggest asset, more so than intelligence or any other ability. It is an essential quality for such ventures.

It's surprising how schizophrenic some investors can be. In their professional life, which might be very successful, they can be willing to invest in a business or new machine and give it time – two or three years – before gauging the results of the project. While at the same time, they expect their investments in listed shares to yield an immediate return. Unfortunately, the qualities which make them good private investors don't translate into their stock market endeavours.

I repeat, patience is the single most important attribute for investing effectively. A patient and reasonably well-informed investor has the philosopher's stone in their hands: the holy grail.

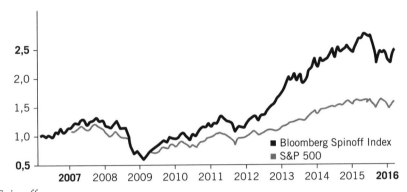

Spin offs
Source: *Value Investor Insight*, Bloomberg.

(8) *Spin-offs or asset separations.* Opportunities can arise which are worth exploring when a division of a company is split off to become its own entity. Over the 13 years from 2002, the Bloomberg US spin-off rose by 557% compared with a 137% increase in the S&P 500.[6] This inefficiency arises from various factors: firstly, with spin-offs the incentives change and executives are financially and professionally motivated to do a better job in managing the new company (perhaps they even managed it before, but the new incentives improve results); secondly, there may be a lack of detailed information on the new business, since we are not talking about a stock market launch (IPO) but rather a placement among existing shareholders; thirdly, the company's existing shareholders may not want to have a position in the spin-off, meaning they will immediately offload their shares, providing an opportunity.

(9) *Free lunches.* These can arise in any of the above cases, or in isolation, and are another way to the tilt the odds in our favour. Free lunches appear when a stable business – which justifies its share price – comes into possession of a tangible asset or an early-stage project with potential to mature and which is not well priced by the market. These amount to free – or nearly

---

[6]'Going separate ways', *Value Investor Insight*, 30 November 2015.

free – lunches, since their remoteness, whether in time or perhaps geographically, means the market tends to overlook them.

They represent one of the most attractive ways to invest, combining security with potential for outstanding upside. What's more, this is exactly the type of mental attitude that we should always look to develop. A clear example for me was the case of Ferrari within Fiat, and under the umbrella of Exor. When I first invested in Exor, investors were correctly pricing its two main assets, SGS (Société Générale de Surveillance) and Fiat Industrial, supporting the overall valuation. However, they failed to take account of Ferrari, which fell under Fiat Auto, a manufacturer of affordable but relatively uninspiring cars and vans. Ferrari was a free lunch waiting to mature. Little by little the market warmed up to it, with the company ultimately being placed on the New York Stock Exchange in 2015 at a bumper price.

The above are some situations which can produce good opportunities, but market distortions can arise in a variety of ways. For example, companies with better than expected growth, or a successful restructuring, or a change of management, etc., or any other potential upside that has not yet been grasped by the market. Rest assured, they will appear and we can find them.

It could be argued that the discounts on conglomerates, family companies, or other situations are something that is more permanent feature than opportunity, but this is not the case. From time to time there will be moments when the discounts begin to close, allowing us to unwind or sell positions, depending on other market alternatives. It's not an absolute certainty, but the probabilities are indeed very high. I will go into this in more detail later on.

Once we have eventually uncovered some quality stocks which we feel comfortable with, we can begin to increase their concentration in our portfolio. However, when investing directly in stocks it's vital to diversify the portfolio among a minimum number of stocks. The exact figure isn't important, although five to six stocks would be a bare minimum. Thereafter, the total number of stocks in the portfolio will depend on how much knowledge we acquire on different companies, but without going beyond a reasonable number, say 15 to 25.

COMPANIES TO AVOID

While there are some areas that are ripe for reaping rewards, there are others which are already overexploited. That's not to say there are no good investments to be found, but the chances of this happening are much lower, increasing the risks of us running into a dud. Some examples are as follows.

(1) *Companies with an excessive growth focus.* Growth is good and beneficial if it's the result of a job well done, which generates resources over

time which are reinvested in increasing the strength of the company, but this tends to be more the exception than the rule. The obsession – because that's what it is – with high-growth targets is extremely dangerous. The goal should be for the largest number of clients possible to enjoy the product on offer but without exploiting loopholes or taking shortcuts. This isn't easy for large organisations, meaning that it's important to be careful when analysing them.

Once again there is an agency problem: who are the company's management working for – themselves or the shareholders? Growth is a hugely attractive call signal, which increases the halo or prestige around managers, but it's only a good thing if it's healthy.

(2) *Companies which are constantly acquiring other companies.* This is linked to the previous point and can make matters worse still. If the acquisition is not focused on increasing the competitive advantage of the main business, it can end up becoming a rueful folly, or what Peter Lynch calls 'diworsification', diversifying to deteriorate. Growth can also bring with it two other problems: first, more complex accounting can more easily conceal problems; and second, each acquisition ends up becoming bigger than the last, increasing the price and therefore the level of risk.

It's worth reiterating how detrimental it can be when some managers feel the pressure or the desire – after selling a substantial part of the company – to buy another of a similar size, instead of returning the money to the shareholders. It brings to mind cases such as Portugal Telecom; Unipapel, Repsol, and Azkoyen in Spain; and Clariant in Europe.

(3) *Initial public offerings.* We've all fallen into this trap and we have to be on the watch for it. According to a study by Jay Ritter, Professor of Finance at the University of Florida, companies who float on the stock market via an IPO post 3% lower returns than similar companies after five years.[7]

There is a simple reason for this: there are clear asymmetries in the information available to the seller and what we know as purchasers. The seller has been involved with the company for years and abruptly decides to sell at a time and price of their choosing. The transaction is so one-sided that there can only be one winner (by the way, somebody received a Nobel Prize for pointing out that there are information asymmetries in the markets!).

(4) *Businesses which are still in their infancy.* Old age is an asset: the longer the company has been going, the longer it will last in the future. In fact, a recent study shows that there is a positive correlation between the age of a company and its stock market returns. That is logical, because it takes a

---

[7] https://site.warrington.ufl.edu/ritter/files/2015/03/IPOs_5years_2016.pdf.

certain amount of time for a business to get on to a stable footing, depending on the level of demand and competition. Until this happens, we are exposed to the high volatility inherent in any new business, with an uncertain final outcome.

Taleb[8] explains this very accurately, applying it to various aspects of our life, even our own life.

Despite the above, I am guilty of having made the error of investing in new businesses, which invariably led to losses. After having had these experiences even Google seems like too much of a whippersnapper, still needing time to become settled.

(5) *Businesses with opaque accounting.* Whenever there's significant potential for flexible accounting, being able to trust in the honesty of the managers and/or owners is essential. Long-term contractors in the construction sector, or in infrastructure or engineering projects, are examples where there is scope for flexible accounting, with latitude to delay accounting for payments or bring forward income.

We could even include banks and insurance companies in this category, where the margin for accounting flexibility is very significant and it's relatively simple to cover up a problem for a while, compounded by having highly leveraged balance sheets.

Prior to investing in these types of businesses, it's absolutely imperative to be certain we can trust the managers or shareholders (to the extent that we are able to determine this). No one forces us to invest in them, so the burden of proof is on the company.

(6) *Companies with key employees.* These are companies where the employees effectively control the business, but without being shareholders (the latter could even be positive). For example, many service companies reportedly have very high returns on capital, but only because capital isn't necessary: investment banks, law firms, some fund managers, consultancy companies, head-hunters, etc.

The creation of value in these businesses benefits these key employees, while the opportunities for external shareholders to earn attractive returns are limited, despite supposedly high returns on capital employed.

(7) *Highly indebted companies.* As somebody once said, first give me back the capital, then return something on it. Buffett also remarks that the first rule of investing is not losing money, and the second and the third... Excess debt is one of the main reasons why investments lose value. We don't need to flee from debt at every opportunity, when it's well used it can be very helpful, but it shouldn't have much weight in a diversified portfolio.

---

[8]Taleb (2012).

By contrast, markets don't particularly like companies to hold cash, rightly fearing that such financial well-being might lead to bad investment decisions. I have always ensured that over half of the companies in the portfolio have ample cash: I sleep well, making the most of incorrect market valuation. I am not worried about excess cash, provided that capital is reliably allocated.

(8) Sectors which are stagnant or experiencing falling sales. While it's not worth paying over the top for growth, on the flipside, falling sales can be very negative. Quite often these companies can cross our radar because of the low prices at which they are trading, but over the long term, time is not on our side with them. Sometimes sales will recover, but mostly the opportunity cost is too high, given that the situation can persist for some time. I have encountered my fair share of these: Debenhams, printing companies, etc.

(9) *Expensive stocks*. It's obvious but worth spelling out. I don't think I have ever tried to buy a stock valued by the market at over 15× earnings. Perhaps it's a genetic disposition, or a habit I've picked up, but in reality, expensive companies have historically obtained the worst results, because good expectations are already priced in and because it's less likely that the price will jump from – say – a P/E ratio of 16 to 21 than from nine to 14.

That's not to say that good results can't be obtained from buying the above types of stocks, but it's an additional hurdle which I have always preferred (and recommend) to avoid.

These aren't the only examples of companies to avoid, but – once again – they are a good starting point.

CAPITAL ALLOCATION

Suppose we have found a good company at a decent price. We have now completed the essential part of choosing our favourite stocks. However, by definition this company generates a lot of earnings, and the managers have significant flexibility in terms of how they allocate this money, with a wide range of options available to them. Therefore, it's important that the capacity to generate value through competitive advantages is also matched by an appropriate allocation of earned profit.

As already mentioned, as shareholders the only thing we ask of the management board is that they give consideration to repurchasing and cancelling shares. We obviously believe the shares to be undervalued – otherwise we wouldn't have invested – meaning that a cancellation would create value. It's not that we're demanding they do this, but it should be on the list, alongside other main options such as dividends, investments in assets for growth, and acquisition of other companies to increase the company's competitive advantage. The board should decide between these options based on the highest expected return and consequent value creation for the shareholder.

The only way we can get a fix on capital allocation is by studying the managers' track record and the company's decision-making processes. It comes down to both a quantitative and a qualitative analysis based on criteria, with experience being assigned a very high weight. As previously mentioned, the greater the extent to which managers have shareholding interests, the more likely it is that their interest will be aligned with minority shareholders, but this step shouldn't be overlooked in any case.

VALUATION

Valuation is the last step in selecting stocks. It involves making the necessary calculations to determine the target price which will serve as our guide. This is the last step and probably the easiest part of the investment process.

On my desk I have a calculator which adds, subtracts, multiplies, and divides. Plain and simple. There's no need for anything more sophisticated, since most of our time will be spent analysing the companies we're interested in. Our goal is to be among the minority of investors, the top five or so, who are best acquainted with a given company and its circumstances. Analysing does not involve building complicated mathematical models with discounted cash flows (and, for example, with forecasts for annual earnings over the next 15 years). Instead, it's far better to have a good understanding of the business and be able to determine a particular company's capacity to generate future earnings. The goal is not to precisely forecast earnings each year, but rather to set out a logical range in which they are likely to move according to the business's characteristics. Doing so requires reading, delving into the companies, asking, learning, and reflecting; not constructing complicated models.

Once we have a figure for normalised earnings (i.e. under stable market conditions – neither boom nor crisis) we can apply an appropriate multiple and arrive at our valuation. Discounting cash flows is a neat stylistic exercise, but adds little to the valuation. I would use it only very occasionally for extremely stable and predictable businesses – motorways, gas or electricity networks, etc., where by their very nature the likelihood of erring is very low – but in other cases it adds practically no value, since the chances of correctly predicting earnings in – say – year seven are minimal. It doesn't tell us enough to warrant the time spent performing the calculation.

The multiple to apply to these normalised earnings will depend on the quality of the business. A very reasonable – and probably the most suitable – approach is to use the stock market average for the last 200 years.

This average is 15, which is equivalent to an 'earning yield' of 6.6% (1 × 100/15), in line with the long-term real return on equities. Setting this as a target return seems pretty sensible. For some outstanding businesses we could apply a somewhat higher margin of between 15 and 20; while for more mediocre businesses, with limited barriers to entry, we should push it down to between 10 and 15. For most businesses, 15 is an appropriate multiple.

Once we have performed the valuation, we should invest where we find the largest discounts relative to this target valuation, calculated according to the multiple. Other qualitative factors will also influence the investment decision, the most important one being the quality of the business and – closely related to that – our confidence in the valuation we have performed. Quality and confidence will help us decide the appropriate weight for each stock in the portfolio.

Overall, the valuation will give us a target price which will serve as a light to guide us in our buy–sell decisions, depending on the available alternatives.

NORMALISED EARNINGS

Normalised earnings are the key to our valuation. 'Earnings, earnings, earnings', as Peter Lynch wrote. Calculating normalised earnings requires us to have an in-depth understanding of the company's business and its market position. The companies' accounts provide us with a first snapshot, although at this point it's not necessary to analyse them in any great detail yet. In this initial approximation, we can limit ourselves to a few headline figures, which will help us determine which companies might end up being an attractive opportunity worth investigating in greater depth.

It will take some time to understand the market and the company's position – days or weeks, depending on how complicated or novel the sector is. Once we have a basic view on the company's position and future (I say 'basic view' because the analysis can take years), we should start to pick apart the accounts. Our initial goal in this part of the analysis is to verify whether the accounts are an accurate portrayal of the company's state of play, enabling us to then move to estimating normalised earnings.

(1) *True reflection of the company's state of play.* As we all know, accounting is a flexible discipline that can be stretched to fulfil a variety of needs. To avoid errors and future problems, we should focus on:

- *Cash flow analysis.* The income statement is important, but the first way to test whether the accounts are credible is by checking whether the cash is real. It's no use if the company is supposedly obtaining good results but this isn't reflected in cash at the end of the financial year. This type of analysis, for example, helped limit our losses in Pescanova: at the end of the year, cash just wasn't rising as it should have been but debt was going up; this led us to pare back our exposure, though unfortunately not completely.

All companies publish cash flow in their annual accounts, and there are various books available on how to focus our analysis of this issue.[9]

The ideal company in this analysis will generate more cash than implied by its P&L account. This is a sign of very conservative accounting and that earnings are being 'stashed'.

- *Credibility of the income statement.* This is the flipside of the cash flow analysis. The main problem arises when accounting is excessively aggressive in regard to income or expenses, reporting income for a year that still hasn't materialised and failing to recognise outlays that have taken place. It's essential to be able to identify either of these accounting tricks.

  Three of the most common problems in recognising costs stem from: provisioning, which can be too low given the company's situation – think of the Spanish banking sector between 2005 and 2011; the company's policy on fixed asset depreciation, which may not reflect real asset depreciation; and, finally, excessive capitalisation of expenses.

  Once again, it's not only about looking at the negative side of the analysis. There are some very conservative companies that conceal part of their earnings capacity, perhaps to hide the underlying attractiveness of the business, or to benefit from a more favourable tax treatment.

  A final problem is the tendency to classify some recurring expenses as one-off outlays. Repeating this year-in, year-out clouds the analysis and makes it harder to discover the real capacity to generate earnings. As Lev and Gu point out (see the chart on the next page), one-off expenses account for nearly 20% of reported earnings.[10]

- *The balance sheet.* Our main responsibility regarding the balance sheet is to investigate whether there are hidden or off-balance-sheet liabilities. These could be pensions liabilities, costs associated with closing down factories, mines, etc., or any erroneous calculation of some type on provisioning for possible future losses.

  An unexplained increase in certain current headings, such as stocks or account receivables, could suggest that the reality is more challenging than the income statement makes out.

[9] A good starting point is Fernández (2017, chap. 2).
[10] Lev and Gu (2016).

The reverse can also be true here: with the existence of hidden assets making the company more attractive, such as real-estate assets not used in the business or subsidiaries not related to the main business, the brand or other intellectual property which increases in value over time, etc.

By going to some effort, we can develop a reasonably accurate impression of the company's true situation.

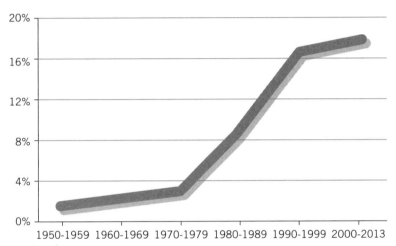

Extraordinary expenses/earnings
Source: Lev and Gu (2016).

(2) *Normalised earnings.* Once we are convinced that the accounts are an accurate reflection of the company's real situation, we can start thinking about the normalised earnings calculation. The company may be going through an unusual situation influenced by temporary factors which obscure its real capacity to generate earnings. We need to delve into this.

- *The economic cycle.* Highly cyclical companies will never be in a stable situation, since the ups and downs of the cycle make it hard to know what 'normal' earnings look like. It's not about predicting the cycle, rather it comes down to understanding where we are right now, which may be an extreme, good, bad, or plain normal situation. There are various different methods we can use to adjust earnings in the face of this difficulty: taking the average of results over the last 10 years, adjusting for inflation; taking maximum and minimum earnings over the last 10 years and using the mid-point; or any other commonsense criteria.

- *Disruption to supply or demand* can bring about exceptional situations, and we know that investors tend to extrapolate the current situation to the future. It's a huge error, since economic agents will react to such problems, and they will gradually be resolved.
- *The company in question might still be in its infancy*, but capable of maturing over time. It's important to consider the potential to generate earnings in the future, which have not yet materialised.
- *The previous issues could affect a part of the company*, tainting the overall valuation of the rest of the business. A normalisation will need to be applied to these 'loss'-making businesses, otherwise we will be damaging the whole company. In the worst-case scenario, we can value the division at zero, taking account of the costs involved in a possible wind-up.

Overall, normalisation helps to refine the valuation, partially mitigating the difficulties involved in predicting the future.

INDEBTEDNESS

Although indebtedness doesn't directly impact on the valuation, it's important to be very aware of a company's debt levels, analysing its capacity to pay back debt: size, term, restrictions, etc. We should steer clear of businesses that are highly indebted, since they can negate our estimates of future earnings. Debt improves the return on capital, but the increased volatility from interest payments can become impossible to bear. The limit for acceptable levels of debt depends on the stability of the business; the more stable – with an easy to predict outlook (motorway toll road, electricity networks, etc.) – the more manageable the debt.

The same applies both to the business world and our own personal situation.

The undeniable advantage of working without debt or other liabilities is that we can withstand any situation with the necessary peace of mind. Debt requires us to be more precise with our predictions than is desirable, especially given the near impossibility of correctly forecasting what will happen and the inevitability of devastating surprises.[11]

The goal of this book isn't to give a lesson in finances or valuation, there's plenty of literature on that; I have simply tried to set out some general rules to enable us to tackle the task of putting together a reasonable valuation. Furthermore, as can be seen, such valuations do not require very sophisticated tools.

---

[11] Taleb (2016).

MARKET RECOGNITION

Some readers might argue that the approach set out in this chapter – and the book in general – depends on the time it takes for the market to wake up to the undervaluation which we have identified.

I don't deny that it can take some time for the market to come to its senses, but if our analysis has been sufficiently rigorous, we should welcome this as it will allow us to increase our positions.

It might also be claimed that we won't have enough liquidity to strengthen these positions, but in reality not all stocks move in sync and these differences can enable us to adjust our portfolio to these relative movements. I am constantly tweaking the weights of my stocks according to their performance. If I have positions in two stocks and one goes up by 20% and the other falls by 20%, I almost automatically sell positions in the first to allow me to reinvest in the second. Therefore, even in the absence of liquidity, we can afford to patiently await future price rises.

The following table calculates the annual return depending on the time it takes for the expected total upside (1.5×, 2×, or 3×) to materialise. As can be seen, if we think our portfolio will go up in value by 50% (1.5×) over time, even if it takes 10 years to get there, we will obtain a 4% annual return. And this is the worst-case scenario, which will improve if the upside is greater or takes less time to materialise.

Annual Return Over Time

Years	1.5× (%)	2× (%)	3× (%)
1	50	100	200
2	22	41	73
3	14	26	44
4	11	19	32
5	8	15	25
6	7	12	20
7	6	10	17
8	5	9	15
9	5	8	13
10	4	7	12

Source: own calculations.

In fact, in the funds I have managed there has never been a period of more than nine years with negative returns. This is consistent with the table above, given that my estimated upside potential has always been above 50%.

In any case, some factors can speed up the process:

- New managers are seldom a quick fix, but they can help catalyse changes, putting companies on the right path and focusing them on their competitive advantages.
- The circumstances which cloud the ability to generate results can change. Currencies, technological changes, or any other event which may have concealed a business's advantages can drop out.
- The economic cycle can change. Nothing lasts for ever and we should be mindful of that.
- Sometimes it just happens: the gap between value and price gradually closes. Experience tells us that for one reason or another, the market always ends up recognising a company's ability to generate earnings.

I don't like talking about catalysts, which by their very definition are unpredictable, otherwise they would be reflected in the price. However, share buybacks will always help. When we come across an undervalued company which repurchases its shares, we are looking at the only catalyst under the direct influence of the company and its shareholders. As investors, we have to make this point to other shareholders.

I feel like I am repeating myself, but patience is the key attribute for investing successfully, and it's what should keep us going during the wait.

THE PERFECT STOCK

In summary, the perfect stock is a preferred share in a medium-size company with a family holding company structure, trading on the wrong market, with a cyclical component and/or long-term investments. A good example of this for me in recent years has been Exor (the holding company for the Agnelli family), which ticks nearly all the right boxes: family company, holding company structure, preference shares, good businesses (CNH, Ferrari, SGS – the latter until it was sold) mixed with less attractive ones (Fiat), trading in Italy, but with global assets, cyclical in nature, and with a long-term perspective. All in all, a real gem which has performed accordingly.

It's not common to find such stocks, but it's possible. In this case I came across it in the weekly *Barron's*, a publication available to everyone. Sometimes you have to investigate a bit more, but with patience they can be found.

How is it possible to find such opportunities? Shouldn't they be obvious to all investors? Is everyone else around us blind? These and similar questions deserve a response before completing our journey through the investment world, and Chapter 9 will address them. First though, I want to sketch out a few key ideas on managing an investment portfolio.

PORTFOLIO MANAGEMENT

Some Ideas on Managing Portfolios

Management is more than the sum of the purchase of attractive stocks. It involves a degree of strategy about the objectives for the portfolio, taking a view on the overall lines of action. It's not always possible to have an overarching strategy, but it is at certain times and it can be very beneficial.

The first step (optional, depending on the circumstances, as we will see) involves trying to acquire some idea about where we are in the cycle. For example, whether we should be moving towards defensive stocks, or – on the contrary – starting to be more aggressive, if we judge the declines to have been sufficient.

This doesn't require having a clear idea of the general state of play in the markets and the economy, but it is helpful to analyse the message coming from the types of stocks that interest us, so as to draw the right conclusions about what's going on. If some stocks in a sector have taken a particular hammering, it's likely we will be at the bottom of the cycle in that sector.

Overall market developments will also give us some insights: if there have been lots of very strong rises, we will be heading towards the end of a cyclical expansion, while after a series of large losses, we will doubtless be close to the bottom.

However, there's no guarantee that our analysis of the cycle will be successful. In many cases the only thing we can say with any real conviction is that the global economy grows by 3% a year, but we don't know whether this year it will be closer to 2% or 4%. If we are able to have some degree of clarity on the overall or sectoral cycle, then the next step is to consider which types of stocks will help us in this context. Obviously, we need to buy the most aggressive stocks during low points in the cycle, even if it can be challenging to overcome the mental barriers to doing so in such a negative environment. And vice-versa at the top of the cycle.

Designing the appropriate strategy for the general or sectoral cycle can be what adds most value to a portfolio. In fact, some 'scholars' believe it's the only thing that adds value as specific stock selection is a zero-sum game, where you don't add value. My experience is that all phases of the investment process contribute, though it's true that it can be easier to add value through portfolio design.

Other relevant factors:

- *Diversification.* The future is hard to predict; situations can arise which hadn't even occurred to us. Often we are prepared for past surprises – no longer surprises as such – but not for the unexpected. And we can be sure they can creep up on us one way or another. As such, our portfolio should be prepared to withstand any situation, be it a market collapse or a boom, inflation or deflation, for all possibilities. It must be agile and resilient against any eventuality.

We also have to insulate the portfolio from our own errors, whether they be our view of the cycle or our choice of companies. We have to envisage how our portfolio would be affected by the opposite scenario to what we are expecting; how it would survive.

Diversification is the clearest way to prepare the portfolio for any eventuality. Having at least 10 stocks gives us a reasonable amount of diversification. If we are managing on behalf of others it can be helpful to hold a few more, creating a portfolio of some 20–30 stocks. After that, there need to be strong arguments for increasing the number of stocks.

In my case, the main reasons come: firstly, from the type of investment vehicle used – public funds – which are subject to relatively strict legislation; and, secondly, a specific seeding strategy based on holding smaller positions.

- *Stock selection should be bottom-up.* Which came first, the chicken or the egg? At the risk of contradicting myself, stock selection is the first step in managing portfolios, except when this selection provides us with enough information to design a strategy straight out of the box before investing. To avoid confusion, suffice to say that if the selection of stocks and the market itself don't provide us with enough information, we can safely disregard having a portfolio strategy and just focus on selecting attractive stocks.

  In doing so, the guidelines set out in this and Chapter 7 will enable us to avoid wasting time on companies which don't stand up to greater scrutiny. Furthermore, in practice, it's important to be very flexible: avoiding slipping into generic asset allocation, both for sectors and regions. If emerging markets are attractive, then we have to invest what we consider necessary. If it's 50%, so be it.

  If we don't understand banks or new technologies, then it is best to avoid them. If we are engineering enthusiasts and we can see opportunities, then carpe diem!

- *Pay particular attention to the weight of stocks in the portfolio.* As already mentioned, over the years we got it wrong on a number of stocks, more than 40, but crucially they were seldom significant investments. We must be very sure of our investment if we are going to assign it a high weight in our fund, never doing so if the company is indebted.

  Bear in mind that it's extremely difficult to discern and accept investment errors: we always end up giving the benefit of the doubt to the company, since after investing so much time studying it, we find it deeply unsatisfying to sell and think that we are throwing it away. One of the ways to get around this problem is by only having small exposures to the more dubious stocks.

- *Changing weights.* One of the ways to add value in asset management is by changing the size of positions in stocks.

In Europe, regulated mutual funds enjoy almost total exemption from capital gains tax. This means that shares can be sold at virtually no cost, especially bearing in mind that brokerage fees have fallen significantly to 25 basis points (0.25%) in the worst case, which is barely noticeable in the context of price movements of 15% or 20%.

As previously mentioned, the argument for continually adjusting is one of simple probabilities: if a stock in a portfolio rises by 10% and another falls by 10%, then there has been a relative movement of 20% which we can capitalise on. The logical thing to do, once we have studied the movements, is to lower our position in the stock that has gained value and increase it in the one that has fallen.

Some investors prefer to wait until the stock has reached the target price before offloading the entire position, or take other approaches. However, it's highly likely that our simple approach increases the potential of the fund, since it's unlikely the valuations of the particular shares have moved in the same proportion.

- *Sectoral effort.* We should focus on attractive sectors. It's impossible to be on top of every sector. As unspecialised generalists we should discriminate between sectors that are worth following – which form the focus of our efforts – while leaving the rest to one side. Not all sectors are equally attractive all the time, and it can take years for the level of interest to shift.

By focusing, I mean devoting the bulk of our resources, especially time, to the most attractive sectors. We should keep an eye on other sectors, being aware of their existence, but they shouldn't eat up our time for the moment.

The same approach applies to choosing sectors as it does when we look for a specific stock: we need to be on the lookout for poor stock market performance, which creates general dismay or even personal disdain about the sector among investors. This is the starting point for us to explore whether it makes sense to invest or not.

Sectoral or regional specialists suffer from a basic problem of being limited to the specific market in which they are able to operate. They have to buy something and they end up doing so regardless of whether it's attractive. The same thing happens with regional representatives in any business: they end up selling, even if not very profitably, because their position is on the line. As the former Chairman of Acciona, José María Entrecanales, used to say: 'Be careful with business representatives in a country, because they always end up taking on work, even if it's not profitable'. He was referring to his main business of construction, with great insight and lucidity as ever.

Finally, when 'experts' talk about sectoral weights in a portfolio, what they are talking about is the relative weight of sectors in the market, which normally don't diverge much. In other words, if the financial sector represents 20% of the market, they might advise investing 15–22% of the portfolio. When I talk about sectoral effort, I'm referring to dedicating resources to it in order to decide whether to invest or not. The decision should be made without prejudice to the sector's weight in the market.

By moving from less attractive to more attractive sectors we avoid wasting time, which is an extremely scarce resource in investment analysis. There will be time in the future to return to sectors left to one side.

A Day in the Life of a Fund Manager

It's almost a cliché to talk up the benefits of consistency, essentially habits, which underpin the achievement of optimal results over time.

In my case, I've been fortunate enough to keep to a stable routine over the years, despite the increasing size of the funds that I manage and the number of clients (not to mention my own family). Nobody can be sure what the ideal path is to achieving one's objectives, it's trial and error for all of us, but I confess I've been reluctant to change my ways having seen early on that they work for me. Here's what I get up to.

I start my day reading the press. Each day for the last 20 years I have read *Expansión* (a Spanish economics and business newspaper published in Madrid) and the *Financial Times* (FT). These two papers are my core reading. I used to also read another Spanish daily economics newspaper, but I gave up in the end as it was too similar to *Expansión*, temporarily substituting it for papers covering other issues that were of relevance at the time, such as the French *Les Echos* or the Chinese *China Daily*.

Among foreign economic press I have always stayed loyal to the FT as a European paper, although I prefer the *Wall Street Journal*'s editorial and opinion columns, which take a less interventionist stance. The FT's 'Lex' column is, in any case, a must read; it analyses companies briefly but in sufficient depth to add value. Nowadays I don't learn so much from the FT, but it gives me a guide as to where market consensus is and how to act accordingly. My core weekly reading consists of *Barron's* and *The Economist*, and it's also worth mentioning *Value Investor Insight*, where a couple of interesting asset managers set out their ideas each month.

Nowadays I don't read general information newspapers or listen to news on the radio or television. I am fed up with their poor understanding of the issues – at least on the topics I know – and their general negativity about a world which every day is offering more people the chance to live a decent life.

After demolishing the press, I get underway with various routines, which can depend on the circumstances: reading company or sectoral reports (I never read reports on so-called investment strategies), company visits or visits from companies to our offices, and contacts with sector exports or people familiar with companies of interest to us. Probably most of my time is spent reading alone – a passion for reading is vital for a good analyst or fund manager. The Hollywood portrayal of traders shouting into their phones is a far cry from our oasis of calm. Coming to our offices is like entering the National Library: Shh, you're not allowed to talk! The true value investor, who deserves my utmost respect, is somebody who devotes their life to their passion of reading. Nobody can spend their life studying for 50 years – which is what we do – if they don't enjoy it.

I have never been a fan of scheduling formal team meetings; I prefer for ideas to be voiced as they arise, or following meetings with companies or expert conferences. In reality, I seldom spend much time with the whole team together.

Until recently, travel was very important, but less so these days thanks to technology. Even so, I will tend to travel once or twice a month, normally in Europe.

I don't follow the markets until they close. I formally took the decision when the Spanish market opening hours were extended from 9:00 to 17:30.

It struck me as being too long, and I didn't want to stop doing other important things to follow what was going on. It was a one-man boycott, which logically hasn't affected the world, although it has implications for me personally, since I spend all my time on analysis.

As I normally like to handle the daily management of the portfolios, the dealers or another team member will let me know if a particular stock has experienced a sharp movement or is closing in on a limit that interests us, so as to make the call on whether to buy or sell.

Generally, I don't have any idea what the market is doing over the course of the day, although I can usually make a pretty good guess based on movements in the stocks that interest us. When the market closes, at 18:00, I review the prices of our stocks and any interesting developments in other stocks that we're following. This information provides the basis for taking decisions the day after.

Some fund managers swear by the need to sleep on decisions. I agree. Giving yourself at least a day helps to fend off unnecessary haste.

I have the good fortune of having completely streamlined my involvement in investor relations tasks, which are the bane of most asset managers' lives. In recent years, my general rule has been not to see new clients, except in exceptional cases, while trying to maintain the relationship with long-standing clients. This increases the importance of annual investment conferences and the work of the commercial team, who I try to ensure are sufficiently well informed.

This enables me to keep a reasonable schedule; I am never in the office after 8:00 in the evening. I think it provides the right balance with family life, also bearing in mind that I use the journey to work and back, an hour all together, for reading. The latter is often quite varied and not necessarily strictly work related, though usually it complements that very well.

Overall, the common element is consistency, combined with a long-term passion for what I do, which together creates a very positive effect, as Angela Duckworth explains.[12] The same basic routine every day, come what may. There have only been two brief moments when I stopped reading the daily news, in the immediate aftermath of my accident in 2008 and after resigning.

This consistency helps develop skills which, as they become refined, give broader meaning to the work beyond myself. These days I don't only do it for personal satisfaction, but also for a wider benefit. For me it's about giving peace of mind and independence to other people in a key part of their life: their savings.

---

[12]Duckworth (2016).

A Case Study in Management: BMW

BMW is a very representative example of my approach to investing and managing. It's a company with an understandable business, with a well-established family serving as long-term reference shareholder. The company enjoys a certain amount of growth and is subject to cyclical fluctuations, but it also has deep cash pockets to defend itself.

The main appeal is its brand, which allows it to sustain much higher margins and returns than most of its competitors, including its rivals in the luxury segment, such as Daimler, the owner of Mercedes. BMW's average sales margin has hovered between 8% and 10% over the last 10 years, enabling it to post a return on capital of 25% in relation to the pure automotive business. This is slightly reduced by lower returns on finance activity, which puts the group's ROCE at between 15% and 20%.[13]

Another factor in originally investing was the enormous expected sales growth in China. Sales to China at the time of investing were limited but set to experience strong growth, given Chinese consumers' preference for status symbols, for which BMW fits the bill (Chinese sales jumped from 44,000 cars in 2006 to 463,000 in 2015). In actual fact, growth was far stronger than I had ever imagined.

I also considered BMW to be one of the most technologically and environmentally advanced companies, offering a wide range of vehicles, with the (at the time) recent launch of the new X-range of multipurpose SUVs.

But the key factor is that it was a company where the Quandt family held control without meddling in day-to-day management. They made a major error in the 1990s by buying the Rover Group, but have since learnt to be more careful about unhealthy diversification – although the upside of the Rover purchase was coming across Mini and Rolls Royce, which have provided good long-term results. This family management is embodied in a 20-year holding of a similar number of shares, around 650 million, financing all growth from cash flow.

We first bought into the company in spring 2005, purchasing common stock trading at 35 euros. This accounted for 0.7% of the international portfolio. At that time we purchased common stock because the discount on preference shares wasn't excessively large, around 10%.

Over the course of that year BMW continued to post record results, while we refined our knowledge of the company by speaking to experts and travelling to Germany to visit them in Munich. We also visited Daimler and Volkswagen. Furthermore, I dusted off my German to read about

---

[13]BMW Annual Reports, 1995–2015; Hendrikse (2016).

the family's turbulent and fascinating story in *Die Quandts*.[14] So, when the share price slipped in 2006, we took advantage to increase our position to 2.5% of the portfolio, elevating it to the status of a significant stock pick. We were still buying common stock, since preference shares were trading at similar levels, even closing 2006 one cent above common stock at 43.52 euros.

I began buying preference shares in the second half of 2007 – at the start of the financial crisis these had fallen more sharply than common stock and were trading once again at around 35 euros – with a 15% discount on common stock. We bought the equivalent of 4% of the portfolio. Despite being much less liquid (around 50,000 shares were trading daily compared with 2,000,000 common shares), we were reassured by the fact that employee incentives were being paid out using preference shares, which also have a statutory right to a somewhat larger dividend. The overall position amounted to around 5%, as I sold off some normal shares to avoid excessively increasing our exposure.

The financial crisis of 2008 and the beginning of 2009 pushed preference shares down to a minimum of 11.05 euros per share, and we took advantage to increase our position to 9% of the portfolio, close to the maximum legal limit, with the average purchase price standing at 20 euros per share.

At that time the company's capitalisation amounted to seven billion euros. This was a steal, bearing in mind that the cash from its industrial activity and the book value of its financial activity were above that amount. Something we pointed out in our March 2009 public presentation. What's more, the company's cash generation was positive throughout these two years. In other words, cash went up during the worst crisis in recent decades.

With cyclical companies the key is to capitalise on cyclically driven price movements. We bought throughout the fall, constantly increasing the size of the position and continually lowering the average purchase price. I didn't know when the share price would touch bottom, but I knew we would be buying on that day, as proved to be the case.

In 2009 the fund was now only holding BMW preference shares and the share price doubled, closing at 23 euros. Throughout the year we sold off shares to avoid exceeding the legal limit and reduce the exposure, which at the end of the year stood at 7.78% of the global portfolio.

In 2010 the share price nearly doubled again, closing at 38.50 euros. We continued selling, but kept the weight in the portfolio at 9% for quite some time. At the end of 2013 we reduced the position to 7.58%, with the share price ending the year at 62.09 euros.

---

[14]Jungbluth (2007).

In sum, during the nine years since our initial investment, the share price had gone up in value by 75%, outperforming the market. But, crucially, by not letting up on buying during the fall, the average purchase price fell and we were able to triple our investment from 20 euros to 62 euros (plus 11.87 euros in dividends, an important amount representing 60% of the initial investment). We weren't anticipating the market crash in 2008, but thanks to Lehman Brothers what would have ended up being a reasonable return of 75% in nine years became something exceptional. As the saying goes among some warped politicians, nothing like making the most of a good crisis...

The factors behind the strong stock market performance reflect BMW's own excellent performance. In 2005, BMW sold 1.33 million cars; in 2013, 1.96 million. In 2005, it posted net profit of 2.2 billion euros; in 2013, 5.34 billion euros. Finally, in 2005 it obtained earnings per share of 4.4 euros; in 2013, 8.10 euros. We are value investors, but there's no reason to turn our noses up at growth when the market doesn't make us pay for it.

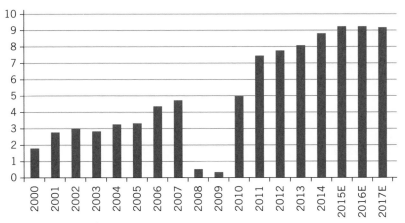

BMW earnings per share
Source: Morgan Stanley.

To conclude, the investment in BMW over 2005–2014 was a classic case of the right type of value investment. It's a perfect embodiment of all the virtues of the 'approach':

1. Ridiculous market prices compared with correct valuation.
    March 2009: Price: €11. Valuation: €100.
2. Mr Market had lost his head in the middle of a crisis.
    Depressed at a time of maximum volatility, he failed to discriminate between companies, senselessly obliterating everyone. BMW was

lumped in with banks and real-estate companies, disproportionately damaging its share price.

3. Mr Market is inefficient in the short term (2009 Price: €11) and efficient in the long term (2015 price: €70).

4. The right mix of ability and value investor personality type led to a good result. In-depth study of the company to determine the right valuation (€100); conviction and courage to swim against the tide (buying when everyone else is selling); maintaining conviction over time (buying at the low point up to the maximum limit); and finally, patience (four to five years of waiting).

5. Getting the valuation right is key. First we study the company and only then do we look at the share price. If the company has been properly assessed and the valuation is correct, then the investment will be profitable provided we are patient. Time plays in our favour.

6. BMW is the ideal type of company for a value investor: sound company; family owned; cash-rich; no debt; powerful brand; subject to certain consumer cycle; durable; natural growth potential (China); focused on what it does well; and in 2009, an absolute bargain!

7. All of this produced a superb result: profit of 300% over four years. Minimum price 2009: €11/Average purchase price 2009–2011: €20/2014 Sale price: €60.

CHAPTER 9

The Irrational Investor Lurking Within Us All

Yes, all of us. Investors, fund managers, even myself; we are all prone to behave irrationally to a greater or lesser degree. We have pretty clear objectives, such as maintaining the purchasing power of our savings, but we're incapable of making rational use of the tools that help us to achieve them. Historically, our irrational behaviour has led to volatility that has little to do with the performance of underlying assets, especially at turning points in the markets.

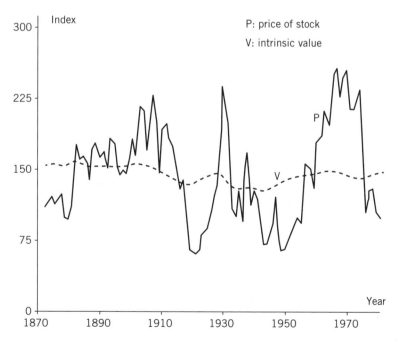

Funnily enough, in our 'business' the customer isn't always right: they invest at the top and sell at the bottom, hampering their ability to obtain returns, which tend to underperform the market average over the long run. This isn't just an opinion. Look no further than mutual fund inflows and outflows.

The goal of this chapter is to get to know ourselves better, with the aim of constraining our dark and crazy side, which drives us to act without thinking, or worse still, to do something which runs contrary to our interests.

- Why do we still believe that fixed income is safer than equities, despite all the evidence to the contrary?
- Why do some investment strategies systematically obtain better results? Why don't we make the most of them?
- Why do some fund managers repeatedly outperform the market?

Responding to these questions requires us to review the research carried out by psychologists and economists, which over the last 50 years has paid particular attention to our irrational behaviour, reaching conclusions relevant to economics and investment, which are our main areas of interest here.

It will come as no surprise to followers of the Austrian School that human beings are not always rational. Although it's true that when we are moved to act it is because we have certain end goals, which – like them or not – are always rational (otherwise we wouldn't act). It's equally true that we don't always choose the best means or apply them appropriately.[1]

Our goal might be to maximise our long-term savings or donate our wealth to people in need, but regardless of the objective, we need to use the right means to make it happen. We won't be able to maximise our savings by donating them to third parties or consciously investing in assets that don't deliver. That's what's irrational.

Before von Mises, Eugen von Böhm-Bawerk explored the topic of irrationality, even though he was an economist and not a psychologist. He was particularly interested in the study of time preference and the errors associated with it, such as the excessive weight that we assign to the present or the time inconsistency of elections.

His interest theory was based on the fact that we assign more value to current goods than future goods, but in doing so we systematically underestimate our future needs and the means for satisfying them.[2]

---

[1] von Mises (1995, p. 24).
[2] von Böhm-Bawerk (1998).

He puts this down to three factors: poor planning of our future needs; a lack of willpower; and the uncertainty and brevity of human life. Each factor will weigh differently on each person and will vary over time.

Von Böhm-Bawerk was the first to analyse our time valuation 'errors' by citing psychological factors, which result in a myopic overvaluation of the present relative to the future and inconsistencies such as assigning a different value to the same time interval at different moments: we assign a lot more value to receiving something today instead of within a year, rather than between receiving it in five or six years' time. In both cases the difference is one year, but our assessment is different.

Twentieth-century researchers studied irrationality in much greater detail. The origins of our problems are to be found in the conflict between our emotional and rational sides,[3] especially when our emotional response unduly outweighs the rational side. As popularised by Kahneman, we have two systems, which we will denote 1 and 2. System 1 operates quickly and automatically, almost effortlessly and without any real sense of control. System 2 pays attention to mental activities which require effort and involve complex calculations.

These systems are very well known to psychologists and we all believe that we act in mode 2, the conscious system, choosing freely and rationally. But that's not the case. System 1, the emotional side, is in the driving seat much more often than we think.

Take, for example, a classic problem to be resolved by intuition:

A baseball bat and ball cost a total of $1.10. The bat costs a dollar more than the ball.

How much does the ball cost?

---

[3] See, for example, Haidt (2006), Kahneman (2011), Metcalfe and Mischel (1999), Ariely (2009).

The intuitive response is $0.10 but it's wrong, otherwise the bat would cost $1.10 and the total would be $1.20. The right answer is $0.05. With a bit of effort, none of us have any problem in reaching the right answer, but we're prone to laziness and we let intuition lead us astray. Over 50% of Harvard, MIT, and Princeton students gave the wrong response to this question, and as many as 80% in less-well-known universities!

The issue is not that we're more or less intelligent, but that we let ourselves be carried away by our more primal impulses without applying our intelligence. We think we are aware of our actions, but frequently we're not. Behaving like this can have very negative financial consequences, so the goal here is to review the problem and find ways to minimise it.

WHY DON'T WE INVEST IN EQUITIES? AVERSION TO VOLATILITY

The first and perhaps most important rational shortcoming is our extreme aversion to risk – confused with volatility in this case – which prevents us from investing most of our savings in equities, which would be logical given the rationale and historical evidence set out in this book. It's true that savers in some Anglo-Saxon countries with a more developed financial culture don't behave this way, and allocate a significant part of their investment to real assets, especially equities, through their pension funds. However, this doesn't happen in most cases. In Spain, for example, the majority of savings go into real assets, but primarily of the bricks-and-mortar variety (78% of total assets).

This aversion to 'risk', essentially volatility, is the most costly error of them all – since it prevents us from taking the clear path to increasing the purchasing power of our savings while taking on a minimal amount of real risk.

The same happens even in the most financially developed economies. For example, according to a survey,[4] only 17% of Americans consider equities when thinking about investing over 10 years with money they don't need. 27% prefer housing and 23% would rather hold liquidity. To put it starkly, more Americans prefer holding liquidity in the long run than shares. The results are similar to those shown in Chapter 5.

If we think logically and consider historic results this is absurd, but it's nonetheless true. Schlomo Benartzi and Richard Thaler[5] provide two reasons for this aversion to risk.

---

[4]Bankrate.com, *Barron's*, 27 July 2015.
[5]Schlomo Benartzi and Richard Thaler, 1993.

(1) Investors abhor losses, putting excessive weight on not losing and doing so myopically, with particular aversion to short-term losses. The joy of a gain is shorter lived than the misery and discomfort of a loss. Furthermore, we give greater weight to effective losses than opportunity costs (foregone benefit). We don't worry about not winning, especially if we don't know that our neighbour has; what worries us is losing.[6]

Such aversion is closely related to what is known as 'frame dependency', which describes how we can end up taking different decisions depending on how the problem is presented to us. Here, the issue is focusing more on the effective loss than the foregone gain.

Consider the following example of risk aversion, which was studied by Kahneman and Tversky.[7]

We are given two options: (a) Accepting a certain loss of $7,500 or (b) A 75% probability of losing $10,000 and a 25% chance of not losing anything.

Both options have the same expected loss of $7,500, but most people choose option (b) because they clearly dislike losing. In option (a) the loss is certain, while in option (b) there's the possibility of not losing.

It may well be that our brain has not evolved as quickly as it should have done and we still attach excessive weight to losing, since the organisms that worry most about threats have a greater capacity to survive. Not only does this lead to a loss of earnings, but it also opens the door to the real possibility of being manipulated by 'perverse' advisors.

(2) We look too often at the results, which restricts us from having a long-term view. If we weren't as focused on them, our results would actually improve. Losses cause us more suffering than the joy we get from a similar amount of gain. When investing in equities, there are many days with losses, even though the final result is very positive over the long term. Therefore, by refraining from reviewing the results so frequently, we will be less exposed to losses and better able to tolerate volatility.

It's a challenge for us to ignore our emotional instincts and assign the right probabilities to the future results of different asset types. The combination of these two personality factors makes it very difficult to accept the volatility and consequent temporary losses associated with investing in equities.

Solving a problem requires us to be conscious of its existence and willing to get to the bottom of it. As soon as we recognise that we are not perfect and that we lack the necessary patience or mental composure, then knowledge should be our first source of support. By increasing our awareness of the

---

[6]Kahneman *et al.* (1986).
[7]Kahneman and Tversky (1979).

underlying realities when we invest, we will help strengthen our conviction to commit a larger percentage of our savings to investing in shares. System 2 needs to be sufficiently well equipped to subdue system 1.

Admittedly, sometimes it's the very same 'experts' who end up making the most errors, but the more knowledge we apply to a decision, the greater peace of mind we will have. Patience can be cultivated.

Patience is key to the investment process, helping us to master our more myopic impulses. As such, anything that helps strengthen it is welcome. A practical tool is to take a systematic approach to investment. For example, investing a given amount at a certain frequency: for example, on the first day of each month, regardless of the circumstances. The amount and frequency are irrelevant, what matters is taking a firm and unshakeable decision to invest regularly. Taking this type of approach can often outperform intuition-based results, or at least equal them.[8]

Another useful approach is to space out how frequently we monitor our portfolios. If it's only once a year or once every three years, so much the better. It might seem like an abdication of responsibility, but if the strategy has been analysed and we are confident in it, then it needs to be left to do the work. I personally have no idea how much money I have invested in my funds. When I have some liquidity I invest that same day in the fund and I forget about it until I have more savings available. Sometimes I look at the monthly statement as a reminder, but other times I file them directly in the bin. The investors or clients who fare best when investing are those who, after having made a well-reasoned investment, refrain from constantly monitoring it.

As an investment professional, I'm obliged to track price movements on a daily basis, but as mentioned I wait until the market closes before firing up the computer and this is the only time in the day when I look at the day's trading. During the rest of the day I don't know what's going on with prices, unless the trading desk or someone in the team warn me that one of the stocks on our watch list is moving in a range that interests us and it becomes necessary to buy or sell. I don't have a Bloomberg terminal in my office; we have a shared one for the whole office.

Some well-known investors go even further and don't look at prices for weeks. Others will only let themselves execute orders after having slept on it. Any system which fits our needs is acceptable; what matters is that we aren't disturbed by day-to-day goings on.

A bit of knowledge and a few tricks up our sleeve can significantly improve our myopic aversion to risk and losses. One of my proudest

---

[8]Kahneman (2011, p. 222).

achievements is having helped reduce the exposure to myopia of a large number of family, friends, and acquaintances, many of whom now realise that stock market volatility is a good thing for their long-term savings.

WHY DON'T WE INVEST USING PROVEN STRATEGIES, OR AT LEAST IN CHEAP STOCKS?

Mean reversion is the clearest conclusion that comes out of O'Shaughnessy's work analysing the performance of different strategies, as discussed in Chapter 6. Expensive stocks eventually become less expensive, posting bad results in the process, and cheap stocks return to average, improving their performance. If some readers remain unconvinced as to whether the market is capable of being efficient, it would seem clear that based on his analysis there is indeed an inefficiency to exploit.

Given the presence of such clear mean reversion in these strategies, it's surprising that they haven't been progressively corrected for by the market and that there's still scope for us to capitalise on them as investors. Once again the explanation lies within us all. The concept of mean reversion itself is very difficult to get a handle on. As Kahneman points out,[9] Francis Galton developed the idea of mean regression five years after the appearance of the law of universal gravitation or differential calculus. It was an effort for him to digest the concept, and it continues to be a problem to this day.

The first problem is that we tend to extrapolate the future based on the past, particularly the recent past. We find it hard to believe that things will change. This is known as the 'representativeness' problem.[10] But things

---

[9]Kahneman (2011, p. 179).
[10]de Bondt and Thaler (1985).

change, and in a somewhat predictable fashion. Consider an example by Hersh Shefrin,[11] which combines both the representativeness problem with mean reversion.

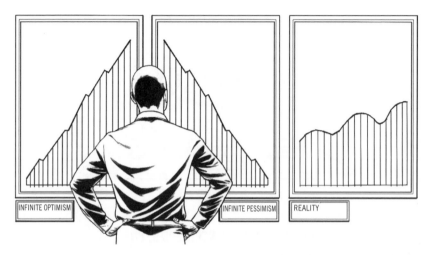

The aim is to predict the grades of university students, given that the average mark for students graduating from school is 3.08. If we have three new students in the university with average school grades of 2.20, 3.00, and 3.80, and we carry out a survey asking what their university grades are going to be, the forecast for the three students is 2.03, 2.77, and 3.46, respectively.

In reality, they obtain grades of 2.70, 2.93, and 3.30. In other words: one tends to think that the bad students will remain bad and the good will stay good. This is true to some extent, but the reality is that there is strong regression to the mean, which is not fully reflected in these forecasts.

School Grades	Predicted University Grades	Actual University Grades
2.20	2.03	2.70
3.00	2.77	2.93
3.80	3.46	3.30

Source: Shefrin (2000).

A particularly interesting instance of mean reversion can be found when looking at the quality of company management. Well-managed companies

---

[11]Shefrin (2000, pp. 14–16).

tend to perform worse in the future and their high returns on capital prove difficult to sustain. In Philip Rosenzweig's book *The Halo Effect*,[12] he explains that the story that is told about the success of a company or the impact of its CEO can be very plausible, but more often than not it's come down to luck, which will then revert to the mean.

The same is true of money managers, who might have enjoyed a good 'run' that's not sustainable in the future. This is why it's vital to analyse their very long-term track record in detail, as well as their philosophy on life and investment. It's not enough to extrapolate from the past.

The second problem arises from the difficulty in going against the prevailing opinion around us: it's very hard to separate from the herd. Once again our prehistoric ancestors are tugging at us: historically, it's generally not been a good approach to leave the group to hunt or live alone; the group is usually right, or at least safer. Circumstances have changed more rapidly than our brains.[13] In fact, when we feel excluded from the group it activates the same part of the brain as when we experience physical pain. It feels painful outside the pack![14]

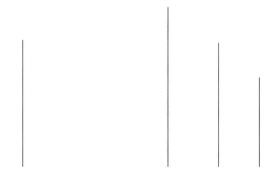

Asch Lines

James Montier[15] provides a famous example from Solomon Asch in 1951. If we are asked which of the three lines on the right (above) is the same as the left line, then the answer is obvious. But if we ask a group of

---

[12]Rosenzweig (2009).
[13]James Surowiecki's book *The Wisdom of Crowds* is an interesting read on this subject, which confirms that diverse groups are more successful than isolated individuals.
[14]Eisenberger *et al.* (2003).
[15]Montier (2009).

at least three people and the other three people who are taking part in the research don't know the subject who is participating in the test, and they respond incorrectly, then the subject will respond in line with the majority on a third of occasions! And if there are various rounds, in at least one of the rounds, three-quarters of us will go with the majority view!

When we buy stock that nobody wants or a group of shares with a low P/E ratio, we are forcing ourselves to do something that feels counterintuitive. We might fully agree on the need to buy cheap stock, convinced that the strategy works, but when we hear the names of the companies we suddenly feel extremely giddy, and we grasp at a thousand excuses not to buy. Nobody is buying them and it's almost painful to do so ...

A way to get around this is by committing to act upfront, applying the same approach as to overcoming our aversion to losing money (with the obvious drawback that we can always back out of it, meaning this strategy won't work). As previously mentioned, it's almost a semi-automatic reflex action for us to always sell when a stock goes up in price and buy when it falls. We look at the cause of the movement and if we think it's exaggerated, as is often the case, we act. When we sell on the rise, we sometimes refer to it as being fooled by randomness – in reference to Nassim Nicholas Taleb and his book *Fooled by Randomness*[16] – because who knows whether we have just hit a lucky break and, as such, the simple fact of a rising price reduces the chances of this continuing. Who knows whether what we are attributing to skill is no more than chance? As Taleb observes, we tend to confuse judgement with luck. A possible solution to this is to assume that luck always plays a part in our success, spurring us to automatically act before it runs out.

A SURPRISING EXAMPLE OF 'HERD' MENTALITY

Climate change is an unavoidable example of 'herd' mentality. The information on offer to us focuses on the negative aspects and distorts reality, creating a mainstream public opinion which drags us along like a strong tide. A healthy dose of scepticism is needed to avoid being pulled under.

I have no interest whatsoever in advocating one thesis over the other: either that mankind is seriously affecting the planet's climate and it is therefore imperative for us to take measures to reduce this impact;

---

[16]Taleb (2007).

or that the impact is small within the context of multiple causes and even if it were to be larger, the costs of acting outweigh the benefits. I am solely interested in understanding what is really going on and how it can be explained. I have invested in CO_2-emitting companies, companies which don't emit, and some which benefit from the war on CO_2, and it appears as though what I regularly hear from the media, which forms public opinion, is not the full story...

If we look at what has happened over the last 20 years, since 1996, global CO_2 emissions have increased from 24 billion tonnes a year to 37 billion, representing a 54% increase, the largest rise in absolute terms in the history of humanity for a 20-year period.

Pollution rises despite accords...

Global carbon emissions
(billion tonnes of CO_2)

Source: *Financial Times*.

If there is indeed a direct causal relationship between emissions and global temperature increases, then a period of 20 years would seem sufficient from a statistical perspective to establish causality. However, if we look at the temperature chart below, calculated by NASA for the low atmosphere (less liable to distortions than land calculations), global temperatures have remained practically unchanged over the period (this might be a misleading perspective, but at least it looks this way from analysing the chart), except during two episodes known as 'El Niño' in 1998 and 2016.

(continued)

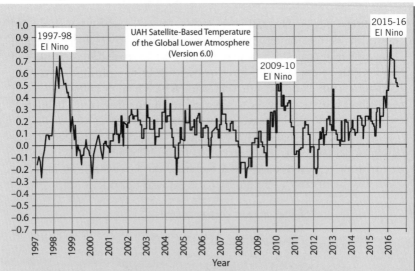

Difference in temperature relative to the 1981–2010 average (°C)
Source: Roy Spencer, satellite temperature of the inner atmosphere.

This may change in the coming years – one way or another – clarifying the relationship between cause and effect, but for now I can't see how it's possible to establish a direct causal relationship between CO_2 and global temperature using this data.

It seems clear that CO2 emissions in the last 20 years are not affecting the planet's temperature. I don't understand what interests are behind the lack of public discussion on this, taking account of other possible causes of temperature variations (such as the intensity of solar radiation). I find it completely unfathomable how the media is not leading sceptical opinion on climate change, nor even reporting the data correctly, nor why scientists are not raising questions given the data.

I guess there are already too many established interests to see through it. It's an inconvenient truth.

In the meantime, a healthy dose of scepticism will enable us to plot a different course from the beaten track, which will bear fruit once somebody eventually sounds the alarm that: 'The Emperor is naked!' An attitude of scepticism, not necessarily cynicism, is the best approach to dealing with the daily news flow, and we shouldn't lose sight of this however much we may appear to be on our own.

The third factor is the point of reference. We have a tendency to immediately take the current price as our point of reference. If Telefónica is trading at 12 euros, we find it hard to think that it's worth 30 or five euros. This is a very common error among stock market analysts, who find it impossible to analyse Telefónica and reach a conclusion that while trading at 12 its intrinsic value is 20 euros. They will normally say 13.5 or 10 euros, because it's difficult to distance oneself from the current reference point (12 euros in this case).

Funnily enough, this seemingly illogical conduct contains elements of both the emotional system, 1, and the rational system, 2.[17] We are indeed able to make a clear and conscious attempt to break from the reference point, but it continues to hold some sway over the result. Some investors get around the problem by first doing the analysis and valuation before then looking at the price. This makes it easier to avoid reference points.

These three traits – extrapolating, herd mentality, and reference points – get in the way of following proven investment strategies or buying stock when they are cheap. Once again the solution to mitigating problems which emerge from emotional baggage when making decisions is to be aware of the problem, knowing it can help to have in-depth understanding of the underlying reality – in this case financial – as well as implementing reflex or semi-automatic investment systems which improve our investment process.

But that's not the end of our problems, our mind can still play tricks on us. Other illogical behaviour can also hamper our ability to take decisions.

Sometimes we are caught in the trap of making rapid decisions on the basis of little evidence, overlooking the need for deeper analysis. As Kahneman[18] explains, we are more attracted to a good, coherent story – or even the most recent one – than the full picture. The automatic emotional system comes to the fore.

The problem can be exacerbated further when we fall into the grips of an excess of confidence after an initial success in our endeavour or investment. This success drives us to double down, losing everything in the end. This is the biggest danger for the enthusiast investor, who gets carried away by gains during a bull market. This bull market is confused with a capacity or ability to invest, leading us to excessively increase the risk of our investments. This is not to deny that non-professionals can't be successful in investing, but it's worth being especially careful in the confusion created by a market with the wind in its sails.

---

[17]Kahneman (2011, p. 120).
[18]Kahneman (2011, p. 87).

It's extremely dangerous to think that we are more capable than our competitors and we are going to get it right all the time. Dangerous but all too common. We must fight to remain within our small circle of competence, as Buffett says. It's a small circle and we have to be conscious of just how small it is. We can gradually build it up over time, but there will always be a line we shouldn't cross.

A particularly disastrous illusion of control arises when we think that we can predict something: the economic or market outlook, or certain short-term market prices. I have already been pretty clear on this point, but it bears repeating that these things cannot be forecast. The best we can manage are some vague long-term estimates, which is distinct from forecasting, making investment decisions on this basis.

We invent the budgets for our company (I expect most readers can identify with this): we don't know how the markets are going to perform, nor what client inflows and outflows will look like, which are all crucial for determining income. Fortunately, expenses are somewhat easier to control, but they're not the key factor in our business. As a result, it's completely impossible to estimate the company's future results.

But what we do know is that we have a good management process in place and that income and profits will naturally follow. We don't set specific sales or profit targets to reach. This isn't applicable to all businesses, but I have already mentioned how the anxiety to meet objectives is one of the biggest errors in today's companies, since it can lead to myopic short-term decision-making. While sometimes targets can be a necessity, we prefer companies that don't have such targets and simply strive to do things well.

This relates to the delusion of thinking that we can explain what took place and that we know it was going to happen. We humans have a very strong tendency to change our understanding of the facts as they develop. If there's a strong fall, we will acknowledge that it was obvious and we'll forget that we had previously thought differently, and this applies across the board.

The somewhat contradictory tendency is to think that whatever's successful is well done. When a stock in our portfolio rises, we think that our analysis has been spot on, even though this increase may have been completely random. In fact, the result itself is not what matters, but rather that it's been accompanied by the right process. If the process is right and we can differentiate it from luck, then we will be able to replicate the success without making unnecessary errors.

Truthfully, the solution to problems generated be overconfidence is to be constantly humble, respecting our circle of competence. It's not usually very large, but this need not be a problem; size is not the key, what matters is respecting it and not venturing outside it.

THE ENDOWMENT EFFECT

Another important and very common problem arises from the special attachment that we have to our possessions, everything that we consider to be ours. We give extra value to an object if we already possess it and we struggle to separate ourselves from it. This becomes more of an issue when it concerns an investment error, since our attachment makes it hard to recognise the error and sell the stock, which probably requires us to accept some losses. I think it's the most frequent error that we have made as investors: Flag Telecom, Portugal Telecom, etc.

An example which is very close to home is Pescanova. At one point we had a very significant holding in this company in our Iberian portfolio, of 4%. Pescanova had a superb position in a growing sector, enjoying some barriers to entry, but every year debt went up and there were no clear signs of cash flow generation or treasury. We had a certain feeling that something was amiss, which is why we gradually unwound our position to 1.5% of the portfolio.

But we weren't able to go below 1.5%. The prices had dropped but we had a mental barrier which prevented us from fully offloading the stock, given the attachment you can build towards an investment. The logical thing would have been to completely sell the position and, clearly, we would have never bought in if we had needed to build a position from scratch at that time, but we were unable to let it go.

Furthermore, there was an added complication because when our investments are losing value, it tends to be a time for great opportunities. If an investment was attractive at a higher price, then it's going to be even more so at 20% lower prices. In such situations, being able to distinguish between strengthening a position, sitting tight, or selling can be one of the most challenging and important decisions we have to make. Our natural tendency is to increase the position, without pausing to think that there might be some major change affecting the investment outlook, with the risk of making an error.

And, in reality, facing up to an error is one of the hardest things for us to do. My experience tells me that the investment in terms of time, resources, and pride makes this one of the most difficult situations in which to do the right thing. You are always inclined to think that they are temporary problems which will resolve themselves. The 'sunk costs of the decision' are what makes it hard to change over time. There might also be some other factors at play, such as the desire to get something out of the weeks spent analysing the company, capitalising on it in some way, despite not being very clear on the specifics.

The way to mitigate the damage is relatively straightforward: we need to take the decision as if we didn't own any shares, as if it were the first time we were making a decision on the particular stock, forgetting about our current positon – would I buy shares if I began the analysis now? The solution is straightforward; the difficulty lies in cutting our losses, with all the corresponding implications.

The positive side of this endowment effect is that it skews us to what we know, and this is no bad thing during times when too many changes are made in search of new ideas. We know full well that limiting movements is a wise decision over the long term: better the devil you know ...

TENDENCY TO CONFIRM WHAT WE ALREADY KNOW

Another danger that constantly stalks us is the tendency to look for evidence that supports our beliefs, avoiding conflicting opinions. It's an innate and almost automatic tendency which our emotional system uses to save time and energy. This can be beneficial when we're supporting our favourite football team or our political party (who we treat like a football team since they can't make errors), but it doesn't make sense when we want to make a rational decision (I don't know if voting is always very rational).

It's true that our beliefs can be very well founded and right (to boot!), which means it doesn't make much sense losing time paying attention to anything that has limited potential to contribute. But, either way, to avoid the danger of isolating ourselves in a bubble, the best solution is to listen to both sides of the debate, the arguments for buying and selling. We can even try to 'intellectually demolish' a company that appeals to us, to see if there is any substance to the arguments against. If we listen to conflicting opinions on a good investment we have found, we will at least be forewarned of where our competitive advantage lies when making the decision to invest.

THE INSTITUTIONS

Evidently, institutions and professionals suffer the same problem as any other investor, exacerbated by the fact that the committees overseeing investments seldom function very effectively.

A report by Bradley Jones of the International Monetary Fund,[19] which analyses the behaviour of large-scale investors – endowments, sovereign funds, central banks, large pension funds – highlights the strong positive correlation that exists between the recent results obtained by an asset and investment decisions to buy what goes up in value. This correlation holds across all asset types, whether bonds, equities, or anything else. This might seem surprising given that the people responsible for managing these institutions are supposedly highly qualified and are meant to have a long-term perspective, but it is nonetheless the case.

The competitive pressures caused by the expectations of bosses, colleagues, and clients generate anxiety and an excessive focus on the short term. And this is even true for successful professionals. Such pressure generates fear of losing money, or even one's job.[20]

Many asset managers weave 'stories' to convince themselves and their clients and superiors, both regarding their investment philosophy as well as specific investments. These stories make it difficult to learn from errors, since they are rationalised in order to confirm the path that has been taken. Others try to lay the blame at the door of the companies they invest in – despite having claimed to be able to correctly evaluate them – or the brokers who

---

[19]Jones (2015).
[20]Tuckett and Taffler (2012, p. 29).

have helped in the decision, without taking their own responsibility. No one faces up to their own mistakes.

Perhaps the best approach is to have a frank and healthy relationship with oneself, ones clients and bosses: investing time in educating them and not yielding to their pressure.

Furthermore, in investment committees, group thinking (group feeling as Tuckett calls it) also comes into play, which increases our dependency on others – with a strong tendency to conform to the group and avoid confrontation. James Surowiecki, in his book *The Wisdom of Crowds*,[21] explains how group decisions prove to be right more often than individual decisions, but this only applies to decisions made by groups formed of different profiles, who are willing to voice their opinions. If this is not the case, we face the risk of group thinking.

Apart from attempting to incorporate a diverse range of views within the group, one way to reduce the risk is for each committee member to write down their opinion before anyone speaks. An alternative is to set incentives based on group results, which is the system that we have always applied.

Another inherent problem is the penchant for wanting to act, to do something, or to appear as though we're doing something, despite the fact that the best thing may well be doing nothing, letting the established strategy run its course. This happens more frequently in institutions, because the professionals who manage them are paid according to their results, and when they aren't up to scratch, they have the urge to explain that they have already taken steps to correct the problem by doing something.

INFORMATION OVERLOAD AND OTHER PROBLEMS

The amount of information we are exposed to has increased exponentially over time. When I started working in 1990 we had to write to companies so they would send us their annual reports, or physically go to the paper records at the CNMV, in order to be able to analyse their results. Nowadays we have all of this information on our computer or mobile at the touch of a button.

Although this might seem like an advantage, it can lead to us being exposed to an overdose of data and opinions that we don't need. Determining what's important isn't easy, but broadly speaking there are a few ways to separate the wheat from the chaff. 90% of the information that we receive on a daily basis from the media, for example, is background noise.

---

[21]Surowiecki (2005).

That's why I recommend limiting our exposure to it as much as possible; as already mentioned, I haven't been regularly watching the television news or reading the general press for some 15 years now. It's enough to read a bit of economics and specialist news.

By the same token, while the Internet offers us an infinite array of information, it's also a source of infinite distraction. A few years back Nicholas Carr explained in his book *The Shallows*[22] that it is incredibly difficult for us to concentrate when reading information online because we are continually being interrupted by distractions, limiting our ability to concentrate, which weakens over time. It's therefore vital to find peaceful moments to read and think, if necessary, physically secluding ourselves.

Moreover, I can't emphasise enough how overwhelmed I am by the negative slant on all the information we receive. Nobody could care less about a family calmly going about its evening meal. This leads us to constantly have a distorted view of the world. For example, in the last 25 years global growth has ticked along at 3–4% per year, with more than one billion people coming out of poverty; similarly, as Steven Pinker points out, violence is at its lowest level since mankind came out of the jungle, but nobody would believe this based on the information beamed to us on a daily basis.[23]

Matt Ridley[24] provides a plausible explanation for this negativity, related to an evolving perspective of reality: all the many good things that have happened over the course of our evolution – economic growth, increasing life expectancy, reforestation in the developed world, reduction in inequality, practical elimination of hunger, etc. – haven't been planned by anyone; we have built them together, slowly but without stopping. This is apparently of absolutely no interest. We only want to know about wars, revolutions, homicides, etc., events which normally have much clearer protagonists than more positive developments.

Such negativity is just another way of expressing our aversion to risk, and is also an inherent part of our nature, since it has produced good results as we have evolved. In marital relationships, for example, doing something bad can only be compensated by doing five good deeds, or when we analyse somebody's character, a murder is only compensated by 25 heroic feats.[25] The media make the most of the impact that this negativity has on our emotions to vie for our attention.

When facing information overload, in countless situations it has been proven that better decisions are made with less information, since in reality

---

[22]Carr (2010).
[23]Pinker (2012).
[24]Ridley (2015).
[25]William Heinemann, cited in Haidt (2006, chap. 2).

we are making the same error as when we are looking at market movements too frequently, which drives us to act when we shouldn't.

Nonetheless, as before, there are approaches which can help improve results in the face of excessive information. One option would be to stick to the same framework for reading (when reading something new, we have to leave what we were previously reading, so as to discourage ourselves from flitting around) or to only make active searches (inspired by our own ideas), avoiding the excessive influence of social networks or other supposed aides.

Taking decisions with small samples, without a suitable statistical calculation, is a problem that we have already cited. Confusing the anecdote with evidence is natural and commonplace, but it still remains a source of rash errors. More in-depth study is required to avoid falling into this type of error.

CONCLUSION

There can be no doubt that our emotional side makes it difficult for us to make the right investment decisions (as in all aspects of life). Overcoming this requires us to make an effort to better understand our flaws and correct them. It's not enough to perform a good competitive and financial analysis, something more is required. Summarising the key points described in this chapter, we can conclude that a proper investment decision should fulfil the following steps:

1. Recognising that there is a problem: sometimes emotions lead us to take unreasonable decisions to achieve our desired goals and it's important to confront them.
2. Analysing the content of the emotional shortcomings which we bring to decision-making. Proposing measures to take.
3. Deepening our knowledge of the investment process through the experiences of other investors.
4. Establishing simple and almost automatic mechanisms in this investment approach to minimise our emotional bias. An additional example which I have already mentioned tangentially, and which I use personally, is investing in funds the same day I have money available, doing so automatically and without thinking about what the market is going to do next.
5. Analysing where we add value compared with other investors before taking a final investment decision. Normally it's not about being more intelligent, but has more to do with having a better understanding of ourselves, which translates into virtues such as patience and, in general, emotional resilience.

Our emotions are the main hindrance to obtaining good results from our investments. This is why it's important to dedicate the necessary time to understanding our weaknesses. Otherwise, there's no point investing since the results will be mediocre.

But there are reasons for optimism: we can learn from our errors. I did so with Nissan and subsequent errors, and we can learn to overcome our shortcomings. I know of countless people who, equipped with the right knowledge and following the example of other investors, have learnt to tolerate market movements and take the right approach to investing.

On this basis, and to finish, we can now sketch out some of the attributes of an ideal investor: somebody who is patient, invests over the long term, enjoying the journey and focusing less on the results, who doesn't get carried away by emotions, with strong convictions but willing to learn. None of us will ever fully become this investor, but it's worth making a continual effort to try and get as close as we can ...

Conclusions and Future

Developing a sound investment process is a personal challenge. My approach has been to look to the best investors in the world, the true masters. I have chosen and studied them with great care; reading and listening to them and trying to glean all I can from them. This is how I have gone about developing my own approach, which is the great 'secret'. This approach has been refined by the experience of day-to-day life, which has helped it to take shape. This is how you develop firm and coherent beliefs, which enable you to be courageous and turn your back on the herd; being patient and accepting uncertainty and, ultimately, keeping your head when all about you are losing theirs.

Armed with an appropriate intellectual framework and having developed the necessary personality traits for a sound investment process, we can attain our goal of preserving and increasing the purchasing power of our savings.

The Austrian School of Economics provides us with such an intellectual framework, offering an accurate description of reality which provides us with a solid foundation for analysing economic developments. It's an economic analysis that won't predict a country's economic growth or consumer behaviour, but will give us a basis for distinguishing the implications of market interventions and prepare us for dealing with them.

The markets work reasonably well since they represent no more than exchanges between individuals acting freely. Some market participant or another will always recognise when there is disorder in the market and, through their actions, address it.

This provides us with the basis for approaching the investment process, which is all about finding value where others won't or can't see it.

Real assets, particularly shares in listed companies, are the best at maintaining the purchasing power of our savings over the long term. The stock market is not the realm of speculators, as I used to think when I was young. Instead, it's a place where all mankind's virtues and miseries play out together – our true selves – and where, thanks to the analysis provided by behavioural science, we can find the irrational (or emotional) side of human beings, enabling us to obtain returns that give us peace of mind and independence in the future.

Indeed, the focus of our analysis is mankind itself. The businesses that we analyse are created and developed by people, who sell their products and services to other people. We're not analysing strange beings or mythical or legendary markets, we are analysing people.

Some people manage to create and develop exceptional businesses, which are difficult to reproduce. Others are unmitigated failures. The former are of more interest to us for potential investment, especially when circumstances mean they can be acquired at accessible prices. These are the businesses that should be the focus of our time; analysing their competitive position and resilience to future developments.

Doing so requires us to have a strong hold over our most primordial emotional urges. We have to be patient, inquisitive, modest, and bold. Patient because it may take some time for others to wake up to what we are seeing, which is why it is necessary to have a long-term perspective. Inquisitive because we have to be attentive to everything that's going on around us. Modest because errors are common but the key thing is to draw the right conclusions from them. Bold because sometimes we will appear like a suicide driver, travelling in the opposite direction to the flow of traffic.

And consistent. Step by step, day by day, like preparing for an ongoing exam which obliges us to be locked in ceaseless study of a continually expanding and shifting subject matter.

ASSET MANAGEMENT

Asset management is shifting towards passive management, buying into an index at low cost and following the markets. Few active asset managers obtain better results than the index and, in the main, most don't deserve the extra fees they charge.

The development of 'passive' modes of investing will create some very exciting opportunities for those of us who believe the market isn't always efficient. I repeat, not *always*. The market tends towards efficiency, but is incapable of always being efficient.

It's affected by constantly shifting consumer tastes and technological innovations which offer us previously inconceivable products and services. This makes it hard to reach a point of full efficiency: the market is always trying, moving in that direction, but it never gets there.

We mustn't forget that the market is made up of people continually making decisions about how to act, and we have seen that these decisions can be absurd, illogical, or simply poorly informed. People make errors; investors are human too, and just as capable of making them.

Therefore, we will always be able to capitalise on opportunities and the development of passive management means a bigger part of the market will be essentially 'brainless', buying by default what everyone else is buying. 'Herd' behaviour just became official. As frequently happens, something that makes sense for an individual to do lacks logic when generalised. The more weight passive management gains in total management, the more opportunities there will be for active managers. And we'll be there aiming to make the most of them.

Stripping this whole story to the bones, there are essentially two ways to take advantage of the markets – one difficult and one easy.

1. The difficult way involves predicting volatility and short or medium-term market movements. We have seen that this is practically impossible in the short term, although it is conceivable to develop some feeling for the long-term trajectory of certain economic factors. An example was Spain's credit and housing market bubble. These long-term predictions require us to acquire a deep insight into economic processes and we can work on improving our knowledge, but ultimately it will seldom be of real use and the chances of success are limited.
2. The easy option involves making the most of volatility. This is quite a lot more attainable for any investor, since it comes down to developing the right personality attributes to capitalise on market movements: pushing the boat out when others are fearful and reining it in when others are being greedy. And, above all, being patient.

The second path ought to be the main approach, with a dash of the first when possible. We will never know how the markets are going to perform, but we must know how to react when the market behaves in a certain way.

MY OWN FUTURE

From time to time one of my children will ask me exactly what it is that I do. My profession isn't very clear to them, since the only thing they see me doing is reading and little else. We rarely ever discuss the issue at home, but when we do I tell them that I am responsible for looking after the savings of people who trust in us, so they can enjoy peace of mind in this area of their lives. I tell them it's a very gratifying job.

Sometimes I am asked in one of our conferences, or personally: How much longer are you going to keep working? Won't you tire of all this? They are fair questions, since we've saved enough to no longer have to work.

However, there's a simple response, as already mentioned. How is it that I'm going to stop 'working' when:

- The work is stimulating and varied, I do it reasonably well, it fits my personality, and it enables me to satisfy an element of temerity that all of us have (or at least I do), with measurable and objective results.
- You are providing clients with a service that they struggle to find elsewhere and which is therefore valued by them. They value it because the returns come with a degree of trust and composure, which enables them to feel that they have this part of their life under control. For me, this pushes it beyond mere work.
- It's valued by clients and therefore extremely well paid, which reinforces the most precious thing that money can buy – one's independence.
- It fulfils a social role, like all companies and people who generate profits.

    It is worth remembering that it's important to offer a service to society using the fewest resources possible; the more profit the better, since either we will be offering a highly valuable service or using very few resources, or a combination of the two.

    When the competition comes alive to these profits, they will do everything in their power to bring them down to normal levels.

    Another 'social' function is increasing market liquidity, acting as a counterparty: we buy what nobody else wants and sell what everyone is after. This liquidity not only facilitates greater price stability, but it also actually supports the process of financing investment, which is key to improving everyone's living conditions.

- With the profits that we gain, we can help other organisations or people who are struggling to achieve their objectives, who our conscience obliges us to help, and who lack the resources to do so.

Furthermore, as previously discussed, I already have a sense of duty to my family, friends, acquaintances, and strangers who have put their trust in what we do. I believe that life needs to have some meaning to it beyond the immediate, and for me this meaning comes from doing a good job, providing peace of mind to people around me with regard to their savings, and using the profits I earn to support those who might be in need.

Moreover, during the most exhilarating moments – when you sense that a very promising investment is within your grasp and that you alone have the right personality type to go for it – a sense of flow descends upon me, time and space melt away; I am convinced that I will keep doing it for a long time to come. At least until I feel the need to write a second book.

26 Small Ideas and One Guiding Principle

1. If you want to know about economics, learn German and study the Austrian masters.
2. We should only worry about the economic environment if we have a clear idea of how it might affect the market. Such clairvoyance might come to us once every five years, at most.
3. Own assets, don't be a creditor. Loans are promises to pay which sometimes are blowin' in the wind.
4. Invest in what you know. The amount isn't what matters, the crucial thing is knowing your limits, even if it's your local housing market.
5. Nobody has to invest in anything. Often it's best to do nothing.
6. If you don't know what to do, invest in indexes. If you are completely bewildered, invest in a cheap global index fund and be done with it.
7. Own shares, using any of the vehicles on offer.
8. If you invest directly in stocks, you need to spend time analysing the competitive position of the company you want to invest in. The rest is market noise, to be avoided at all costs.
9. It's about studying companies, not the stock market. Buying a share should be like buying the whole company. If we are not up for buying the whole company, we're not ready to buy a single share.
10. Businesses with a long track record have more chance of surviving than new ones. Focusing on them will save us a lot of problems.
11. Make sure that the business is more or less capable of sustaining the same position over the next 10 years. If you're not sure or think new technologies or new consumer trends could affect its market position, better let it go.
12. If a company is creating value each year and improving its results, don't worry why the market hasn't cottoned on to it. It's another opportunity to keep investing at a good price.

13. The lower the price of a well-researched stock, the greater potential upside on the investment and the less risk involved. The reverse of economic theory is true: the higher the potential return, the lower the risk.

14. Acquaint yourself with the past, but be careful about extrapolating. Things change and future problems can emerge from the least expected places.

15. Speculators and volatility are dear friends: the more, the better our long-term results will be.

16. Lack of liquidity is also an ally. Other investors pay too much for liquidity.

17. Understanding what motivates others to act and how they do it, and our own rationale for what we do, is the essence of prudent and successful investment.

18. If we don't have the right personality for investing, it's better not to get involved. Alternatively, work on it. It's not easy but, with the right guidance, it's possible to improve our attitude towards investing.

19. It's important to have firm beliefs (preferably the right ones!), but we must remain open to new ideas and ways of doing things. When we stop learning, we have one foot in the grave.

20. Investing in listed shares involves the greatest information asymmetry possible between buyer and seller. In the private market the seller knows how much the asset is worth (all homeowners know how much their house is worth). With listed shares, small investors spend too little time on analysis and institutional investors are subject to the restrictions of their institution.

21. Getting it right is not only about foreseeing what a company will do; more importantly, it's about knowing how to distinguish between what the market thinks will happen and what will really happen.

22. Take the less trodden path. Buy what nobody else is buying. In the words of the Italian songwriter Fabrizio de André: be headstrong and go against the grain!

23. Enjoy the process. The journey is more interesting than the final destination.

24. Think. Don't build models.

25. Read.

26. Cheer up. It's much better to have been born in 2016 than in 1963.

Guiding Principle: Invest all the savings that you don't need for the immediate future in shares.

Reading Material and Wealth Creation

It is disheartening to peruse the shelves of the average bookshop, even those that are specialised in economics. Most books favour interventionist approaches, which is surprising since, during the twenty-first century, a large part of the planet's population has left – and is continuing to leave – poverty behind, with more people enjoying a decent life than at any point in history, thanks to the widespread market formed of all of us making decisions.

It is difficult to explain such negativity in the face of such an obvious reality, although we might find an explanation in von Mises' arguments on intellectuality. However, I think we should focus on explaining what's before our very eyes. The sun rises in the morning and sets in the evening, and the improvement in our living standards is due to mankind's own ingenuity: engineers and innovators, those who uncover them, and those who finance their endeavours with their savings.

This increase in living standards is definitely not attributable to the businessmen who lurk in the shadows of political power in order to maintain privileged market positions. Nor have living standards improved as a result of trade unions, whose struggles look after the well-being of their own. If this were true, we could raise living standards by creating such organisations in countries like Zimbabwe or Haiti.

Living standards have increased due to the efforts of people whose innovations have contributed to improving the productivity of our work and endeavours, supported by savers who have sacrificed present consumption of material goods in order for these projects to enjoy future success. In sum, living standards have improved because the accumulation of all forms of capital increases the value of labour: the more capital that's created, the less value it has and the more valuable the work that uses the capital.

That is why in places where there is more capital – think Switzerland – workers have higher salaries and higher standards of living. If wages could be decreed by law, or raised under the influence of trade unions, any undeveloped country would do so immediately. Let's increase wages from 100 dollars a month to 500. Or, as some people argue in certain developed countries, let's put up the minimum wage to 15 euros an hour. Why stop there? Why not 25 or 50 euros?

This isn't possible without having accumulated capital, and it's this capital which makes such increases possible, as has always been the case. And capital does so reluctantly, since it always prefers to remunerate work as little as possible, but the momentum of events causes this to happen: with greater capital accumulation, there is no other option but to pay higher relative wages.

Therefore, we should all be fighting for the greatest amount of capital accumulation possible: firstly, to spur technological developments, which help improve everyone's living conditions and help protect us from the dangers that stalk the planet (meteorites, destructive viruses, climate change, etc.) and secondly, to improve the absolute and relative positions of workers compared to capital.

Perversely, limiting capital accumulation will lead to the impoverishment of the labour factor, which will lose value relative to the scarcer capital factor.

We should all stress this point, which is as self-evident as it is simple, and as optimistic as it is sincere. We mustn't allow intellectuals to distort reality from the side lines.

The following references and further reading list not only include experts on a range of different issues, but also various thinkers who have railed against interventionism. Carefully absorbing what these texts have to say will enable the reader to grasp the subtleties of economic development from a perspective that provides an accurate portrayal of our planet and the human beings that inhabit it. It's a realistic, albeit somewhat utopian vision, seeing as it doesn't correspond to mainstream interventionist thinking (don't forget that public spending in developed economies is now up to around 50% of GDP).

These texts have helped me be able to enter into bookshops or read the press with a critical spirit, which has saved me from many an upset and freed up my time to spend on more interesting reading.

Finally, the books I am particularly fond of in relation to the investment process are marked in bold. Some have had a direct influence on the process while others have influenced me more indirectly, clarifying my view of reality. My sincere thanks to all the authors.

References

Acemoglu, D. and Robinson, J., *Why Nations Fail*, Random House, New York, 2012.

Ariely, D., *Predictably Irrational*, HarperCollins, London, 2009.

Asness, C., Frazzini, A., Israel, N. and Moskowitz, T., 'Fact, fictions and value investing', *Journal of Portfolio Management*, 42(1), 2015, DOI: 10.2139/ssrn.2595747.

Bagus, P., 'Five common errors about deflation', *Market Processes*, III(1), 2006, 105–123.

Benartzi, S. and Thaler, R., *Myopic Loss Aversion and the Equity Premium Puzzle*, National Bureau of Economic Research, 1993.

Bogle, J., *Common Sense on Mutual Funds*, John Wiley & Sons, Hoboken, NJ, 2009.

Bosset, P., *Investment Companies. Look Beyond the Discount to NAV*, HSBC, December 2015.

Bregolat, E., *The Second Chinese Revolution*, Ediciones Destino, Barcelona, 2007.

Bryan, A. and Li, J., *Performance Persistence Among U.S. Mutual Funds*, Morningstar Manager Research, 2016.

Buffett, W., 'The superinvestors of Graham-and-Dodsville', *Hermes, Magazine of the Columbia Business School*, 1984.

Carr, N., *The Shallows*, W.W. Norton and Co., New York, 2010.

Credit Suisse, *Family Firms, an Opportunity for Minority Investors?*, July 2015.

De Bondt, W. and Thaler, R., 'Does the stock market overreact?', *Journal of Finance*, 40, 1985, 793–805.

Dimson, E., Marsh, P. and Staunton, M., *Equity Premiums Around the World*, CFA Institute Research Foundation, 2011.

Duckworth, A., *Grit. The Power of Passion and Perseverance*, Vermilion, London, 2016.

Eisenberger, N. I., Lieberman, M. D. and Williams, K. D., 'Does rejection hurt? An fMRI study of social exclusion', *Science*, 2003.

Fama, E. and French, K., 'The cross-section of expected stock returns', *Journal of Finance*, 47, 1992, 427–466.

Fernández, P., 'CAPM, an absurd model', *Business Valuation Review*, 34(1), 2015, 4–23.

Fernández, P., *Valuation and Common Sense*, IESE, Madrid, 2017.

Fernández, P. et al., *Profitability of Investment Funds in Spain, 2000–2015*, IESE, 2016.

Fisher, P. A., *Common Stocks and Uncommon Profits*, John Wiley & Sons, Hoboken, NJ, 1996a.

275

Fisher, P. A., *Conservative Investors Sleep Well*, John Wiley & Sons, Hoboken, NJ, 1996b.

Fraser-Jenkins, I. *et al.*, 'The state of fund management: Quants have destroyed the active–passive distinction', *Bernstein Research*, 9 November 2015, pp. 21–28.

Gawande, A., *Being Mortal*, Metropolitan Books, New York, 2014.

Graham, B., *Security Analysis* (5th edn), McGraw-Hill, New York, 1988.

Graham, B., *The Intelligent Investor* (4th edn), Harper & Row, New York, 2009.

Grant, J., *The Forgotten Depression. 1921: The Crash That Cured Itself*, Simon & Schuster, New York, 2014.

Greenblatt, J., *The Little Book That Beats the Market*, John Wiley & Sons, Hoboken, NJ, 2006.

Greenwald, B. and Kahn, J., *Competition Demystified*, Penguin, Harmondsworth, 2005.

Guerra, A. L., 'Performance of actions in inflationary contexts: Empirical analysis of the Argentine stock market', Rosario Stock Exchange, 2012.

Haidt, J., *The Happiness Hypothesis*, Random House, London, 2006.

Hayek, F. A., *The Road to Serfdom*, University of Chicago Press, Chicago, IL, 1994a.

Hayek, F. A., *Hayek on Hayek*, University of Chicago Press, Chicago, IL, 1994b.

Hayek, F. A., *The Fatal Conceit*, Routledge, London, 1998.

Hendrikse, H. C., *Will BMW Celebrate the Centenary?*, Morgan Stanley, March 2016.

Hessler, P., *Country Driving*, HarperCollins, New York, 2010.

Higgs, R., *Depression, War and Cold War: Studies in Political Economy*, The Independent Institute, Oakland, CA, 2006.

Hoppe, H.-H., *Democracy, the God that Failed*, Transaction Publishers, Piscataway, NJ, 2011.

J. Huerta de, Soto., *Money, Bank Credit and Economic Cycles*, Ludwig von Mises Institute, Auburn, AL, 2006.

J. Huerta de, Soto., *The Austrian School*, Edward Elgar, Cheltenham, 2008.

Jones, B., *Asset Bubbles: Re-thinking Policy for the Age of Asset Management*, IMF, February 2015.

Jungbluth, R., *Die Quandts*, Campus Verlag, Frankfurt, 2007.

Kahneman, D., *Thinking Fast and Slow*, Farrar, Straus and Giroux, New York, 2011.

Kahneman, D. and Tversky, A., 'Prospect theory: An analysis of decision making under risk', *Econometrica*, 47(2), 1979, 263–291.

Kahneman, D., Knetsch, J. L. and Thaler, R., 'Fairness as a constraint on profit seeking: Entitlements in the market', *American Economic Review*, 76, 1986, 728–742.

Laidler, B. *et al.*, *The Small Cap Handbook*, HSBC, February 2016.

Landes, D. S., *The Wealth and Poverty of Nations*, Abacus, London, 1999.

Lev, B. and Gu, F., *The End of Accounting*, John Wiley & Sons, Hoboken, NJ, 2016.

Lewis, M., *The Big Short*, Penguin, Harmondsworth, 2011.

Lynch, P., *One Up On Wall Street*, Simon & Schuster, New York, 1989.

McCloskey, D. N., *Bourgeois Equality*, University of Chicago Press, Chicago, IL, 2016.

Mehta, P. K. and Shenoy, S., *Infinite Vision*, Collins Business, London, 2011.

Menger, C., *Principles of Economics*, Ediciones Orbis, Barcelona, 1985.

Merino, J. B., 'Theory of exchange. Proposal of a new theory of interpersonal exchanges based in three simpler elements', *Market Processes*, XII(1), 2015.

Metcalfe, J. and Mischel, W., 'A hot/cool system analysis of delay gratification: Dynamics of willpower', *Psychological Review*, 106(1), 1999, 3–19.

Moncada, I. and Rallo, J. R., *Inequality in Spain*, Institute Juan de Mariana, Madrid, 2016.

Montier, J., *Value Investing*, John Wiley & Sons, Chichester, 2009.

Olbrich, M., Quill, T. and Rapp, D. J., 'Business valuation inspired by the Austrian School', *Journal of Business Valuation and Economic Loss Analysis*, 10(1), 2015, 1–43.

Olson, M., *The Logic of Collective Action*, Harvard University Press, Cambridge, MA, 2000.

O'Shaughnessy, J., *What Works on Wall Street* (4th edn), McGraw Hill, New York, 2012.

Pabrai, M., *The Dhandoo Investor*, John Wiley & Sons, Hoboken, NJ, 2007.

Pinker, S., *The Better Angels of Our Nature*, Penguin, Harmondsworth, 2012.

Rallo, J. R., *Los Errores de la Vieja Economía*, Unión Editorial, Madrid, 2011.

Reinhart, C. M. and Rogoff, K. S., *This Time is Different*, Princeton University Press, Princeton, NJ, 2009.

Reisman, G., *Capitalism*, Jameson, Ottawa, IL, 1996.

Ridley, M., *The Evolution of Everything*, Fourth Estate, London, 2015.

Ritter, J. R., 'Economic growth and equity returns', *Pacific-Basin Finance Journal*, 13, 2005, 489–503.

Rosenzweig, P., *The Halo Effect*, The Free Press, New York, 2009.

Rothbard, M. N., *History of Economic Thought* (Vols I and II), Unión Editorial, Madrid, 2000a.

Rothbard, M. N., *America's Great Depression* (5th edn), Ludwig von Mises Institute, Auburn, AL, 2000b.

Rothbard, M. N., *What Has Government Done To Our Money?*, Ludwig von Mises Institute, Auburn, AL, 2010.

Shefrin, H., *Beyond Greed and Fear*, Harvard Business School Press, Cambridge, MA, 2000.

Siegel, J. J., *Stocks for the Long Run* (5th edn), McGraw Hill, New York, 2014.

Simon, J. L., *The State of Humanity*, Blackwell, Malden, MA, 1998.

Skousen, M., 'Who predicted the 1929 crash?', in Herbener, J. M. (ed.), *The Meaning of Ludwig von Mises*, Kluwer Academic, Amsterdam, 1993.

Smith, A., *The Wealth of Nations*, Penguin, Harmondsworth, 1982.

Spitznagel, M, *The Dao of Investing*, John Wiley & Sons, Hoboken, NJ, 2013.

Stiglitz, J. E., Orszag, J. M. and Orszag, P. R., Implications of the New Fannie Mac and Freddy Mae Risk-based Capital Standard, *Fannie Mae Papers*, Vol. I, Issue 2, March 2002.

Surowiecki, J., *The Wisdom of Crowds*, Abacus, London, 2005.

Taghizadegan, R., Stöferle, R., Valek, M. and Blasnik, H., *Austrian School for Investors*, mises.at, 2015.

Taleb, N. N., *Fooled by Randomness*, Penguin, Harmondsworth, 2007.

Taleb, N. N., *Antifragile*, Random House, New York, 2012.

Tuckett, D. and Taffler, R. J., *Fund Management: An Emotional Finance Perspective*, Research Foundation of the CFA Institute, 2012.

Vishny, R. W., Lakonishok, J. and Schleifer, A., 'Contrarian investment, extrapolation and risk', *Journal of Finance*, 49(5), 1994, 1541–1578.

von Böhm-Bawerk, E., *Shorter Classics of Eugen von Böhm-Bawerk*, Vol. 1, Libertarian Press, Grove City, PA, 1962.

von Böhm-Bawerk, E., *The Positive Theory of Capital*, Ediciones Aosta, Madrid, 1998.

von Mises, L., *Theory and History*, Unión Editorial, Madrid, 1975.

von Mises, L., *Human Action* (5th edn), Unión Editorial, Madrid, 1995.

von Mises, L., *Socialism*, Ludwig von Mises Institute, Auburn, AL, 2006.

White, M. V. and Schuler, K., 'Who said "debauch the currency": Keynes or Lenin?', *Journal of Economic Perspectives*, 23(2), 2009, 213–222.

Woods, T. E., *Meltdown*, Regnery Publishing, Washington, D.C., 2009.

Further Reading

Adams, J., *Risk*, Routledge, London, 1995.

Anderson, B. M., *Economics and the Public Welfare*, Liberty Press, Indianapolis, IN, 1979.

Armentano, D. T., *Antitrust. The Case for Repeal*, Ludwig von Mises Institute, Auburn, AL, 2007.

Bastiat, F., *Economic Harmonies*, Instituto Juan de Mariana, Madrid, 2010.

Baumol, W. J., *The Free-Market Innovation Machine*, Princeton University Press, Princeton, NJ, 2002.

Bernstein, P. L., *Against the Gods. The Remarkable Story of Risk*, John Wiley & Sons, Hoboken, NJ, 1996.

Boldrin, M. and Levine, D. K., *Against Intellectual Monopoly*, Cambridge University Press, Cambridge, 2008.

Bresciani-Turroni, C., *The Economics of Inflation*, Routledge, London, 2003.

Brooks, J., *The Go-Go Years*, John Wiley & Sons, Hoboken, NJ, 1998.

Brooks, J., *Once in Golconda*, John Wiley & Sons, Hoboken, NJ, 1999.

Buffett, W., *Berkshire Hathaway: Letters to Shareholders* 1977–1983, 1984–1988, 1989–1995, 1995–2015.

Chang, J., *Wild Swans*, CIRCE, Barcelona, 2006.

Christensen, C. M. and Raynor, M. E., *The Innovator's Solution*, Harvard Business School Press, Cambridge, MA, 2003.

Clews, H., *Fifty Years in Wall Street*, John Wiley & Sons, Hoboken, NJ, 2006.

Cunningham, L. A., *Warren Buffett's Essays*, Valor Editions, Hendaye, 2015.

Dawkins, R., *The Selfish Gene*, Oxford University Press, Oxford, 1999.

Deci, E. L., *Why We Do What We Do*, Penguin, New York, 1996.

Diamond, J., *Guns, Germs and Steel: The Fates of Human Societies*, W.W. Norton & Co., New York, 1999.

Dorsey, P., *The Little Book That Builds Wealth*, John Wiley & Sons, Hoboken, NJ, 2008.

Epstein, G., 'The Fannie and Freddie Chronicles, cont.', *Barron's*, 7 January 2012.

Feynman, R. P., *Six Easy Pieces*, Penguin, London, 1998.

Frank, R. H., *Choosing the Right Pond*, Oxford University Press, Oxford, 1986.

Garrison, R. W., *Time and Money. The Macroeconomics of Capital Structure*, Routledge, London, 2002.

Gawande, A., *The Checklist Manifesto*, Metropolitan Books, New York, 2009.

Glaeser, E., *The Triumph of the City*, Penguin Press, New York, 2011.

Gordon, D., *The Essential Rothbard*, Ludwig von Mises Institute, Auburn, AL, 2007.

Greenspan, A., *The Age of Turbulence*, Penguin, New York, 2007.

Greenwald, B., Knee, J. A. and Seave, A., *The Curse of the Mogul*, Portfolio, Penguin, 2009.

Hagstrom, R. G., *The Warren Buffett Way*, John Wiley & Sons, Hoboken, NJ, 1994.

Hagstrom, R. G., *The Warren Buffett Portfolio*, John Wiley & Sons, Hoboken, NJ, 1999.

Hagstrom, R. G., *Latticework*, Texere LCC, New York, 2000.

Hayek, F. A., *The Foundations of Freedom* (6th edn), Unión Editorial, Madrid, 1998.

Hayek, F. A., *Law, Legislation and Freedom*, Unión Editorial, Madrid, 2006.

Hayek, F. A., Ashton, T. S., Hacker, L. M., de Jouvenel, B. and Hutt, W. H., *Capitalism and Historians*, Unión Editorial, Madrid, 1974.

Hazlitt, H., *The Inflation Crisis and How To Resolve It*, Ludwig von Mises Institute, Auburn, AL, 2009.

Hoppe, H.-H., *The Economics and Ethics of Private Property*, Ludwig von Mises Institute, Auburn, AL, 2006.

Huang, Y., *Capitalism with Chinese Characteristics*, Cambridge University Press, Cambridge, MA, 2008.

J. Huerta de Soto., *The Mystery of Capital: Why Capitalism Triumphs in the West and Fails Everywhere Else*, Basic Books, New York, 2000.

J. Huerta de Soto., *The Theory of Dynamic Efficiency*, Routledge, London, 2010.

Jay Nock, A., 'The criminality of the state', *The American Mercury*, March 1939.

Kindleberger, C., *Manias, Panics and Crashes*, John Wiley & Sons, Hoboken, NJ, 1996.

Klein, P. G., *The Capitalist and the Entrepreneur*, Ludwig von Mises Institute, Auburn, AL, 2010.

Kuan Yew, L., *From Third World to First: The Singapore Story: 1965–2000*, HarperCollins, New York, 2000.

Leoni, B., *Freedom and the Law*, Unión Editorial, Madrid, 1974.

Lev, B. and Gu, F., *Intangibles*, The Brookings Institution, Washington, D.C., 2001.

Lindsay, B., *Against the Dead Hand*, John Wiley & Sons, Hoboken, NJ, 2002.

Loomis, C. J., *Tap Dancing to Work*, Penguin, New York, 2012.

Lynch, P., *Beating the Street*, Simon & Schuster, New York, 1993.

Machlup, F., *The Stock Market, Credit and Capital Formation*, Ludwig von Mises Institute, Auburn, AL, 2007.

Mackay, C., *Extraordinary Popular Delusions and the Madness of the Crowd*, John Wiley & Sons, Hoboken, NJ, 1996.

Marmot, M., *Status Syndrome*, Bloomsbury, London, 2004.

McGregor, R., *The Party*, HarperCollins, New York, 2010.

Moon, Y., *Different*, Crown Business, New York, 2010.

Murray, C., *Coming Apart*, Crown Forum, New York, 2012.

Neff, J. and Mintz, S. L., *John Neff on Investing*, John Wiley & Sons, Hoboken, NJ, 1999.

O'Driscoll, G. P. and Rizzo, M. J., *The Economy of Time and Ignorance*, Unión Editorial, Madrid, 2009.

Pinker, S., *The Blank Slate: The Modern Denial of Human Nature*, Penguin Press, London, 2002.

Porter, M. E., *Competitive Strategy*, The Free Press, New York, 1980.

Porter, M. E., *The Competitive Advantage of Nations*, The Free Press, New York, 1990.

Poundstone, W., *Fortune's Formula*, Farrar, Straus and Giroux, New York, 2005.

Proust, M., *In Search of Lost Time*, Gallimard, *Paris*.

Rand, A., *Atlas Shrugged*, Penguin, New York, 2005.

Riedel, J., Jin, J. and Gao, J., *How China Grows*, Princeton University Press, Princeton, NJ, 2007.

Risso-Gill, C., *There's Always Something To Do. The Peter Cundill Investment Approach*, McGill-Queen's University Press, Montreal, 2011.

Rogers, J., *Investment Biker*, Random House, New York, 1994.

Rogers, J., *Adventure Capitalist*, John Wiley & Sons, Chichester, 2003.

Rogers, J., *Hot Commodities*, John Wiley & Sons, Chichester, 2005.

Roth, B., *The Great Depression. A Diary*, PublicAffairs, New York, 2009.

Rothbard, M. N., *The Essential von Mises*, Unión Editorial, Madrid, 1974.

Rothbard, M. N., *The Ethics of Freedom*, Unión Editorial, Madrid, 1995.

Rothbard, M. N., *The Panic of 1819*, Ludwig von Mises Institute, Auburn, AL, 2007.

Rothbard, M. N., *The Mystery of Banking*, Ludwig von Mises Institute, Auburn, AL, 2008.

Rothbard, M. N., *Towards a New Freedom*, Unión Editorial, Madrid, 2013.

Rothbard, M. N., *Power and Market*, New York University Press, New York, 1977.

Scherman, H., *The Promises Men Live By: A New Approach to Economics*, Random House, New York, 1938.

Schroeder, A., *The Snowball. Warren Buffett and the Business of Life*, Random House, New York, 2008.

Seely Brown, J. and Duguid, P., *The Social Life of Information*, Harvard Business School Press, Boston, MA, 2000.

Serrano García, J. B., *The Calm Investor*, Ediciones Diaz de Santos, Madrid, 2013.

Shearn, M., *The Investment Checklist*, John Wiley & Sons, Hoboken, NJ, 2012.

Smithers, A. and Wright, S., *Valuing Wall Street*, McGraw-Hill, New York, 2002.

Sowell, T., *Applied Economics*, Basic Books, Philadelphia, PA, 2009.

Steely Gordon, J., *The Great Game*, Suribner, New York, 1999.

Thaler, R. H., *The Winner's Curse*, Princeton University Press, Princeton, NJ, 1992.

Thornton, M., *The Economics of Prohibition*, Ludwig von Mises Institute, Auburn, AL, 2007.

Train, J., *The Money Masters*, Harper & Row, New York, 1980.

Train, J., *The Midas Touch*, Harper & Row, New York, 1987.

Train, J., *The New Money Masters*, Harper & Row, New York, 1989.

Tsai, K. S., *Capitalism Without Democracy*, Cornell University Press, Ithaca, NY, 2007.

Vogel, E. F., *Deng Xiaoping and the Transformation of China*, Harvard University Press, Cambridge, MA, 2011.

von Mises, L., *Bureaucracy*, Unión Editorial, Madrid, 1974.

von Mises, L., *The Ultimate Fundamentals of Economic Science*, Unión Editorial, Madrid, 2012.

Walter, C. E. and Howe, F. J. T., *Red Capitalism*, John Wiley & Sons, Hoboken, NJ, 2011.

Welch, J., *Jack, Headline*, London, 2001.

Wilson, E. O., *Consilience*, Abacus, London, 2003.

Wu, J., *Understanding and Interpreting Chinese Economic Reform*, Thomson/South-Western, Mason, OH, 2005.

Index